Memoir Of A Psychic

I0149853

AMANDA McHUGH

Light Feather Publications

MEMOIR OF A PSYCHIC: TRUST YOUR INTUITION & THRIVE!

http://www.amandamchughauthor.com

Front Cover Design A. McHugh

Book & Cover design by A. McHugh & S. Eadie.

Author Photo: M. McHugh

ISBN:9780648163503

First Edition: November 2017

First Published in Australia by Light Feather Publications

DEDICATION

To my beloveds Mick, Kia and Orin, and my family and
friends for believing in me and letting me be me
so I could let you be you...
and to our spirit family for loving us unconditionally
and teaching us that love is everything.

PREFACE
By Mick McHugh

I met Amanda in Dublin, Ireland in 2002 and was instantly in awe of her. I knew this was a person who could and does live and strive beyond the reach of everyday normal human existence and common beliefs systems. In our fifteen years together, I've seen her do some incredible things. A lady walks past us, says, "Good morning", and Amanda replied, with a smile that eases a person, "Good morning. Who's Lizzy?" The lady burst into tears saying Lizzy was her favourite aunt who had passed away.

The depth of the conversation, connection and the healing that ended up taking place between Amanda and the lady for the next few hours was something beyond anything I had ever experienced before. The other thing that struck me was how Amanda worked altruistically in that moment in order to give the lady the message from her dead aunt.

In 2004, I listened to Amanda as she told me Madrid was going to be bombed in three days' time. Three days later I stood there in shock as my work colleague exclaimed, "Madrid has just been bombed."

In our fifteen years together, I've continued to see her do countless amazing similar psychic acts that have blown mine and other people's minds.

I've seen the incredible change in people from before and after a psychic reading with Amanda. Words almost don't do it justice, it's like a light bulb has been switched on in them! They have this glow, sense of knowing and empowerment.

To our family, these psychic events have become common place! It is simply a natural way of life for Amanda and for our family. Amanda really lives to helps people with her natural gift and it is just that, a natural gift.

I hope her stories that she shares in this book will touch your heart and soul, and ultimately inspire you to trust your own intuition.

CONTENTS

INTRODUCTION

I wrote this memoir to tell people about my extraordinary life experiences as a psychic medium. I also wrote it because I want to help people use their intuition to make their own lives wonderful!

Being a psychic medium means sometimes I 'know' or 'see' things in the past, present or future. I also talk to spirits, angels, ancestors and deceased people. You may use other terms to describe these beings – there's no right or wrong. I've found it's best not to judge other people's terminology but to accept that we all use terms that we are personally comfortable with depending on many things like our culture, education, religion, upbringing and our family's beliefs. I use all of these terms depending on the energy that I feel when I am sensing or communicating with the being.

The definition of intuition is the ability to understand something instinctively, without the use of conscious reasoning. Intuition is often an immediate, gut feeling or hunch that appears quickly in our minds, without us being aware of the reasons for it.

We can all think of situations where we have experienced intuition ourselves. We might have a feeling that something is wrong with someone we love, even though they are at school or work or live some distance away from us. Then we find out that they were in trouble or sick. We might just know who is ringing us on the telephone before we answer it. We can feel that someone isn't telling us the truth, only to find out later that we were right. We might hear a warning in our head that helps us avoid an accident or we might have a dream that subsequently comes true.

I have been using my intuition, like you, my whole life. In my twenties I decided to use it consciously and regularly and by doing so, I made my life amazing! I found true love, I gave important messages to people from their deceased loved ones, I predicted bombings, weather, pregnancies, death, illnesses and spoke to angels, animals and more!

If you have ever wanted to awaken or enhance your intuitive abilities, then this book is for you. By showing you what is psychically possible, the stories in this book might inspire you, and, if you wish, combined with the targeted exercises and meditations at the end of several of the chapters, help you open up and enhance your own psychic field.

This book can help you learn how to connect in with people who have passed over (died) if this is what you wish. You will learn how to read their signs, listen to their messages and interpret what they have to tell you. It will help you trust your instincts and what you hear, rather than doubt yourself. Because we are not taught anything like this, we can tend to doubt what we are sensing, however after many years of trusting myself and spirit, it becomes second nature to hear what spirits are saying or see what they are trying to tell us through feelings, physical sensations, thoughts, images, ideas, and dreams.

I share wonderful stories in this book about connecting with our loved ones who have passed over to the 'other' side. It is incredibly healing and inspiring to hear about such human and spirit encounters and is another step closer to proving that there is continuing life after death.

I hope my stories will help you as much as they have

helped me, providing answers to life's biggest questions, peace of mind and purpose in life. Through learning about our innate intuition, we discover the incredible spiritual world that exists both within us and around us, as we continue to build a bridge between this world and the next.

Our intuitive psychic abilities can really help us here in this world, especially if we decide to use and develop them over time. I invite you to explore this fascinating journey into intuition and the spirit/earth world connection with me and thrive in your life...

CHAPTER 1

Intuition Defined

"The most beautiful thing we can experience is the mysterious.
It is the source of all true art and all science."
Albert Einstein

THE TERM 'PSYCHIC' IS ABOUT HAVING SPECIAL MENTAL ABILITIES, where we can know about things without knowing how we know them. This is also known as intuition. It's that quick, powerful gut feeling you get when you just know something.

We use these extra intuitive senses and not just our standard five senses, to get information about the world and everything in it and also, beyond it. Using my psychic sense, I have experienced some truly incredible things in my life. Things that I had been told were impossible or only existed in the realm of movies and science fiction.

I have used multiple psychic abilities. Some of these include:

- Seeing pictures or movies of the past, present or future play out in my mind (clairvoyance);
- Knowing that something is going to happen, such as an impending pregnancy, death, car

accident, etc.

- Connecting with deceased people, angels and spirit guides (psychic medium). This includes seeing them physically, sensing their energy or thoughts in my mind, and hearing their voices in my left ear (clairaudience).

- Gleaning information off objects about the owner of the object or something that happened to the object (psychometry) or getting information about a distant object (remote viewing);

- Sensing medical issues that a person has (medical intuition);

- Psychic smell and taste abilities, for example, smelling roses or tasting a favourite food or drink because the deceased person loved these things when they were here;

- Empathic abilities, feeling other people's emotions;

- Telepathy, hearing other people's thoughts and sending my thoughts to others (examples in this book include experiences with my children);

- Shaking or feeling oncoming bad weather formations such as a tsunami or acts of terrorism before they occur.

I look in more detail at some of these abilities below.

Mediumship

I am a psychic medium, which means I communicate with other beings including people who have died, spirits, guides, angels and ancestors. I can feel, sense and hear when they are present. I often see them in my mind's eye (my thoughts) and I have seen them with my physical eyes also. They have looked as real as you or I, standing right next to me in a room.

Even though many people can't physically see spirits, they do often feel, hear and sense them (just like we can't see radio waves or Wi-Fi but we know these exist). Spirit people exist at a different dimension or density to us.

People in spirit form can let us know they are here. They might make the hair on our arms or on the back of our neck stand up or they can tickle parts of our body! Many a time I have felt my hair pulled or stirred.

Unfortunately, because we haven't been taught about spiritual beings or to trust that we can sense them, we often discount what our senses are telling us. Just because we don't see the spirit person with our physical eyes, we doubt what we are feeling, thinking and knowing. I've known many grieving people who say they feel their loved ones but they don't know if it's true.

I have some beautiful young friends who died and when they have visited me in spirit, light bulbs have blown in the room I was in! On several occasions I sensed their presence, I've seen them in my mind's eye like picturing a photograph of them, then heard them tell me a message about their mother, and then the bulbs have blown. If you ask me this is a brilliant and clear communication strategy to get their message across and demonstrate that they are definitely here!

People in the spirit world tell us profound messages. They seem more aware of what is happening around them and assure us that life continues after death. There are so many books about this, many people have written about their loved ones returning from spirit and telling them or showing them the love and beauty on the other side. They tell us not to worry here, nor to worry about death and dying. They say it's just back to a state that we already know.

So while I see and hear messages from the other side, I also feel or sense an altered state of energy simultaneously. Every soul has an energetic footprint or signature; you could call it a personality. It is this energy that you can feel and it tells you lots of information about the spirit person. It is distinct and different for everyone. You might feel all manner of things about the deceased person, such as if they are male or female, a grandparent, parent or child, funny or serious, and if they loved cooking, flowers, writing or sports or some other hobby. You might sense illness they had when they were alive or the manner in which they died.

It's just like sensing somebody nearby in the physical world. Like you know how when you are standing alone at your kitchen sink and suddenly you can feel someone looking at you from the other side of the room? When you turn around your housemate, partner, child or even your pet is there just looking at you? It's that knowing and feeling another person's energy, even though you hadn't heard them come into the room or seen them physically yet, you just 'felt or 'knew' someone was looking at you!

It's true that we just know things sometimes, without knowing how we know them, we just do.

A Beautiful Example of Mediumship

There are many ways to begin a memoir, from defining what psychic means, to telling you more about who I am. For me, I find that real life examples of things really help me to grasp an idea and that's why this memoir is packed full of examples and stories. We learn mostly through observation, so by hearing these stories and knowing what is possible, in theory this should open or enhance your own psychic field, if this is what you wish. And so, I thought the best way to introduce myself to you

4

would be through a powerful example of my psychic experience.

The following story is one of the most beautiful examples of my psychic gift and one of my favourite stories because of the profound meaning that it has imparted on my life and the lives of the people involved. It sets the scene for how magical our lives really are. I'm skipping my life story ahead a bit; I was about thirty-two when the following event happened.

The Twins

This story begins in Ireland when I was doing readings for a professional, travelling, holistic fair. Some of the country's best psychics, natural healers, naturopaths, massage therapists, tarot and angel card readers and crystal and light healers travel with this fair so I felt very privileged to be a part of it.

There is a great sense of love and spiritual power emanating from this fair; and no matter your belief, you can't help but feel there is a God like presence. The energy in the room is just incredible.

A middle-aged woman named Claire saw me giving readings at the fair but I was very busy so she took my card. Claire called me afterwards to arrange a group reading at her house in Drogheda (north of Dublin). She said she didn't know why but for some reason it was important to see me and not any of the other psychics who were there that day. When I turned up to her house there were eight people who wanted a reading. I had been expecting about five people but I took it in my stride, although I knew it would go well into the night.

It was a bright, warm, summer's evening and they were all enjoying drinks and food on a lovely wooden deck extending off the side of the house. One of my favourite things in the whole world are the long, glorious summer evenings in the Northern Hemisphere, where the sun doesn't set until 11pm in the height of the season. There's nothing like that wonderful feeling of enjoying a late evening picnic or stroll in a park, seeing the kids out playing football and the joy as people are out and about, shaking off the long winter months. My husband, Mick and I used to love getting hot chocolates or mocha lattes from Butler's Chocolate Café on Grafton Street and going into St Stephen's Green, a beautiful park right in the heart of Dublin city. We'd have a lovely walk in the park and then lie on the green with all the other summer revelers soaking up the warmth and light of the glorious summer sun.

That particular beautiful afternoon however I wasn't enjoying the sun, rather I remember feeling nervous about 'putting on a good show' for the people who were each paying good money to see me. I also had a strong feeling that it was really important that I be there for them and do what I had come to do. I worked through my nervousness and was focussed and ready to do the readings. I had been praying and talking to the angels for days beforehand leading up to the psychic party to help me do the best possible readings for the people present.

Claire was a lovely lady, so well-spoken and well dressed, with a beautiful light-filled, newly decorated home. She wasn't rich by any means but her life was comfortable. In the boom time of the Celtic Tiger many Irish people were enjoying such comforts and their homes were newly built, spacious and modern. There was a lot of building and construction going on in the country.

Claire introduced me to a few people around the table and then to her young teenage son. She led me to a small but cosy office that was the perfect place to do readings.

I created a sacred space for myself in the office using candles, prayer, crystals and the scent of lavender oil. I saw three of her friends first. They were happy with their readings, and in between seeing these people; I was playing a fun peek-a-boo game with Claire's twin daughters. They were really cute, little blonde girls about nine years old, poking their heads around the office door and smiling at me. Although no one had told me, somehow I just knew they were Claire's daughters.

Then Claire came in for her reading. I will never forget her reading because it was so beautiful and so profound. Often the best readings are the simplest, straight to the point and as natural as breathing. My eyes often well up thinking about this beautiful experience. Perhaps because I am a mother, I feel extremely grateful for it.

She made herself comfortable and we were facing each other and smiling. The first thing I said to Claire was actually all she needed to hear. It was the reason she had invited me to her house in the first place, and having her friends there only seemed to give her courage and perhaps a sort of emotional cushion.

Only a few seconds after she sat down I said to her, "On the way into the house you introduced me to your son, but you didn't introduce me to your twin girls that have been playing with me around the outside of the office door this evening. Where are they?"

Immediately, Claire broke down crying.

Sobbing, she bent over in her chair and held her hands in her face. She appeared to rock back and forth a little for a few moments. She cried out, "That's all I needed to hear! That's all I needed to hear!"

When she composed herself again, she was smiling, though tears were still streaming down her face, and emotions were running high in the room.

I knew I'd said something really important but I didn't know yet how important or incredible it had been. I was smiling but I had no idea why!

Through smiles and tears, she turned to me and dropped her hands from her face. In an amazing moment that I will never forget, her eyes shining so brightly, she said, "My twin girls died at birth. They died at birth!"

To me, at that house, that evening, those blonde-haired, pig tailed twin girls were as ALIVE as their mother sitting before me! I saw them at the human age they would have been had they survived. Strange, but at the time I remember smiling and laughing so much with the girls, I hadn't noticed that no one else could actually see them.

Claire told me that she had always felt them around her, especially when she was in the kitchen cooking, but this was the first time anyone had confirmed that they were actually with her. The girls came back into the room; this time I couldn't see them physically but I could feel them standing there and see them in my mind's eye. They spoke into my mind and said they were being raised on the other side with their elder relatives and that there were a lot of children for them to play with. They assured their mother they were very happy and had always visited her and would continue to do so.

We could both feel them in the room as they spoke to me. It was a beautiful, heartfelt reunion. Claire would never doubt again; she knew that when she could feel them, they were with her. After this, we discussed that she would be able to have a relationship with them and carry on conversations and trust that she was heard and that her love was always felt by her beautiful twin girls. That death was only an illusion was clear to us that beautiful, long summer's evening.

Several chapters of this memoir are devoted entirely to messages from our loved ones on the other side just like this story.

Life After Death

What deceased persons tell us about life after death is

very inspiring. Obviously this means a lot to us living people, as one day we will be on the other side. This knowledge can have a huge impact on how we live our day to day lives.

Death can give life a whole new perspective. We can more appreciate our lives now and also embrace what is to come. We can also deal with our grief for our loved ones in a healthier, real and spiritually aware way because we understand that they continue to exist after the passing of their physical body. We can keep in mind the spiritual perspective that there is a lot more going on behind the scenes in our universe that we are just not privy to yet.

All evidence (from all cultures, over centuries of history) points to the fact that we live on in an afterlife where our souls, our personalities, our thoughts, continue to exist with many other souls in a multi-layered existence. There is also much accumulated information and scientifically validated accounts of reincarnation, where the soul moves onto a new human life after completing another.

We can prepare for our continuing life in the now, by being fully aware and conscious of our continued state of being. We have nothing to lose and everything to gain if we do this.

Because of my own experiences talking to deceased persons and angels/spirits/guides and reading about thousands of other people's accounts of their experiences with other worldly beings also, I wholeheartedly believe that we continue to exist, thrive, grow and love when we shed this particular body. This book contains so many of these wonderful stories and I'm sure that you can probably think of many of your own stories or stories from people you know or books you have read.

This is a very little but sweet story that happened one day in 2016 when I was in Byron Bay; I live twenty minutes inland from this coastal town. I was going for a walk but had left my hat at home. I felt a spirit voice tell me to go to a particular opportunity shop in town, one that I hadn't been to in years. She told me that there was a hat just perfect for me on a hat stand to the left of the entrance and that it would be $1 and that I would know it immediately.

I could see in my mind's eye that the hat was pink and that it had a word on the front of it, but I couldn't see what the word was. Spirits often leave details out of visions so we that can uncover things in the real physical world. They have their reasons for this, which we are generally not privy to. I get the sense that they enjoy giving us happy little surprises as much as we enjoy receiving them. They also like it when we listen to them, it validates our connection to them and to our own spiritual nature.

I parked my car and walked a few minutes to the shop. When I got inside there was a hat stand to my left and on it I saw this lovely pink hat that stood out to me. It's hard to believe but not only was it in excellent condition for a second hand item, the big bold hot pink words on the front of the hat said, "Heaven!" complete with a love heart after the word! That was definitely the perfect hat meant for me! The spirits have such a wonderful sense of humour!

But they also come through for us when we need them and in serious and sad times. Mick and I had taken our two children, Kia and Orin, roller skating, but Mick doesn't know how to skate and he isn't learning because he's a full time musician and has to protect his hands and arms so that he can play guitar for work.

I was skating around with the children, enjoying the popular music they play there, when Mick's best friend from high school, Neil, who had just passed away recently, suddenly came into my mind. He told me to go straight over to Mick who was sitting on a low sofa, just out of my line of sight because of the walls surrounding the skating rink. A song had come on that I didn't know but it was really nice. I felt Neil tell me that it was something to do with the song.

At Neil's insistence, I went over to Mick and he was literally crying his eyes out. Mick told me that the song we were listening to had been played at Neil's funeral. We hadn't been able to attend the funeral as Mick is Irish, the funeral was in Ireland and we live in Australia. Mick's friends had told him all about the service and what songs were played and although I didn't know that the song was relevant beforehand, Neil made sure that I knew the song was important. He also made sure that I was there to hold Mick as he shed all the tears that had been waiting for the right moment to come.

If Neil hadn't have told me, I would have been skating around happily oblivious to my husband's pain. This is what connecting to the spirits can do for us, help us, help each other, in such a beautiful, true spirit-way. They tell me they come to us all the time to help us help each other, it's just that I can hear them clearly and feel their energy so strongly that I can put words to these incredible experiences. Many times they help us but we don't realise they are the ones who put a thought into our head that directed us towards helping someone.

By reading this book, spirit tell me that others will be better able to hear them more clearly also.

Telepathy - Picking up on People's Thoughts

As a psychic, sometimes I can hear what people are thinking and will know what they are going to say before they say it. Recently I was driving home and thinking of my neighbour and I heard the words, "I've got a present for you!"

On arriving home, I was walking into my house when he came into my yard calling out to me, "I've got a present for you!"

Another recent situation was where I was trying to pick a gift for my friend but I kept seeing that she needed pillows. I did not want to buy her pillows! I text her and said, "Weird question, I've been looking for a present for you this week and I keep thinking you need pillows lol is that true?"

She messaged me back stating, "Omg… how did you know… I just picked up a pillow in the shop… cause my pillows have gone missing again… lol… I didn't buy cause it wasn't firm enough…"

We live twenty hours' drive away from each other so I couldn't have actually seen her doing this or known by any 'normal' means.

As psychic beings, we have a radar that works continuously reading the environment around us, but that environment is not limited to the direct space or time within our immediate vicinity.

The range of our psychic radar is expansive and nonlinear. It transcends what are accepted as general physical laws (such as time goes in one direction – in fact physicist's now say that time in non-directional).

For example, I had been seeing all week that my friend needed pillows, and thought of texting her, but chose not to text her until it felt right, which meant I actually sent the text to her a minute after she had just looked at pillows in a store, when the text would be most relevant and have the most impact. Also, in what could be considered an amazing 'coincidence', my mother just also happened to be in the store that day and my friend had seen her at the same time also!

*Seeing Things Before They Happen
and Getting Information off Objects*

I am also a psychic or clairvoyant so I see things before they happen. For example, even though my friend's car appeared to be driving well, I once predicted the exact day that his carburetor was going to break down on his car.

I have predicted many things before they happened including acts of terrorism, bad weather and natural disasters, pregnancy, illness, death, accidents, etc. I have also talked to unborn babies in their mother's wombs who told me what was going to happen in the future and incidentally, I have also heard the thoughts of animals both deceased and living.

The way I see things about to happen in my mind, is much like seeing a photograph or a mini-movie clip. These premonitions can come in my waking life, in a state of meditation or when I am asleep and dreaming or just waking up from sleep.

Sometimes the messages come through to me when I am involved in automatic type activities, such as driving or washing the dishes. I have found that spiritual beings can get through much more easily when the mind goes into this relaxed, altered and automatic state. The mind is more open to messages when it is relaxed.

When I am in focused gentle meditation or mindful prayer, spirit can get through easily also; and when I hold an intention and ask them to come through for someone and I am very focused on that, the spirit can also come through clearly.

Thus our consciousness can open to other realms when it is less preoccupied with thoughts or everyday worries. This is why I work on my own positive mental and physical health so that I can unmistakably hear the voice of spirit talking to me. It is important to me; I don't want to miss the messages because those messages can really help us here.

An example of this is when recently I thought of a friend after not thinking of her for many months. She used to live near us but moved far away to another state many years ago with her family. Her daughter was best friends with my daughter and we could go for six months without contact. One day I thought to myself I must message her today and ask if they are coming for a visit soon. I forgot to contact her as I was busy and that night I received a message from her saying that they were coming the next week and asking if we would we be around to catch up. The next morning my daughter Kia knew none of this and said to me that she wished to see her friend soon! I then said, "Oh I forgot to tell you that I got a message from them last night and they'll be here next week!" We can feel or hear messages from each other despite long distances!

Some other examples might be when I might think of messaging someone a minute before they message/text or call or I can feel that a certain person is about to ring me and then they do. Often I am thinking of someone and I go to dial their number and they ring me at that exact moment. I can have my mobile phone on silent but still 'feel' a text come through any time night or day.

My husband is a musician and often he will text me from a gig in the middle of the night, and even though my phone is on silent or do not disturb mode, I will wake at the exact moment he sends it! It is like I can feel a subtle vibration in my own body or in my ear or in my mind before the text message actually comes through onto the phone. Many people have described similar experiences to these, especially in relation to knowing that the phone is just about to ring and who it is.

Perhaps we are like antennas and receivers for such energy, be it thoughts or phone vibrations. It's all energy.

Just how strong this ability is, is anyone's guess. But for me it's constant. It can happen anytime, anywhere, and be related to almost anything!

We took our children to stay at a lovely beachside hostel in the Australian coastal town of Coffs Harbour and we met some nice backpackers travelling Australia. The night before we left I kept thinking I must get our uneaten bananas down to the communal kitchen and I kept seeing the face of Bito, a young Indonesian man we had met. The next morning, we were late to the breakfast table, and I said to Bito that I kept thinking of giving him these bananas. He said that earlier that morning one of the other residents was looking for a banana and then it made sense why I really wanted to take the bananas to the kitchen the night before, because someone would need them the next morning! And I felt I had to ask Bito because he was the only one around who could tell me this fact!

We were at a library book stall sale. I wanted to buy this children's book on Egypt for Kia, our daughter, and said to Mick that I didn't know why but we were going to need this book for her shortly. A week later she told us that she had an assignment to do on Pharaohs!

In another example, my friend came over and she was distressed about something that had happened in her life. She was having a bit of a panic attack in my lounge room and suddenly this book came into my mind. I pretty much jumped up into the air and started running to my room and said to her, "Come with me, I know what you need!"

I found the book on my bookshelf and handed it to her. She started smiling and her eyes went wide and she looked super happy and excited! She said, "That's my favourite book in the whole world! I lost my copy of it and I've been looking for it everywhere! I just took all the books out of my bookshelf looking for it! They are still on the floor!" We laughed and hugged and I told her she could keep it!

This story and stories like it make me so happy and so grateful for my gift of sight. I'd actually only ever been into that particular friend's house once and only for a brief moment many years ago, so I had no idea what sorts of books she was into. Our children are friends so we usually get to see each other when she picks her son up from my place after a play date. I adore her and want the best for her, and so does spirit and that is why the image of that book suddenly and powerfully came into my mind.

The book I gave her was an inspirational paperback by the awesome life coach Tony Robbins, whose work is helping millions to live their best possible lives here on earth. I love his spirit, he's helping us all to shed fears and blocks and move on to become the awesome, empowered beings we are meant to be here.

Psychometry & Medical Intuition

We can pick up energy and information off everyday objects. This is called psychometry. Objects can 'tell' us something about the owner of the object or about the environment in which the object has been in.

I was at my friend's house watching her two adorable children use home-made maps to find hidden 'treasures' around the house (i.e. toys they had wrapped up in newspaper and hidden around the house so they could then find; just so cute). While we were laughing and chatting about their game, I was looking at one of the maps and I was unexpectedly transported in my mind to a particular family fun park on the Gold Coast in Queensland, Australia.

In my mind I saw the family having fun following a map around the park. I could see it and feel their experience, almost as if I was there on the day! My friend's eyes lit up as she said, "Yes! That is where they first learnt to use maps as we were completely lost when we went there!"

I can also feel other people's illness and disability in my own body (often called medical intuition). I sometimes sense it in their bodies or I will actually feel pain or changes in my own body alerting me to their condition.

One day I was standing in my kitchen at the back of the house when I suddenly felt my right eye go funny, at the exact same time at the front of the house something flew into my son Orin's eye and Mick had to wash his eye out. There was nothing in my eye, but I had felt the thing fly into Orin's eye. I didn't know that this had happened to him at first, I was standing in the kitchen rubbing my eye when Kia came in and said, "Something just flew into Orin's eye on the deck, Daddy's washing it." My eye was suddenly completely fine.

It makes sense that I'm very connected to my own children. Funnily enough, the most practical thing has happened with my psychic gift and Orin's shoes! Twice now, several years apart, I have been grocery shopping and I felt I had to buy Orin new shoes. He hadn't needed them, but on two occasions I felt I should get them that day. On both those two occasions, when he got home from school, he walked in the door and announced that his shoes had just broken that day and that he needed new shoes! So twice, I was able to pull out the new shoes that I had just bought that day! A very practical and useful skill for a mother to have!

So while that was a very present and in-the-moment thing to do, I can also see things in my mind that have happened in the past to people, although I wasn't present at the time or didn't know the person then and didn't have any information about the event.

Ten years ago I had this excellent book on alternative

health that contained very useful information about nutrition, herbs and supplements, however every time I read it I felt extremely stressed out and anxious. My tummy would be doing belly flops reading it! One day, after many weeks of feeling uncomfortable when I read the book, I flicked to the author's prologue at the back of the book. In her closing statements she shared that while writing the book she was very stressed as she was on a strict and almost impossible deadline from her publisher! Then my feelings made so much sense! What a shame because it really effected the quality of the book for me and I stopped using it because of how it made me feel.

You don't have to worry about that with this book, it took me over six years to write it at my leisure, with no one but myself and spirit to monitor where I was at with it. I've always known it would be published, I just always also felt that spirit and I would do so when the time was right.

A Strong Receiver

I have been this intuitive all my life, but I truly and fully embraced it in my twenties and I travelled the world doing readings for people. I love to call myself a spirit walker, this seems like an apt title to me.

Some people say the intuitive sense is like having a strong receiver, like a radio, picking up waves from the air. Waves such as thought waves that create a type of energetic pulse that can be read by people with in-tune intuitive receivers – we have so many other types of invisible waves in the air, such as radio, electromagnetic, sound, ultraviolet rays, gamma rays, kinetic energy, x-rays, microwaves, heat, colour and light, and scientists believe more will be discovered. We cannot see these waves, just like we can't see psychic energy or thought or emotional or spiritual energy, but we can receive, transmit and feel these waves.

As we've established, we can be very sensitive to these thought and energy waves that are in our world. So I can feel that the house phone is about to ring a second or two before it does, as if I can pick up on the electrical or energetic vibration before the devices alert me to the incoming communication.

I can also pick up on the exact thoughts of the person who is about to make a phone call to me. I will see the person in my mind and hear exactly what they are going to tell me, and then my phone will ring and that exact conversation will then ensue.

I believe that we all do this to some extent. This is a part of our brain that we use all the time but are often not aware of it. The following incident supports that we can hear other's thoughts. One night I wasn't tired and I stayed up reading on my phone until late. I was squinting, closing one eye and not the other and the next day I had severe pain down one side of my face. It's silly I know, but I was in a lot of pain and I said to myself, "I better be careful not to have a stroke." That next night when putting my son Orin (aged 7 at the time) to bed, I was thinking about the pain in my face again as it hurt. I thought I must be more careful reading in bed so as not to have a stroke. Simultaneously, I was giving him a big hug and he said to me, "Mummy what is a stroke?"

In another example, my daughter Kia, 13 at the time, was at school one day and her good friend told her that she had just written a new story. Without thinking, purely instinctually and naturally, Kia struck her hand into the air and exclaimed, "A gift from above!" With a look of surprise on her face, Kia's best friend announced, "That's what the story is called!"

So yes, these stories are proof we must be aware of what we are thinking! We are often aware of what we say to others, but we also need to be aware of what we think, because even if we don't realise it, these thoughts are out in the atmosphere and are apparent to others.

Of course some people are excellent blockers and can block others from seeing what they are intending and thinking until it is too late and the other person has been duped in some way. However, the more you use your intuition, the more you can see past these masks and pretenses and unless you are really tired or sick or the person is very skilled at pretense, you will not be easily fooled. You might have an inkling or a gut feeling that all is not as it seems. Whenever I've ignored this feeling, I've usually ended up learning a valuable lesson the hard way!

We are spirit walkers, energy sensors, and thought readers, we live in this realm but also in the other realms that we can sense around us, and often we go to these realms in our dreams. When we fully embrace these facts, and learn to master our abilities, we will go forward into a new generation of being here on earth, as spirit will be able to manifest more clearly alongside us, like in the story about the twins whose physical bodies died at birth, but whose souls are very much alive.

CHAPTER 2

My Psychic Background

I'M STANDING IN MY KITCHEN AND A WOMAN IS TALKING TO ME. This is a normal everyday event for us all, except in this case, she is talking to me in my mind. I can't see this lady at all, but I know she's there because I can hear her and I can feel her presence beside me, just like you would feel another human close by. She is whispering to me in my left ear.

She asks me to think about the women in my community that I know. I start to think about them, and I feel a bit spacey, a bit far away, like my mind is travelling away from my body, like the two are distinctly separate.

When I get to a particular woman, Amy, I feel I am meant to stop, like I have found the right person. The invisible lady says to me, "Last night we got through to Amy, and if you contact Amy as well today she will listen to you and you will save her son from drowning in the pool."

I hadn't been to Amy's house in a few years. I recalled that years ago she didn't have a fence around her pool. She now had a toddler about eighteen months old so I knew I had to contact her immediately.

I sent Amy a concise text message and told her about the spirit lady's message. I explained that they got through to her last night, that her pool needed a fence as soon as possible, and that her son was in danger of drowning this week. I explained that if I contacted her then she would get the message and she would save his life.

Amy rang me back immediately. She was in a state of shock and amazement.

The night before she had experienced a powerful dream in which she saw a baby lying face down in a full bathtub of water. She pulled the child out and she saved the child in the dream. She felt that it was her child but she didn't want to face it at the time.

I told her that I was shown exactly what happened if he was to drown - the sorrow, the pain, and the intense heartache that would never end for her and her family. I was shown the family would move house and never, ever get over the loss.

Amy told me that she and her husband wanted to buy a fence for the pool but it was a big expense on their wish list and they kept saying they were going to do it soon. She said she always kept a close eye on her baby son, but she had fears about the pool. She confided that she had thought to herself that if anything happened to her child in the pool she would move house and never forgive herself.

Because of our timely warning this child is safe and sound. I saw them recently, and Amy and I now have a unique and special bond built on gratitude and love, and of course on a shared, powerful, spiritual experience.

I feel so grateful that I could pass on such an important message and save a lot of people from the pain of this child's unnecessary loss.

As described previously, with my psychic sense, sometimes I will see things, other times I will hear things or I will feel things. In this instance I heard the woman's voice in my ear and I was also shown what could happen to the little toddler if my friend didn't act on her dream and my message. Like other psychics, I act as a psychic bridge, and can readily move my awareness from this world to the next so that I can help us humans here in the physical world.

One thing that I know for sure, without a smidgen of doubt – We are not alone.

Growing Up Psychic

I know that I was always psychic. When I was a child, I used to be scared at night. I would hide under my covers, terrified to take a breath, praying to God that the spirits wouldn't harm or scare me. My mother said that when I was little I spoke about some interesting things that freaked her out a little. She said it was like my brother and I were recounting past lives. While I was a natural psychic, it wasn't openly encouraged or talked about. In fact, my Mum was a very devout Catholic and she told me not to speak about such things as I got older. She said that authorities would put me away if I spoke about what I could do. As the ancestor of an English convict, and a strong Catholic, I know my mother was just trying to protect me.

As a child however I begged for help with what I could sense but there were never any answers from the adults. I was told to relax and that I was dreaming or that my imagination was making things up. All the while, I could sense energies close by but I didn't understand them. I could feel and hear spiritual beings trying to speak to me, but I didn't want to talk to them and find out what they wanted. I would see and sense them at the foot of my bed and I was so terrified they would scare the life out of me like in a clichéd thriller movie.

The spirit at the end of my bed was my deceased great grandmother. I knew it was my great grandmother, because I could sense her energy; her distinct personality and physical shape but I was still scared. She wouldn't have hurt me at all, she was always such a loving, funny woman, but I was young and just didn't know what to say or do. I didn't know what she wanted from me. I would run into my mum and dad's bedroom, sometimes screaming, always out of breath and terrified!

In that old house where I grew up there was also a male spirit who used to walk around with big clomping boots. He would walk through the house and stop at my doorway. When I opened the door, he wasn't there but I could hear him walking and breathing and I could sense his thoughts. He didn't have bad thoughts at all, but just a presence that stood out as being aware and alive and conscious. He seemed protective but as I was so young, I still felt utterly terrified.

So many nights he woke me by walking up the stairs near my bedroom window and along the corridor to my closed bedroom door. I always had it closed because I felt safer. I would tell myself that at least I would hear if he was to try and open the door. Somehow I knew I wasn't in danger but I was still freaked out! I also knew it wasn't my father because Dad had a wooden leg which made a distinctive sound when he walked through the house.

When I was about twenty-two years old, I lived and worked in a town three hours away from my parent's house and I was visiting them for the holidays. My mother and I were in the lounge room watching late night television when the clomping man suddenly started walking through the house! He was so loud; he stood in the kitchen just on the other side of the curtain that separated the lounge room from the kitchen.

My mum nervously opened the curtain but there was no one there! He was so loud walking around out there, only a metre from us! We could feel him there, a distinctive masculine presence. He wasn't angry or aggressive or threatening at all, but of course we were both spooked!

It was then that my mum finally told me that she had always heard him in the house as well, but had never wanted to acknowledge him to me in case it scared me even more! I had been talking about him since I was young, and when I would run into my parent's room, terrified because he was walking in the house, she would tell me to settle down and that I had been dreaming. I know she did the best she could at the time, she just didn't know how to cope with a psychic child.

I have learnt when my own young children have intuitive moments, to be honest and calm and truthful with them. I want them to have faith in what they intuit and not fear their gift of seeing and sensing spirits.

Interestingly, one day not long after my mother and I heard our stomping man in the house, a friend of mine Tina came over. Tina was a natural psychic, as was her grandmother before her. Tina said, "There is a man here in the house, he doesn't want to hurt you, but you hear him?" I told her I did hear him and I tried not to be scared but his heavy male footsteps had always frightened me.

Tina reiterated that he wasn't there to hurt us and that he was just visiting and looking out for us. This did help me to relax and not worry about him so much after that.

A new brick home stands there now, as the old house was destroyed in a cyclone, and no one has ever heard him walking on the tiles - he seems to have gone with the old house. Sometimes I wished I had had the courage to speak to him and I have wondered what he would have said to me. I will never forget him though, he was a peaceful spirit, he never meant any harm, it felt like he was looking out for me, for my family, and somehow, through his gentle thoughts and peaceful actions he was able to let me know this.

School Years

When I was in grade 3 our teacher introduced us to long division mathematics. When he asked the class for the answer, he wasn't expecting anyone to know. But I knew the answer and put my hand up and told him and the rest of the class. As my mother had taught me how to read numbers and letters by the time I started school, my teacher asked me if my mother had taught me how to do this type of mathematics. I said no. What happened was that the answer popped into the front of my head, as if it was just placed there and I could read it. I used to sometimes feel the presence of tutors or guides helping me as I wrote a paper.

I also had an incredible photographic memory. I could write out verbatim pages and pages of textbooks that I had read. In university, I could read many articles about a topic and then just write a ten or twenty-page essay from memory because in my mind's eye I could see every single word I had read about the topic. I would do this for university exams also. For most of my life schoolwork was so easy for me and I never really had to worry about it. I feel that I had a lot of help with it from the other side!

I remember a powerful incidence when I was eleven years old and in grade six. In my mind, I saw a simple scene involving my classroom and some of the boys getting into trouble between two rows of desks that separated the class into two. I kept seeing it a few times in my head over a period of time and then one day it just happened in real life, in the exact same way I had seen it. In my mind/vision, I had felt the anger of the teacher, which was the prevailing emotion he had expressed when the event actually occurred in real life.

The teacher was frustrated with these particular boys and they were always pushing him to his limit. This day they pushed him too far and he really let his anger fly which wasn't like him. That's probably why I had experienced it beforehand, because it was an intense, uncharacteristic emotional outburst that was going to leave a strong energetic imprint.

I remember being amazed but not telling anyone. I had witnessed an entire scene play out in my mind way before it actually happened in real life. How does a child put such a thing into words?

Teenage Years

I went through several years of spiritual, physical and emotional turmoil from 12 years of age. My carefree and happy childhood was interrupted. A young man hurt me emotionally and physically. I found myself in a solitary, lonely and scary place, that I had to learn to deal with and ultimately, move on from.

Throughout this experience, I felt very alone and I really didn't know how to heal and get through it. I was at a very low point in my life, I was truly at rock bottom and just wanted give up. I used drugs and alcohol to escape sometimes. It's clichéd, but I got in with the wrong crowd.

I also got bullied by other kids. I didn't know who they were, but some girls rang me at home and told me they hated me, they actually gave me a long list of their names and told me they wanted me to die or kill myself. Another young man rang me and told me what he wanted to do to my body. This is over twenty years ago, bullying has no doubt been a long term social problem for us humans.

At the time I felt very hurt inside and I couldn't stand how I felt about myself and my life. I didn't have the vocabulary or skills to ask a trusted adult for help. My parents were so caring, but I didn't want to get into trouble or make them feel bad. I just couldn't tell them what was really going on for me. I had been such a smart and happy child previously, so my tender, young ego was trying to save face, and I pretended to others that I was okay.

Sadly, at the time, I saw no other way out of what I was going through and I tried to take my own life. I was in hospital for several days after the attempt and feeling very sorry for myself. I was in the children's ward, crying non-stop, thinking of how I was going to succeed at the next attempt on my life when I got out of hospital.

It's not his fault, I'm sure he cared very much for his patients, but the male doctor on the ward said to me, "We hate your kind in here." Now, being a child I didn't understand what he was trying to say to me and I thought he hated me. I thought the nurses hated me because he said the word 'we'. I saw the nurses talking in the nurse's station and looking over at me. I felt so alone and exposed and very embarrassed. Still yet no one asked me what was wrong with me. My mum just cried and said, "Why did you do this to me?" It was a lot for a 13-year-old to take on.

So I just kept crying and crying and thinking about leaving so everyone's lives would be so much better. I really believed this at the time. Now of course I just want to tell every person who feels that low to please wait and to talk to someone. To delay the act of hurting yourself because you are beautiful and you are loved. And because it's amazing just how people will show you and tell you that you are loved and wanted and it's also amazing what might be waiting for you in your life and what you can create for yourself and how you can help others!

Like me, I went from being that low to finding true love and having the most wonderful children and to absolutely loving my life! If only we just give ourselves time to heal and remake our lives and weave a new path for ourselves, we can find the spiritual resolve to shine and thrive again!

At that time however, I was very down. I didn't feel that anyone was truly connecting with me because I was in so much pain.

One late afternoon, I was alone in the hospital ward room, crying. It was dusk and the lighting in the room was changing to a warm golden colour. Out of nowhere a man appeared by the side of my hospital bed. He literally seemed to materialize out of the golden light. He took my right hand in his. I remember just looking into his soft, caring face and gentle, compassionate eyes. All he said was, "Amanda if you don't make yourself happy then no one else will."

In my mind he showed me a stack of books and I knew that I would write these books and that they were going help others and the world heal. Then he enveloped me with the purest of love and healing light. I felt it encompass my whole being. The love shown to me was like no other. I call him my guardian angel.

This incident with him completely turned my life around. It helped me heal, at a time when no one could have foreseen such a turn around. I can only describe the feeling of him as Christ-like - the way Christian people might explain their conception of modern day Jesus.

As I stared into his eyes, I knew without a doubt that he loved me. This overwhelming feeling of love was so powerful and so healing and it has always remained with me. I think it is one reason I am able to project so much love to people when they come to me for readings. I have such as sense of overwhelming love for people. It is unconditional and entirely non-judgmental.

After I got out of hospital, I completely changed my life. I became an A Grade student again, stayed healthy and fit and strong, and got my life back on track. Sometime later, I had a really lovely boyfriend who was my age and we had a wonderful teenage romance. I had several close, kind and loving friends and a part time job at a shop that I loved.

This period of my life was very healing for me and I remade myself with the help of the love of my guardian angel, to whom I am forever grateful. There was such a profound feeling of healing and light within myself, I knew I was special and I was going to help others because of who I was and what I had been through.

I felt connected strongly to spiritual beings, I always spoke to God (to the source), it was just a natural thing for me to do. I felt very light filled and very special. I wanted other people to feel this. Sometimes I would meet people and they would tell me that there was something different about me. Some could sense this great joy within me, while others could sense my psychic sight.

It's true that every moment of our lives we can make this choice, to see the light and to be a bringer of light. This is the beautiful gift that my guardian angel gave me and that I hope to pass on to others. And I beg all people who are thinking of leaving this world by their own hand to know that you are not alone. Please believe me when I say this, there are many of us who would hold you so tight if we could. Hold on and please reach out for help. We deserve a life filled with light, joy, promise and love, this is what is wanted for us, this is what is ours if we just ask for help.

In My Twenties

I went to university to do writing and journalism but somehow I became a psychologist! I loved the subjects at university and I realised there was a lot to learn about human behaviour. So in my twenties I became a fully registered and practicing psychologist and, perhaps because of my own past, I loved helping people who needed support and strategies when they were going through dark times and couldn't see a way out by themselves. I liked teaching positive life coping skills like relaxation and rational thinking exercises and assertiveness communication training.

However, when I wanted to study mindfulness and psychic phenomenon, my university professor said I would have to travel to England where parapsychology was seen as a legitimate branch of psychology.

I was taught to be a 'scientist' of human behaviour. It was our duty only to provide psychological treatments that were based on empirical evidence and 'proven' statistical studies. I was taught that sometimes what we think and feel is based on irrational beliefs that we develop in childhood.

We learnt that people use inappropriate or unhelpful coping strategies (alcohol, drugs, anger) to deal with their problems and that psychologists could teach people more appropriate, helpful and empowering ways of seeing the world and oneself. We were shown that people have picked up damaging and negative ways of seeing the world, themselves and others, and that we could work on helping people to change that negativity and learn how to view things rationally and positively.

While the psychological techniques were helpful, especially for some people, over time I found that they were lacking in depth, spirit and overall foresight into the bigger picture of human spiritual life on earth. Something was missing for me in the psychological theories about life.

When I was seeing people as a psychologist, I could sense things within their bodies and minds. Often I would just know how they felt by feeling it within my own body and I would hear important words or sentences to say to open the person up. I seemed to just know what had happened to them and that knowledge would help me formulate the appropriate questions to ask them. I would sense things strongly with my intuition. For instance, I would know if someone had cancer or relationship or money problems. I would read it in their bodies just like one reads a book.

There was nothing about medical intuition in the so-called comprehensive psychology textbooks about human behaviour! And yet I knew things without knowing how I could know them.

One day I was in training as a clinical psychologist and my supervisor had to sit in with me as I undertook an initial interview and counselling session with a new patient. The client was an older man from Yugoslavia. He had severe back pain and was feeling irritable. My supervisor had an anxiety condition of his own and often sweated profusely. He also spoke with anxiety in his voice, using big psychological words and the Yugoslavian client was having none of my supervisor's textbook based jargon! But somehow I managed to get the Yugoslavian man to talk and he knew that I was really listening to what he was saying. I was empathising with him and working out a good therapy protocol for him and I felt that my energy and his were in sync. He could feel this and he actually told my supervisor that he was a stupid man and to shut up because only I knew what he was talking about!

I wouldn't step out of the boundaries of psychology with my clients, I was careful not to. I found that as I treated more clients I could put words to the energy I was feeling and I was careful about the energy that I was giving out to people. With practice, I was able to read the energy signs clearly and sense illness or disease in a person's body. I didn't tell them outright but it helped me make sense of what they were dealing with. People were also helped because they could intuit that I had empathy for them and cared for them.

Another supervisor saw an older female patient giving me hugs at the end of sessions and asked if I was sticking to the cognitive-behavioural treatment plan. I was sticking to the plan and I was teaching people the strategies because they are so useful for improving our mood and the way we think, but I was also giving them lots of unconditional love and respect. Sometimes I think that was just as effective as the strategies themselves!

Another time I was doing counselling with a lovely young woman who had slight brain damage and some residual physical issues from a serious car accident in which her whole family had died. She said to me, "You love me. I can feel you love me."

I agreed with her and said that I did care greatly for her and sincerely wanted the best for her. This helped her because she knew that the strategies I was looking at with her were only coming from the best possible place from my heart and mind to help her. It was still professional, it was just also a very caring and unconditional place of love and acceptance for a fellow human being who was going through so much in her life. She knew I genuinely cared for her and this was the biggest healer of all.

Another man came to a session when I was working in alcohol and drug treatment and he said to me, "You are different to the others."

To which I replied, "Yes I am."

He said, "We are spiritual beings having a human experience."

To which I also agreed.

The patients could sense that I wasn't just there as a psychologist who had a job to do. I treated them like human-spiritual beings and gave them the upmost respect and love. It is this unconditional love and connection that I believe probably does the most healing in a counselling situation. It helps people to be present in the situation and feel validated and valued. This helps them shift their mood, because they know they are not being judged, which enables them in turn to see that moods can be shifted with positive thoughts, behaviours and intentions. True connection with others, positive social support and good relationships are being hailed as extremely important factors in people's healing and also in maintaining long term wellbeing. While there is a lot written on unconditional positive regard (love, acceptance, respect) for patients in healing and treatment, I love the book called 'Zero Limits' by Joe Vitale and Dr Hew Len which is based on a Hawaiian healing technique called Ho'oponopono, it is such a beautiful technique and message about using the power of forgiveness and love in all aspects of life.

In terms of my psychic evolution however, I had no loving guidance at the time to help me cope with what was happening to me. All around everyone seemed to be getting on with life and seemed so 'normal', but I was seeing and doing things that psychology didn't mention anywhere! I was about 24, and working as a psychologist still, I was attending a social event one evening with my health professional coworkers. We were playing a game whereby a person would have a famous person's name on their forehead that they couldn't see, but they had to guess who it was. This person had to ask other people, who could see the name on that person's forehead, questions to try to determine the celebrity's identity.

Well, in my mind's eye I immediately saw that I had the Queen Mother on my forehead! My psychology supervisor was one of the people playing with me and the first question I asked was something like, "Is it a royal and a mother?"

She gave me a very strange look, that seemed to quiz whether I had cheated or not as she said, "Yes."

I asked if it was the Queen Mother and my supervisor just looked at me and said, "Did you see the answer?"

I replied, "Yes I must have."

She was still looking at me strangely.

I wasn't yet able to tell her that I had seen it in my

mind's eye, like in my forehead, like a word flashed across a screen. I wasn't yet fully aware of what I could do, it was just so natural to me, and I'd never been taught the vocabulary to describe my ability to use my extrasensory perception in such circumstances.

Being 26

When I was twenty-six, I felt like I woke up out of a bad dream. For some time, I had lost my way. I was stressed, overworked, in an unhealthy long-term relationship, not truly living my life purpose, and feeling extremely overwhelmed by all the work in my life.

I was working several jobs as a psychologist for the state health department, as well as running my own private practice and studying a combined post-graduate degree, a Clinical Coursework Masters in Psychology and a research PhD! I was also tutoring first year psychology students, supervising clinical master's student's work placements and marking assignments for first year postgraduate psychology master's students!

All I seemed to do was work! I was so engaged with doing all the time; I had forgotten how to just be. I had lost sight of who I really was. I had stopped doing all the things that I loved.

Not surprisingly, living a life like this, I was sick quite a lot with allergies and sinus infections, which was not like me at all. I had always been very healthy and fit, energetic and strong. I was certainly not living the life that I had dreamed of as a teenager – which involved travel, helping people, writing, dancing, singing, fun and lots of laughter!

I hadn't been listening to myself or paying attention to the signs in my own life that were telling me things weren't right – like ill health, low energy, feelings of stress and tension, and one or two panic attacks due to university exam stress, and weight gain.

After a period of an exhausting illness and great soul searching, I completely changed my life. Sometimes a big mistake, like not looking after yourself, can lead you to the best thing that could ever happen to you, although it's hard to see it at the time. I had reactions to medical treatment for my allergies that made my health worse. It led me to seek the help of a naturopath, which was the beginning of my journey with alternative and spiritual health and a wonderful new chapter in my life. Also, taking a break from work to rest and heal, my intuition really kicked in.

Probably because I wasn't so busy all the time, I could clearly hear my spiritual guides again! But this time, I was older and I realised I could use my psychic ability all of the time to help myself and others. I finally understood that my psychic sight was essential for the rest of my life journey. I realised that I could use it consciously and regularly, it wasn't just an occasional magical thing that happened. It was a natural part of who I was.

My naturopath sent me to a healer named Lynn, who had been trained by medical intuitive Carolyn Myss. Lynn pointed out some big things in my life that needed addressing. I went into the session with a horribly irritating cough that had lasted for months and when I walked out of just one session with that wonderful woman, I was cough free! She pointed out that my throat chakra was blocked because I wasn't speaking my truth or asserting my own will. Chakras are energy centres in our bodies that have been written about for centuries in very ancient Asian healing texts.

Chakras are situated throughout our body and when they are spinning freely we are healthy and well, but when they aren't because of things like abusing alcohol, overworking or giving our power away to others, they can get blocked or dirty. She did a chakra healing on me as well that was extremely energizing. I had been in a bad relationship for many years with a man who was an atheist, and who, among other things, worshipped money. This relationship was not good for me. I finally had the confidence to leave him.

After seeing Lynn, I read Myss's book 'Anatomy of the Spirit' and from that moment on I devoured natural health and spiritual books that helped me reclaim my health and personal power. They also taught me how to embrace my psychic abilities and helped me change my life for the better.

While I had always seen spirits, I had never developed the confidence to tell people what I could see. With newfound wisdom and because I had just gotten through this massive healing crisis, I began to tell people what I could see for them and I began to feel and show an inherent shamanic psychic wisdom.

I stopped work and I started travelling which was something I had been dreaming of for a long time. A spirit voice told me my friend was going to America and that I should go with her. So I asked my friend if she was going to America and she said that she was and I knew I had to go.

I went to America for a three-month holiday with her and I began doing readings for people everywhere I went. I would see a person's deceased loved one and give them messages from the other side. I did so many different intuitive things that I had never read about or heard about before. I didn't know it was possible to do what I was doing!

Going to the United States of America (USA) in the summer of 2000, is the beginning of an amazing journey of intuition, seeing things before they happened, learning how to give readings, how to interpret symbols, speaking to dead people, spirit people and angels, talking to animals through thoughts, and all manner of miraculous things that I have documented in this book.

At twenty-six I went from working long hours testing people's memory and intelligence on standardized psychological instruments and writing detailed neuropsychological reports, to giving people incredibly accurate messages from their deceased loved ones on the 'other side'.

I felt so alive and so aware of everything around me, including the usually hidden spiritual world. I felt like I'd been walking around half asleep for many years!

On one occasion, I met a lovely young lady on a little boat while holidaying in Miami, Florida, USA, and while we were relaxing looking up at the beautiful bright blue sky, her recently deceased grandmother came to me. I told the young lady that I could see a lovely, large, brown smiling woman in a long flowery dress, who felt and looked like a grandmother. She confirmed that her grandmother had just died a few weeks before.

I saw what her grandmother looked like, what she wore, how she talked, how she cooked all the time and how she was trying to sew but couldn't really do it yet, like she appeared to be struggling with it. The young woman confirmed that this was because her grandmother was always cooking for the family, however was only just learning to sew when she died in her human form!

Her grandmother was able to give her beloved granddaughter important messages to help keep her safe and happy for her future. This young woman was going into the modelling industry and had a lovely, sweet boyfriend that the grandmother confirmed was a grounding and loving influence for her. Her grandmother was able to tell her to not fall into any of the modelling traps such as ego or drugs. She was also able to warn her about a particular person that didn't have her best interests at heart.

I was able to tell other people things that were going

to happen in the future, past or present, that I could have no knowledge of by 'normal' means. My American friend, Walt, asked me to do a reading for him and I saw and felt that the carburetor on his car was going to break down in nine days' time.

I had returned to Australia and he emailed me and confirmed that his carburetor did break down when I said it would! He asked me if he would get into the college of his choice, and I was able to tell him that he would have his choice of colleges. When his offers came back he was accepted into several excellent universities, including the one he really wanted to get into, which he was very pleased about.

On a more serious note, I saw that a friend, Jim, had a blockage in his throat vein and that he should visit a doctor as soon as possible, because I felt the possibility of a stroke. Sadly, my warning was too late and a short time afterwards he had a major stroke that paralysed one side of his body. I met Jim's wife a few times briefly over the years that I had known him and every time I saw her I felt this thickness on my tongue. I knew something was wrong with her tongue but didn't understand what the feeling meant. I found out later she was diagnosed with tongue cancer.

Also, while in the U.S. I was able to help save a woman's life. I was travelling around, seeing the Florida countryside with Paul, who was an American friend that I'd made. He introduced me to Trish, a woman in her late fifties, who also just happened to be a professional psychic. Because she was a psychic, the connection to the spiritual side was incredibly powerful. Spirits came into my mind almost immediately for her! Within moments of meeting her, I was able to tell her that her deceased Aunty Margaret and Aunty Mary were there. They were her favourite, much loved Aunties as a child and she hadn't seen them in a long time. Her Uncle Tom was also there.

I was also trying to say another name, like Ger... Ger... Ger-tru... I couldn't get it out and I said to her that there was another woman with us; with a stutter or something that I couldn't totally understand her. It sounded like she was saying her name was Gertrude. Trish confirmed that her cousin was Gertrude and she may have had a stutter as a child but also that she was German, and English was her second language and she was very difficult to understand in this life. Therefore, she had showed me this by being difficult to understand in the next life!

I was also able to say there was a Bob, who was different to the others, not family, who appeared to be there only recently. He said he was her friend. She confirmed that her dear friend Bob had just passed on. Then after the introductions were done, her whole angel-spirit mob bombarded me with health warnings for her! They didn't let up. My God they were so loud in my head and my body!

They implored with me that she would soon get a pain in her chest and must immediately go to the hospital whereby she would receive a simple treatment that would save her life. Trish actually disagreed with me on this one, saying that she was very healthy and that I was picking up on her emotional pain in her heart because her son was very unhappy with her choice of career as a psychic and he was not speaking to her.

She said she had previously felt pain in her heart but it was emotional pain and that was that. I didn't want to scare her, but I did reiterate the warning, to appease her spirit family and friend, and I asked her to humour me and call the ambulance if that pain did come back. I was very tactful when speaking to her about it and didn't push the issue. Years of psychological training has taught me to generally speak cautiously and calmly to people about important matters, because if you push your energy and ideas onto people, that's often when they reject your advice or your help.

A week or so later, my friend Paul said to me, "Why didn't you tell me you were that psychic? I had no idea that you could do that."

He then proceeded to tell me that Trish had indeed felt chest pain, and normally would have just let it pass, but my advice came into her mind and she thought she had better listen since it was evidently from the spiritual realm.

She rang the ambulance and was raced to hospital where doctors confirmed that she got there just in time as she had a heart problem. She told Paul to tell me that she was given a simple treatment that saved her life. She said that without the warning, she would not have gone to the hospital, she would not have had the treatment her heart needed and she would have died.

Another day, when I had returned to Australia, I felt called to go to a beach one morning as if there was something I had to do there. I was sitting quietly reading my newspaper, when an Aboriginal man and his friend came to sit next to me. They looked around forty-five years old. They had been out the night before and they had slept up under the palms bordering the beach. I felt no fear at all, I knew that they were the reason I had felt drawn to the beach.

We struck up a conversation on the beach and in my mind's eye I saw an arrow through the Aboriginal man's heart. I felt his pain in my own heart. I started to channel an Elder ancestor from his people, I could see and feel him in my mind, he was very old, wise, and caring and his skin was the most beautiful glowing black.

Though I could see this image in my mind, I also knew the Elder was indeed ageless and timeless, he was a representative of the Aboriginal people who had passed on and he enabled me to speak truthfully to the Aboriginal man by coming through me. My voice changed, I was speaking with an Aboriginal accent and with masculine tone and energy. I was very aware of this energy coming through for him; I let it come through.

I boldly asked the Aboriginal man, "Why you wanna kill yourself?"

He looked at me, up and down, as tears welled in his eyes he cried out, "World don't work like that no more sister, world don't work like that no more."

He was crying and shaking his head.

I said to him, "Yes it does because I am here. I can do this. I can see you. They can see you. They are talking through me."

I got him to discuss his problems with me, which as I felt, turned out to be about a girl who he loved but who was causing him much grief.

His Caucasian friend sitting with us was speechless; he just sat there saying nothing. I left a few minutes later, having opened him up to the fact that the ancestors had seen him and knew of his pain and that he should not kill himself but should work through it instead.

I don't know what happened to him but I hope that it gave him the strength to keep living. I got the feeling he heard them clearly talking through me and that he was affected enough by their message to listen.

Looking back, I have helped a lot of people through my gift and I can honestly say that without the guardian angel's intervention in the hospital none of that would have happened.

A respected Reiki healer, naturopath and counsellor once told me that the reason I might be such a powerful psychic is because I crossed over to the other side when I was a teenager. I was always a spiritual and fairy like child, however meeting with my guardian angel might have strengthened my psychic link to the other side. Because I have been there, and come back I have retained a powerful connection.

After becoming a full-fledged psychic medium, I then went on to my toughest role yet and became a mother!

Reading the Energy and Signs Around Us

I have learnt to read the signals and signs that I see or feel in my own body and mind as best I can – sometimes new ones throw me a bit, although I'm used to many of the different sensations now. Like the arrow through the heart for the Aboriginal man, that was a new one at the time but through the Aboriginal Ancestor who came into my mind, I knew exactly what it meant. They give you the feeling of what something means and somehow explain it to you without using words, somehow you just understand and know what they are trying to say. This knowing transcends words.

I also came to learn that if something is going to be bad for me, I feel a loss of energy or a flow or release particularly leaving my groin, stomach area or chest (these are the sites of several of the major chakra centres in the body as taught in ancient Asian medicine; they are bases of power and security, so it makes sense I would feel losses there). Sometimes I feel a sense of heaviness down my leg if something will be bad or not right for me and my energy. If something is going to be good for me or someone else, it can feel light and positive when I touch it or think about it.

I have a sensitive body and have to be careful what I put into it. When I am picking a new herbal supplement or a multivitamin, I do a kinesiology test, sometimes using my fingers as I was shown by a kinesiologist but other times, just holding the item will lead to an energetic weakness in a part of my body or a feeling of nausea. The item 'tells me' that it will not be good to put it into my body.

My friend asked me to buy him a bottle of

multivitamins from the chemist. I did a kinesiology test on the bottle while thinking of him and I felt it would not be the right type of multivitamin for him. On first sight the multivitamins looked like they would be good for him, but after the test I looked more closely at the fine print and realized that shellfish was listed as an ingredient. He was allergic to shellfish and without the energetic testing I might not have realized that the multivitamin would not have suited him.

These little snippets of information and awareness in my own body are vital to me and to my understanding of what is going on for other people. While in this instance, I used my own body to give me the information I needed, when I require information I often do distinctly hear a different voice, a male or female and sometimes see their physical shapes beside me. Sometimes I see what they look like in my mind and sometimes I just hear them speaking to me. It is often in my left ear. My mum and grandmother had inner ear balance problems and I have them too. My daughter, son and I also have very sensitive hearing and we have all shown high levels of intuitive abilities.

There were times when I didn't tell people important information that I had heard or sensed. When I knew I had missed an opportunity to help someone it hurt me inside my body, mind and soul. I would get this horrible sinking feeling in my stomach like I had messed up and missed out and so had the person. When I did share the information, the energy felt amazing, a sense of positivity, love and great joy permeated the space around us. We would all feel connected and energetically charged and things were changed, like something powerful had happened and things would never be the same again.

I realised that I had to continue to share my gift with others because it felt like the right thing to do, both for them, and for me - and of course, for those who were/are trying to get through to help us. I learnt that angels really are 'messengers' and they are here to help us through our lives here on earth.

By my late twenties I had become a fully-fledged psychic medium. I was no longer afraid of my abilities and I identified as a conscious empath, clairvoyant, medical intuitive, remote viewer, and spirit communicator. I had come to fully believe in and see angels, spirit guides and the deceased. I could sense a great feeling of pervasive and powerful, all-encompassing love, and I felt like this is what 'God' might be like, this loving being of light that spread through us all.

I once read that twenty-six is a pivotal age for people, where their life changes drastically and begins to lead in the direction it is meant to go. It certainly did for me!

Now

I am a mother of two, Kia a girl aged 14 and Orin a boy aged 8. I've been married for 15 years to a lovely Irishman named Michael (Mick). I am the secretary of my child's school parent and citizen's committee and my family have an endearing little miniature Maltese Shih Tzu dog named Sparkles who is the grand age of 11 and two loveable cats named Minty and Kitty. We live in a rustic farmhouse near Byron Bay in New South Wales, Australia.

I have been an out-of-the-closet psychic medium and clairvoyant for over seventeen years. One moment I am a counsellor, mother, wife and homemaker, the next minute I am speaking to those on the 'other side'.

Often when I am relaxed and daydreaming or involved in a mundane task, my consciousness wanders off and gathers information from the future. The most incredible readings have come to me in my kitchen when I am washing or drying up the dishes! Often on my daily meditative walk down my long country driveway, admiring the birds and the trees and the sky, I can clearly hear and see my beloved friends who have passed over into the other side. I think it's important to let yourself daydream and unwind in meditation/relaxation or alternatively, be in complete mindfulness of your surroundings. The mind is altered; a different state is reached and I believe many incredible things are possible and these things can get through to our altered mind.

I feel very blessed in my life to have developed my psychic sense as strongly as I have and to be as aware of it as I am, to listen for it and use it to help people in my life. While I might not always be able to prevent things that happen, I find that knowing in advance provides a sense of great comfort because it means that things in the universe are going as planned.

While we might not always understand everything that happens, there is an overriding power that does. There is a sense of something miraculous and more amazing than we can ever truly comprehend. I have seen many things before they happened - from impending health issues, cancer, pregnancies, car accidents, cars breaking down, bad or unusual weather patterns such as tsunamis/floods/hurricanes, terrorist bombings and death - which opens up a whole world of questions and philosophizing about our world and the next, and what we are a part of. There is this tantalizing feeling that something truly remarkable is at play.

Our intuition is a part of that remarkable higher power to which we are all connected. Quantum physics tells us that we live in a field of unlimited potential, and it makes sense to me that some of us would be more highly attuned to these potentialities (sometimes I might be highly attuned, at other times other people will be).

We are all a part of this whole, all connected, all in a synced existence. Physics tells us we are all composed of the same basic material and the more we become conscious of it, the more of us 'wake up' to this feeling of interconnectedness. It engenders a great feeling of peace when one feels this interconnected living field, the feelings of universal oneness. I love this feeling and try to spread its message and love wherever I go.

Despite all that we know in science and technology, religion and spirituality, my own experiences highlight that we still have so much to experience here on this earth, and definitely a lot to learn. When you have experienced these wonderful connections between us and the other side, your life is never the same. It is changed forever and for the better.

Just like in 'The Twins' example that I discussed at the beginning of the memoir, this book contains many examples of psychic ability that we can receive inspiration from. The following chapters outline many examples which I hope inspires you to share your own stories with the world.

Chapter 2 Exercise:
Revitalising Angel Light Meditation

This is the perfect, gentle, angel meditation exercise.

I do this sort of exercise regularly to give me strength and revitalize me and keep me connected to the love of the 'other side' and to the angels. This is a simple exercise to bring in cleansing, healing, love, energy and light from the angels.

You can do this type of exercise for a few seconds or a few minutes, for as long or short as you please, whatever it takes to make you feel loved, calm, joyous and full of this beautiful angelic light. You can do it sitting at a bus stop or in your kitchen, standing in line at the bank or grocery shop, when you go for a walk in a park and take a moment's break or in bed when you wake up in the morning or just before you go to sleep at night. They are always available to us any moment of the day or night.

- Just imagine that light is pouring into your body from the sky, from the divine creator that you pray to. See a beautiful group of angels (you might see these as guides or ancestors) sending the light, praying for you, sending you love and beautiful positive energy. Know that there is no right or wrong way to see your angels, just know that they are full of love and healing for you. You might see your loved ones who have passed on amongst these loving angels.

- Feel yourself filling with this love, with this light and it surrounding you in a bubble of pure white light or a colour that you feel you need at the moment. My favourite is soft pink pearly light as it softens the heart and is the colour of love. You can even go through the colours of the rainbow if you like or use gold or silver, or the all-powerful ultra-violet light but it will be what makes you feel the love and strength of the angels at this moment in time.

- This beautiful light is strengthening you and cleansing you. It is filling you with power, love, and all the energy that you need while you are here on earth. Your angel brothers and sisters are happy because they have been able to get through to you and help you to strengthen your body, mind and spirit. If you want to you can talk to them, ask them their names and ask that they help you and thank them for everything they do.

- Sometimes a beautiful larger than life big

white female angel is holding me in her arms as she fills me with love and light and other times I am lying on my back or side and many beautiful beings are standing around me pouring this energy into my body and helping me strengthen and heal body, mind and spirit. You might like to try visualising these types of experiences also.

Grounding Exercise

After each of the divine meditations in this book, please ground yourself afterwards. You do this by grounding to the earth that sustains us. In your mind's eye picture that you have beautiful tendrils or tree-like roots connecting you to the earth.

These energizing tendrils can be any colour or form you wish; they could be green like tree roots or silver thread or red soil or even pretty ribbons. Whatever helps you to ground to the earth while you simultaneously feel the love and joy and energizing light of the angels is the right thing for you.

We feel the breath as it slowly goes in and out of our body. We draw beautiful energy and breath from the earth up into our feet and into our bodies, it goes up through the top of our head to the divine, then the divine sends the healing breath and light back into our bodies and down into the earth.

This type of meditation is often called the pillar of light meditation as light flows through us into the earth and the divine. Do this several times and finish when you feel centred and calm, grounded and peaceful.

Open your eyes and feeling grateful and calm, thank the universe and the angels for this wonderful loving, healing, calming and energizing experience.

AMANDA McHUGH

CHAPTER 3

Connecting With People Who Have Crossed Over

I RARELY WATCH TELEVISION, but I can suddenly get the feeling or hear in my mind that I should turn it on, only to find important information that I have needed to an issue or problem.

I have been singing a song in my head and felt compelled to turn on the radio, only to find that song is being played.

Sometimes I am thinking of a person I haven't seen in ages and I will see them that day or the next. I might be thinking about my husband and he will text or ring or we will write each other a text at the exact same moment. I will know when he is drinking or even thinking about drinking a coffee even if he is in another country!

Psychic connections are made easily when I'm relaxed or in an altered meditative or automatic state. I will be doing something mundane, like washing up dishes or driving my car, and people who have died will get through to me with messages for their loved ones. I also connect with spirit and angelic beings through focussed prayer, like when I'm doing a reading for someone and I invite the spirit person to come and speak to their living loved one.

I particularly love connecting people with their loved ones who have crossed over. Their bodies may have died, but their personality and spirit are very much alive. Sometimes deceased loved ones might get me to do something unusual, like dance a certain way or do a certain thing that is uncharacteristic of me but very characteristic of the person who has died. The spirit person can get me to give very relevant and specific advice or messages or even gifts, items or conduct ceremonies (such as sharing a pot of tea) that make sense to the person and connect them to their deceased loved one.

We can clearly help each other through this spiritual communication pathway. Whenever I have received a message from the other side it has always been for the good of those for whom the message was intended. They always have messages of love for us and I am often asked to pass this love onto their relatives and friends who are still here on earth. They also want us to know to make the most of it here and make our lives count. They understand we are hurting for them, but they don't want us to dwell on that. They always want us to make the most of our time because one day we will be on the other side and there is so much to experience, love, learn and grow from here. They appreciate life and want us to fully embrace it.

Just like those on the other side, we create our world through our thoughts and connect and communicate through thought form. We are just slightly different because of our dense physical bodies, but we can still communicate with each other and still influence each other's worlds with our thoughts. We are richly connected to each other in the subtlest of ways. There is powerful evidence accumulating about the power of our thoughts and their influence on the world such as research by Bruce Lipton for example, a developmental biologist who has shown that our thoughts effect our DNA, our genes and our cells. There's also research about how water molecules are affected by thoughts and how plants grow at a different rate because of thoughts directed at them!

I'm so lucky as a dear friend of mine is a medium and so I have also benefited from receiving messages from spirit. She often channels my Dad and has given me beautiful messages, things that only his spirit could have known at the time. I've found such comfort in this, just as I know many others have, when I have channeled their loved ones for them.

This next section looks at some of the experiences I have had connecting people with their beloveds on the other side.

Her Father is a Saint!

I want to share a beautiful example of being called upon by a man, newly deceased, to help his daughter, Angie, cope with his quick and traumatic death. A few years ago, after dropping my husband off at the airport, I heard a male's voice come through. He requested that I go to a particular shopping centre to meet his daughter. I rarely go to this shopping centre because it is far from my house, however it happened to be on the way back from the airport. Although I had never met him, I knew through a recent social media post that Angie's father had died.

I was driving along the highway when I saw an image, in my mind's eye, of Angie at the supermarket in front of the cash registers. I also saw her asking me over for a cup of tea at her house. And, this is what happened. I went to the shopping centre, found her in front of the cash registers and she asked me over for a cup of tea.

I had been speaking to her deceased father in the car

and he had set up a meeting with her so that he could speak to her through me. Of course I did not have to follow through with his wishes, but I knew it was important for them, as he had died tragically and quickly a few days before and they didn't get a chance to say goodbye.

And speak with her he did! We went to her house and he came through and gave her messages of hope, healing and love. I won't go into the private details except to share one amazing statement that he made that was unique to his particular life and that provides clear identifying information of him in life and in spirit.

Angie's father said to me, "John Joan of Arc."

I had no idea what this meant at all, but I relayed it exactly as I heard it. I have found this is important because often what makes no sense to me, makes absolute sense to the person for whom the message is intended.

As I relayed the message to her, I realised I didn't even know her father's first name.

Angie then said that her father's name was John, and that she had been saying to her other friends that, "People who die on their birthdays are saints!"

Her father was letting her know, that he John, was now indeed a saint having died on the actual day of his 75th birthday! He was a very special man with a wonderful sense of humour and talking to him as a spiritual being was an absolute delight.

His visits didn't stop there; a year later I sat down to have my cup of tea one morning in peace. My children weren't up yet and my husband hadn't started his workday.

The heater was warming the kitchen and the early morning sun's rays were streaming into the room. I was quite relaxed and content, not thinking about anything in particular and the next minute Angie's father started telling me things to tell her.

He showed me wildflowers along beautiful country paths, beaches, views, and an ocean expanse. I knew that Angie had gone to England on holidays but I had pictured her in the city. I contacted her with his messages using social media and she confirmed that she was staying by the beach, with ocean views and that she was walking pathways filled with those beautiful wildflowers he had shown me. Angie's son had said a prayer for his grandfather when they visited a local church. John heard this prayer and relayed his thanks to me, which in turn, I relayed to Angie.

He was able to remind her to watch her health at a festival that she was going to and also he wanted to let her know that he wanted to write a book with her about their relationship both with him living and 'dead'.

Most interestingly, he also told me to tell her that she would use her healing abilities and not to be concerned, that this was part of her path here. He showed me she would make use of her first aid skills but not to stress about it. She was nervous because the last time she had used those skills was the day that he had died. He had collapsed on his birthday and she had performed CPR until the ambulance arrived. However, despite her efforts he had died instantly.

A day after his message, Angie was involved in a bus crash and had to put those first aid skills into practice. She said she was calm and serene as she applied her healing knowledge and helped to calm and give first aid to an injured older woman on the bus.

She said she could feel her father by her side as she helped the woman. Having her father's pre-emptive warning before the event helped her to cope and to react calmly in the situation. John came to give his daughter help even though he has crossed over - he was her strength and her rock in this life and he continues to be there for her.

A Story About A Powerful Unborn Spirit

When I was travelling the East Coast of America I was introduced to a man named Peter. Upon meeting him I said, "There are babies all around you, babies, babies, babies."

My hands made sweeping gestures over the front of his body and I later found out his girlfriend was four-months pregnant.

When I met Peter's girlfriend, an amazing thing happened. The baby came to my mind as a powerful ancient being. I cannot explain the sheer magnificence of this spirit, except to say that he felt ancient, powerful and strong. A male essence at this incarnation, the baby told me that his physical body would die during birth - he would be stillborn to teach his mother and father important life lessons.

His father, Peter was a womaniser, who 'played' the field, i.e. he had sex with many different women, disrespecting the women who cared for him and wanted him to like and choose them. The baby's mother was nevertheless infatuated with Peter, and had fallen pregnant believing that this child would be a way to keep him.

After imparting this information about his death, the unborn spirit told me that I couldn't tell Peter or his pregnant girlfriend. He assured me that it was an important part of their life journey to experience his short in vitro life and subsequent early death. He explained that his parents needed to go through this experience in order to learn an important lesson about love, and the impact of their choices. They had to learn not to hurt or use other people because ultimately, they would end up getting hurt.

There were probably other complex karmic influences involved in this situation but the unborn spirit did not share anything more with me. However, he did give me this message to share with his parents, "You will experience the greatest love, but also the greatest pain and disappointment you have ever known."

Peter knew I was psychic and when he asked me what would happen when his baby was born I relayed the spirit's message to him.

At the time, Peter thought that this meant he would be trapped in a loveless relationship, because his love for his baby would keep him connected to this woman he did not love and in fact, felt controlled by.

Five months later when I was back in Australia, Peter called to say they had just buried his stillborn son. He said they heard the baby's heartbeat only an hour before birth but then his heart stopped and he died unexplainably just before being born. He then asked me if I had known that his baby would die.

I felt a strong spiritual presence assuring me in this moment and I was then able to tell Peter the truth of his son's life and death, and the lesson that his powerful spirit had hoped to impart. While we can try to hide the truth from ourselves and from others, the spirits know exactly what we are doing and they will find a way to help us learn those lessons we need to learn – no matter how painful they might be.

Sometime before Peter's baby died, I shared the story with a friend, Sean, who did not know Peter. I had possible prior knowledge of a death and I wanted to make sure that I was doing the right thing - I needed support with this decision.

Not all things are clear-cut when it comes to the spiritual realm but both Sean and I felt that warning Peter could potentially do more harm than good. It would certainly break a special bond with the spirit, and there was also a slight chance that interfering could create a self-fulfilling prophecy. For instance, if I warned the mother about what I knew, she could feel that I created stress within her, which caused the baby to die.

I honoured my agreement with the spirit, because he could see the bigger picture and I was in no position to make this about my own human needs, fears or desires. This was a big lesson for me, being able to listen and trust their divine wisdom. I was only twenty-seven years old at the time, but through experience I had learnt that they wanted the best for us, so I put my faith in the spirit and abided by his wishes.

Each of us has a significant part in this incredible, divine journey. Peter's baby was a wise spirit who had given his life in order to impart these important lessons. And while I do not take lightly that this baby died, I have learnt that the spirits and angels are involved in every aspect of our existence and they know infinitely more than we ever could about our learning journey here.

Though the thought of losing a loved one is difficult emotionally, I acknowledge that we do not die, that we just pass from one realm to another, that we continue to exist. We are here for each other, for each other's growth and learning. We may not all remember this and may not be able to verbalise it like the unborn baby spirit did, however our souls and those in the spirit realm know.

My Friend's Father Comes Through

My dear friend Carol's father passed away and he was such a lovely family man. Needless to say she was very sad. I had never met him because he lived eight hours south of Byron Bay and she often visited her parents, not the other way around.

Carol's mother came to stay with her a few months after his death, and I was going to visit with them. They knew that I was a medium so there was every chance that he would come through to see them.

On the way there I was so excited, I was almost jumping out of my own skin. I was shaking in my chest and I was in such a rush that I had to focus on driving carefully and safely. I just couldn't wait to get there. Those feelings I felt were not my own, but I didn't realise that until later.

When I got there her mother was obviously grieving. She missed her husband so much. In her 60's now, she had been married to him her whole life. She loved him dearly as he had loved her. He had doted on her. I listened to stories about him and let them speak about him for several hours. It was a beautiful heart-felt afternoon, but he hadn't come through and I had to leave because my husband's family, who were visiting from Ireland, were waiting for me. Just as I was leaving he was able to come through!

He showed me that his friend had saluted him at the funeral and he told me his friend's nickname. It was a very unusual name to me, Chucky, and I had never heard his name before. I relayed this information to his family, and his wife and daughter were overjoyed and the look on their faces said it all.

I knew I had done it – I had heard him and I felt ecstatic for them!

Carol and her mother confirmed that his friend, with that quirky and unique nickname, had saluted him at the funeral (and was the only one present to do so). They were in the navy together and the friend had come to the funeral at the last minute. Initially he had not been able to attend and Carol's father was acknowledging how touching it was to have this particular friend there.

He also said a few other things, including that Carol's mother had taken some cream out of the fridge and forgotten to put it away before she left home. He said it had spoiled because of the heat in the closed-up house. She confirmed that she had taken a tube of prescription cream out of the fridge and left it on the kitchen counter before she left.

For me this is substantial evidence of how our loved ones still look out for us when they make the transition over.

He showed me that he was in the house with her, often beside her, often still sitting in his favourite chair. I was able to tell her that she had moved the table that sat by his chair and he thought that it was better in the other position where he used to like it! She moved it back when she got home.

He wanted her to use it and keep it the way it was because it was so comfortable and would help her to relax more. She was a very busy lady, actively helping in her community and a town councilor for many years. He wanted her to look after herself now that he was gone. He kept saying that she needed apples and spinach as well as nettle tea. He said clear blood and good blood circulation is very important for us in human form.

He was also able to show me that at his favourite club there was a picture on the floor and broken glass. When I questioned my friend's mother about this she looked amazed and confirmed that in their local club they had hung a photo of him but that it kept falling to the ground and smashing. I assured her that was no accident. He didn't like the picture and kept knocking it off the wall! She couldn't believe it! She thought it was a lovely picture and had chosen it herself thinking he would have liked it. But she agreed that she would look at putting a different photo in the frame, one that he would have chosen himself.

He was also able to warn her about her use of a ladder, that she wasn't very steady on it and had to be careful. She confirmed that she had indeed used a ladder and that it wasn't very safe at the time. She said she wouldn't do it again! He was no doubt watching her and still looking out for her!

As I drove home calmly and serenely, I realised that my friend's Dad had actually come through just before I had left my home and that was why I had been so excited. As I drove away I left him there with his family, his excitement was gone from my body entirely.

Another day Carol's Dad came through and showed me something special. He showed me that he had controlled a moth when Carol was putting her young son to bed. He made it gently flutter around Carol's face as she bent into the bottom bunk. I asked her if this was the case.

She said there was a moth and this made her so happy because she could feel her father around her at the time (she's very intuitive herself). She said she went to carefully remove the moth but when she went to touch it, it seemed to disappear as if by magic.

Her father showed me that he was able to control the moth to get her attention, in effect he became the moth and she could feel him in the room.

Then he was able to show me the occurrence so that he could confirm it with her afterwards, for otherwise she would not have mentioned it to me, it would have seemed insignificant, which it certainly was not.

A Father and Loving Husband Pays a Visit (or Two!)

One afternoon I was washing up after lunch when I felt my friend's deceased husband behind me. I felt him before I saw him; he was a massive man in life and in death. I had never met Markus when he had a human body but I met him in spirit not long after I met his partner, Lucy, though he had already been 'gone' for several years by then.

He had given me messages for Lucy before, but this day things were different. He was really solid and present, like a big massive dark shape of a very large man – in fact I was reminded of a big gorilla!

After I got my breath back and managed to calm my nerves, I said, "Okay I see you Markus, I know you are there... what is your message for her?"

He said a few words that made no sense to me really.

He said, "He's old but he loves you, oh he loves you."

And with that he sent me the most beautiful warm feelings of love and comfort. I thought about it for a moment until I thought I knew what he was talking about but I still didn't know why he was saying it. Lucy had a dear friend named Thomas who had been her friend for over twenty years. Thomas was a lot older than Lucy and he had been a great comfort to her since Marcus's death.

Later that day Lucy came over for afternoon tea. As she sat at my kitchen table I told her that her husband came that day and I relayed what he said.

Lucy burst into tears. Unbeknown to me she spent the morning talking to Markus herself and she had asked him a very important question. She asked Markus whether she should pursue a loving sexual and life partner-type relationship with Thomas even though he was much older than her. She couldn't hear her husband's reply at the time, but he got through to me instead so that I could tell her and she would have no doubt in her mind whatsoever.

He gave her his blessing to move on and have a relationship with another man who loved her and whom she loved. What a gift to be able to receive! And I felt blessed to be able to give the gift to her, and I'm certain Markus did also, for it is a gift for both sides that we can all be heard.

He also had some other messages that day, in fact he came back while we were sitting at my kitchen table, only this time he just spoke to me in my mind and didn't appear like a big ape! One of the words he said was 'rubber'. I asked if this meant anything to Lucy but it didn't at the time. We thought perhaps we better check the rubber on her car tyres! But there was nothing wrong with her tyres or mine.

The next day I was at her house standing in her kitchen, when Katrina, her eldest daughter, brought out some of her school drawings. She said, "This is my rubber drawing."

I instantly recognized the word and so did Lucy!
Simultaneously Lucy and I squealed, "Rubber!"
We had the biggest smiles on our faces!

Fathers Have Important Messages for Their Children

I was at a friend William's house and I heard the name Jackie. Sarah, William's wife and I were discussing my psychic gift when I said to her that I could hear the name Jackie in my mind. Sarah said that Jackie was the nickname of William's father who had just died recently. I was aware his father had died however I had never met him nor known his name. I also didn't know his actual name, which was John. Sarah said the family never called him John, only Jackie. Jackie was able to make his presence known to me and I could feel how much he loved his son.

William later told me an amazing story about his Dad hiding his watches from him. William never lost his watches because he always kept them in the same place. However, after his father died both of William's watches disappeared, one after another, and despite extensive searches he ended up finding the watches in places where he'd already searched.

Finally, William realised that his Dad was trying to get a message through to him so he asked his mother if there was a reason that his Dad would be hiding his watches. His mother said there would definitely be a reason and it was that they hadn't found his watch in his belongings yet and he would want that watch to go to someone special in the family.

His mother had been putting his Dad's belongings in a bag for charity, so it was lucky that William got the message to her in time. She searched through his belongings more closely. While in hospital, to keep it safe, Jackie had hidden his watch in his hearing aid case, that was in a jacket, that was in the bag, that was ready for the charity shop! Luckily William is a sensitive soul and his Dad was able to get through to him, that watch is an important heirloom to the family. Another fascinating twist on the story is that William's second watch that went missing, turned up only after his Dad's watch was found.

The Sister

Several years ago, Rhonda, a middle aged woman from Byron Bay, contacted me for a reading. When I was on the way to Rhonda's house I had similar feelings of excitement like when I was on my way to visit my friend Carol and her mother.

A female on the other side spoke the entire way to Rhonda's house, a journey of half an hour.

Normally I don't go to people's houses for readings, but this spirit had been so excited from the moment I began talking to Rhonda on the phone that I felt compelled to do a house visit. The spirit told me that she had recently died of cancer and that she was Rhonda's sister and best friend. She was so excited to speak to Rhonda through me, just like my friend Carol's Dad. She managed to get through clearly that day to Rhonda.

Rhonda confirmed that her sister, Jane had passed

away and she asked me to prove that Jane had been present in Rhonda's life during the few days before my visit. Jane showed me Rhonda cutting a loaf of homemade bread with her daughter the day before. Jane showed me that Rhonda had made a joke to her daughter that Jane would have loved the bread and said she might have even helped cook it!

Jane was indeed impressed with the bread and had been with her sister and niece while they were cooking and eating it. Jane was able to tell them that she was there, which was a wonderful gift to Rhonda. Rhonda said that although she could feel sister around her, she missed her terribly.

Rhonda confirmed that this is exactly what happened. She had indeed made the bread with her daughter the day before and had made that exact comment about Jane when they were making the bread!

Jane was then able to pass on a message for their cousin. She told me the cousin's name and that she wanted her to have something from her estate that looked like a lovely leather handbag. Rhonda confirmed that the following weekend they were dividing up her sister's estate and that they were trying to decide what to give that particular cousin. She said that the cousin had wanted some sort of item but they couldn't find it, so it was nice that Jane was able to tell her what to give her instead! Rhonda confirmed that there was a bag, fitting the description I gave, that they could give to their cousin.

Aunty Elizabeth/Lizzy

Many years ago, I met a remarkably humble and devout woman named Katie, who has since become a dear friend. In fact, she was actually Matron of Honour at my wedding to my Mick. At the time of our meeting, I immediately asked Katie if she knew Aunty

Elizabeth/Lizzy?

Instantly, Katie started crying and confirmed that her favourite aunt, Elizabeth, had passed over some time ago. A moment later I began to dance strangely and I felt compelled to sing in a funny sort of way as well. Katie confirmed that her aunty was seen as a bit strange because this is exactly what she would do! But she was just a fun person who loved rocking the boat here!

I also felt a strong desire to keep staring into the bottom of a nonexistent teacup in my hand. I didn't know why but it turned out that Aunty Elizabeth was a teacup reader. I was trying to read the leaves but not understanding what I was trying to do. Aunty Elizabeth was a very powerful person in spirit and she was Katie's favourite family member who had sheltered and cared for her in her youth. Because of their close relationship to each other, it made perfect sense to us that she came through as strongly as she did.

Dennis

Sometimes, like with Aunty Elizabeth, I will hear a name come through so loudly and clearly, it's as if we were being introduced. In fact, it's happened a few times where I have called a person by the wrong name because I have such a strong urge to call them something else. Usually I find out later that they had a very close deceased loved one with that name. I feel it's their angelic loved one getting through to me! The following little story is a most perfect example.

When I first went to live in Ireland, I used to go into this lovely little health store/cafe in Waterford City. There was a friendly chef named Steve, who worked at the café and I always enjoyed chatting with him and having a laugh. One day I said to him, "Steve, it's the strangest thing but whenever I see you, even though I know your name, I want to call you Dennis ... I just can't get the name Dennis out of my head."

He looked at me, amazed.

With a very astonished look on his face he told me that before he was born his parents had a son named Dennis who died at the age of two! I felt that Dennis was saying hello to his little brother.

The Brother

Brothers and family members really do love to get through to their living relatives.

When I was doing readings with the travelling holistic fair in Ireland, a man in his late twenties sat down in front of me. He looked very uncomfortable as he sheepishly said, "Do you see dead people?"

I replied, "If you are talking about your younger brother who died in an accident last year, then yes."

He was taken aback. He looked to be in shock.

I was able to tell him that his brother was a cheeky larrikin who loved making jokes and teasing everyone. He was the fun one, the life of the party. His death had left a horrible big hole in his brother's life and he was having trouble coping with the loss.

I explained that his brother was happy and enjoying his new 'work' on the other side, helping other people cope and adapt to their new environment. I sensed his brother had died in a work accident and this was confirmed. He was a builder and had fallen from a height. It all felt so senseless to the living brother, and I had to reassure him that it was his brother's time to go.

An hour or so later, a man and a woman sat down with me, and the lovely young man who had died in the accident returned to my mind. I immediately sensed the connection and said, "You are the parents of the boy; his brother was just here, and he has returned into my mind, you must be his parents."

The boy's father was obviously a disbeliever; it was almost impossible to get through to him. His mother wanted to believe so much but she was so grief stricken it was very hard for her.

Their son had died a year before but it was still like it was yesterday to them.

I was able to see him standing behind her in the kitchen and I saw how he used to pull lots of jokes on them and he really made their lives happy and joyous when he was alive. He showed me he was still there and that his mother thought he was around but she was so full of grief she couldn't hear him. He was able to tell me his pet name for her, which she confirmed and that seemed to brighten her up a bit.

It was more like a counselling session than a reading.

He tried to tell me other stuff but their grief was like a big brick wall blocking the channel between them. But there was enough information to lift them just enough and I am sure they went home knowing that he was present with them in their lives, just not in the same way as before.

I felt that he was going to be able to contact them through other psychics when their grief dissipated a little. I saw in my mind that they would seek another medium when they were ready. This precious young man was so funny, cheeky and happy; I can see why they missed him so.

But they weren't able to get on with their lives, and they weren't able to enjoy their living son. They also weren't able to hear their deceased son who was trying to get through to them. They couldn't hear him telling them that he was feeling alive and wonderful and that he loved them and wanted them to be happy! They couldn't appreciate his continuing life - though I hope that following the reading they were able to try to do so just a little. Grief is such a powerful thing; it can cut us off from living our life if we let it. Healing our heart starts with facing that grief and then using positive affirmations to start rebuilding our lives when the time is right for us. We can't rush it, the process of grief, but we can make it easier on ourselves by not making it harder with negative thoughts and statements such as "it's not fair", "he was too young", etc. In life there is so much we don't know about, his soul had a journey all its own, and we must all accept this for each other, for the ones that we love so much, including ourselves.

A Loving Son Contacts His Mother

Mick and I went to our friend's 60th birthday party. We sat with another couple, approximately twenty years older than us. Mick knew the man well through work and we both met his wife for the first time that night.

We were getting on very well with this lovely couple. I went to the bar to get Mick a drink, and while I was there I felt compelled to buy a certain drink that I had never heard of before. It was an imported brand of light beer, and though Mick had asked for Guinness (being Irish), I purchased the beer and went back to the table. Mick drank the beer and said it was an okay drink but he asked me not to buy it for him again. It wasn't totally his cup of tea as they say.

However, when I went back up to the bar, I felt like I had to buy that particular drink again. I actually found myself touching the middle of my forehead, the third eye, which I often find myself touching when I am sensing something. I told the bartender, "Something's telling me to get this drink, but I don't know why."

The bartender looked at me with a very perplexed look on her face and replied tentatively, "Okay."

It was only later, after purchasing the second drink

that the nice woman at my table told me it was her deceased son's favourite drink. He was a bartender/bouncer at a club and sadly he was murdered the year previously, protecting a young woman and her child from her angry ex-partner. During a confrontation, the woman's violent partner stabbed him directly in the heart.

She told me his name was Stuart, but I kept seeing love hearts in my mind's eye. I said, "He is saying his name is Luv... Luvy... Luvee?"

She couldn't believe it, because that was his nickname.

Apparently, when he was 'alive' he insisted on being called Lovee and love hearts were his thing. He showed me that at his funeral, butterflies were released and his mother confirmed this. Butterflies had become another sign for her that Lovee was around her.

She was a very spiritual woman and she always felt that he was with her, despite the death of his body. He was actually able to reminisce about old photos - very specific photos that he described to me, and tell her he was okay. She confirmed that these photos were real.

I was able to see him sitting next to us; his arm draped around her little shoulder. He was a very happy young man and he too was doing 'work' that he loved on the other side. He loved helping people when he was human and he loved helping them as a spirit.

He was also having a lot of fun; he just really enjoyed himself wherever he was! He loved the freedom that he had now as a free spirit. He was experiencing great things and loved the wind and the ocean and the feeling of a breeze as he could literally just fly through it. He gave me a feeling that he was the wind now. His mother and I shared that drink together, the second drink that he had influenced me to purchase. She said not only was it his favourite drink, but when he was out with his friends, he would never be seen without it! I had never even heard of it before that night so the chances of me buying two bottles of his favourite beer without his intervention were very slim, and like I said it was not the drink my husband had asked me to buy!

I said I could see a flashing blue light in her house and she confirmed that she did have blue lights but that they were on the blink as they kept flashing on and off. I assured her that they were not on the blink; that he was turning them on and off to get her attention!

When I visited her house for the first time sometime after first meeting her, he told me his mother had purchased a new dining table and chairs and showed me that he wouldn't be able to put his feet up on the table anymore. I meant to tell her but I forgot to say it straight away and then her husband told me that they had just bought a new dining table and chairs. It's somewhat disappointing for me when I see or hear something from spirit, but don't get to say it first before someone mentions it. It's a missed opportunity to let the family know the deceased person is actually hanging around.

This precious young man exists on the other side. While they will always miss him, this family is very spiritual and they have been shown the proof of Lovee's life after death and this helped them cope with his transition. He has not just come through to me but he also came through to another psychic woman that his sister visited.

His acceptance of love here while he was a human is also indicative of his beautiful angelic spiritual nature, he never forgot that love was the most important thing of all while he was here in his physical form.

Man! Husband!

Andrea, a woman I had never met before, rang for a reading and asked me if I could speak to people who had died. As she was asking me, a man was literally yelling at me inside my mind saying, "Man! Husband! Man! Husband!"

I told her that I was a medium and asked her if it was her husband who had died, because there was a man here yelling at me, "Man! Husband!"

We did the reading right then and there on the telephone. I couldn't remember most of what was said afterwards because I let him talk through me the whole time. I was present but removed somewhat, in a meditative trance, as I let him take over the conversation. Later Andrea said I told her what his name was but I had no recollection of doing that myself. I remember that he was talking about their writing and that she should continue doing it. They wrote about political matters and community concerns and he wanted her to make a difference to the world. She was following through with a lot of their projects and he was able to connect in with this.

When she visited me some time later for a reading at my house I had the strongest urge to have a pot of tea with her and set out a cup for him. It was not like a normal urge, but a spirit push. It was such a powerful feeling; it is hard to describe. It's similar to buying Luvee's brand of beer in the above story. When I said it to her she told me that her husband loved to have a pot of tea with her. He did it regularly throughout the day so it made perfect sense to her that he would get me to set it up.

Another time, just before she came in for a reading, he told me that she needed a massage. He asked me to give her shoulders a rub for him. We got into the reading and I told her what he said. She started crying because he was the only one in her life who would give her a little shoulder massage to ease her tension! From beyond, and through me, he was still able to give her one.

The Spitting Image of Her Mother

When Mick, Kia and I lived in Dolphin's Barn, Dublin City, we lived next door to a couple called Margaret and John. They were the salt of the earth, hard working people and while John's health kept him from working in his later years, Margaret still worked and would go off every day to catch her bus.

Margaret and John were very kind to us. They doted on our little girl Kia and they were excited when we brought her home from the hospital after she was born. They watched her grow and she often played in their back garden with their grandchildren.

Margaret had a wonderfully nasal inner-city Dublin accent and she would laughingly call Kia "Nosey Rosey" because Kia loved to look over the fence and get their attention. John kept pigeons, which Kia found fascinating.

On the day I told Margaret that I was a psychic, her mother came through to me. She was the spitting image of Margaret; they were like two peas in a pod. She spoke exactly the same way as Margaret did too and they were both hard-working women. In fact, they were almost like twins in manner and looks - they were so similar!

Margaret confirmed this with tears in her eyes, and there was a brief reunion of mother and daughter. It was so special to be able to do that for her because Margaret missed her mother so very much. There wasn't much to tell Margaret, as her mother had been gone a long time, but I felt blessed that her mother was able to get through to me that day. It wasn't so much the words that I could hear, but rather, feelings and impressions of their similarity, which enabled Margaret to recognise that it was her mother. I was able to share my gift and in turn, Margaret could feel her mother's ongoing love for her.

The Grandfather Visit

On the way to my friend Jill's house for a much needed massage, I saw Jill in my mind's eye. She was in her kitchen and standing to her right was a Black African man doing some sort of dancing ceremony. He looked like an elder medicine man powerful and strong. This was interesting as Jill is a Caucasian Australian, with Italian and Irish ancestry. I had no idea why this man would be next to her!

When I got to Jill's house she was in the kitchen as I saw in the vision. However, standing beside her, to her right, was an African woman that I knew. Her name was Salina, but I didn't know that Jill knew her, and so did not expect to see her there at Jill's house.

Later when we sat and spoke, I described my vision. Salina told me that the man I described was her Grandfather who was indeed the leader and medicine man of their tribe. He had come to visit her that day to give her strength for her challenging journey ahead.

On the way to Jill's that day I also kept thinking, "I have to go to Ballina." Ballina is a town located 45 minutes away from where I live, and I didn't actually need to go there but as usual I knew that I would probably find out why I was thinking and feeling the way I was.

When I got to Jill's, not only was Salina's grandfather getting through, but her thoughts had gotten through to me as well. While we were sitting at the table she said, "I have to go to Ballina."

I looked at her and said, "Oh that is why I thought I had to go there. Even though I don't have to go I will take you if you need me to."

She didn't take me up on my offer, but I just wanted to include this example because it makes me wonder how often we are influenced by other people's thoughts!

Readings Help Heal Grief

A friend asked me to see a young woman, Melanie, whose boyfriend had suicided. Melanie was experiencing profound grief and had feelings that she should join him. It was a difficult situation for everyone involved. The young man, Sam, was, by everyone's account, a happy, fun loving and vivacious person. He got in with the wrong crowd and went overseas with them on a holiday. He got involved in activities that he was ashamed of and he came home and couldn't live with what he had done. There were drugs and alcohol involved also.

Melanie knew that Sam had been about to propose to her before he left for his trip, but when he came back he was a changed person, haunted by things he had done while on holidays. She couldn't save Sam and he wouldn't talk to her about his problems.

I went to her house to visit her and I let Sam take over my body during the reading so he could let me know how he felt and what he was doing that led to his death. He was a very active spirit because he was an active person. He had a beautiful brightness to his spirit, a happiness that was delightful. But he showed me his pain and shame over his behaviour. It involved sexual activities and a sexually transmitted disease contracted while on his holidays. This is a very difficult thing to share of course and he couldn't talk about it with Melanie when he was alive he felt so awful about it all.

He was going to make amends on the other side he told us. He was working hard to help her and to help others. He had to work through what he had done. He didn't want Melanie to suffer but he knew she was. He needed her to know it was not her fault. He shared some stories that only she could know about. I actually can't remember them well enough to recount them because I didn't write them down straight afterwards and I was in a completely altered meditative state.

I continued to support Melanie for some time after that until she was able to regain her life back. She learnt to live without him, though she would never forget him. She had a new job, new friends and new purpose in life. To cope with her grief, she had to let herself experience it, feel the pain of loss. With time, and love and support from those around her, and the adoption of new ways of thinking and coping with life, Melanie found her way.

There was a little bit more to the story however. Not long after seeing Melanie the first time I was driving along on my way home when suddenly I felt different. Although I drove along that particular stretch of road all the time to get home, I did not recognise it. It felt like I was somewhere completely new and exhilarating! I was euphoric and super excited. I looked at my hands on the steering wheel and they felt foreign. Suddenly I knew what was happening. I felt Sam's thoughts and energy. I saw him in my mind and I knew that he had come into my body unannounced to experience life in a body again.

He had enjoyed inhabiting a physical body during the reading with Melanie. So when I was driving, he did it again, but this time I had not invited him to do so.

As soon as I realised what had happened I spoke to him in my mind and told him that it was not acceptable for him to come into my body and use it for himself without my permission or awareness. He did not realise that it was inappropriate to do so. Perhaps he thought I wouldn't realise that he was there and he could go on a joy ride in my body. However, I was very aware of his presence.

Sometime later, I can't remember exactly how long, a month or two later, I was again driving when I had the same sensation. I felt completely unfamiliar with my whereabouts and felt the same feelings of excitement like I'd experienced previously. I felt so happy to be alive! I realised it was Sam almost immediately, but before I had a chance to communicate with him, he left almost as soon as he came in. I could feel that he realised it was wrong and he left me alone. I felt he wouldn't do it again. It's been years and I have never experienced this sensation again.

My Father Helps Me Make a Decision

A few years after his physical passing, my father came strongly into my mind. I had been asleep but was on the verge of waking when he came directly into my consciousness to tell me something important.

He was very serious and he showed me a cross in front of him, not like a spiritual catholic cross but an X, like a no. Just prior to his visit, I had been trying to decide whether or not to post a particular letter. My father was able to tell me that it would be the wrong thing to do and in fact, he was absolutely right. To send the letter in that particular form would have invited trouble into my life and he was able to strongly discourage me from sending it. It was such a relief to have his guidance and wonderfully reassuring that he is still able to help me from the other side.

My father passed away in December 2008 though he often visits me, particularly in my dreams. Although his physical earthly body is gone, we still have a very special and important continuing relationship.

He also came through to let me know my mother was sick and needed my help! While gardening, my mother had gotten a bite or a scratch on her leg that had turned bad.

The wound would not heal and it appeared to be turning into a flesh eating disease. It was festering and constantly infected for months and months. Medical treatments and antibiotics were not working.

As I live twenty hours or so away by car, I don't get to visit my mother very often (Australia is a huge country!). On the phone she had downplayed just how bad the wound was, as mothers do about anything to do with themselves! She didn't want me to worry about her.

Without my father's reminder in a very powerful dream I would have believed that everything was okay. He showed me that he would be meeting her when she went over the cliff on a tractor (he was a mechanic in this life)! I knew then that she was ill and it would be her downfall if we didn't act.

When I rang her after the dream, she confirmed that everything was not okay. I jumped immediately to action to help her and did not delay because he made me realise just how important it was that I provide help to her.

I went straight to the local Herbal Store in Mullumbimby and asked them what might help her. They said if it was a spider bite it was a very dangerous thing to happen and that it needed attending to as a matter of urgency. They recommended a potent tree sap containing a mixture of powerful antiseptic, antifungal and antibiotic properties. It was called Dragon's Blood, though obviously not real dragon's blood but just as powerful!

My mother didn't use much of the ointment because she felt it was burning her leg – she hated the stuff! Nevertheless, after using only a small amount, the wound did heal up! Now she just has a nasty red scar, which is much better than a festering flesh eating wound!

Without my Dad's intervention I don't know what would have happened to my Mum, but I have an inkling the ending wouldn't have been so positive. I'm so grateful to my Dad for getting through to me and I'm also grateful to myself for listening.

Another time I asked my father to give me guidance on my work and what I should be doing. That night I had the most powerful dream that contained him and several other powerful spirits I had known when they were alive. One being the amazingly gifted neuropsychology professor I had at university Dr Jocelyn (Jo) Wale, who passed away quickly following a late-stage cancer diagnosis. My Dad said that he would be there for me while I started working again, Jo was looking at me from across a table where she was doing neuropsychological testing like she had taught me twenty years previously. He said they would look after my youngest son and make sure he was looked after when I went to work. He walked up a long flight of steps and I asked if he could get up them ok? When he was alive Dad had lost his left foot in a motorbike accident in his twenties, and in later life found getting around difficult even on his wooden leg. He assured me he could and he would get up them to help me. I woke up crying that morning it was so real, and then my mobile phone rang and it was a woman asking for a counselling session. I had lined up to do my counselling at a practice that had a long flight of stairs. My Dad came to tell me to do it, re-start my practice up. So I did.

More About My Dad
And His Messages From The Other Side

Sometimes if you speak through your thoughts to a loved one who has passed, they can give you messages in interesting ways. One day when I felt my father in the room with me, I started a dialogue with him in my mind. I felt him urge me to open a book that I had recently borrowed from the library but hadn't read yet. I actually had the book in a bag with lots of other books that I was returning as I had borrowed too many and didn't think I'd get a chance to read them all. He told me to look through the books and when I got to the book in question he told me to stop and open it.

I started flicking randomly through the book until my energy told me to open it to a particular page. I read no other stories in the book prior to this story. On the page I opened to was a story about a father who died. He went through a tunnel and was met by loved ones, but then was revived by the medical emergency team. When he woke he was able to tell his children not to be scared to die. When he did die sometime later, they knew not to be scared at all and they knew he was still with them and with his loved ones in the afterlife. Of all of the pages for me to open this was the most significant for me as no other stories in the book were like this.

This was the story my father wanted me to read. I got the message, loud and clear and it really helped my heart and mind so much. I listened and then I acted, I followed through with his prompting. Had I failed to go with my strong feeling to open the book, and ignored or doubted that he was present and what he was telling me to do, I would have missed this beautiful message. So although the doctors didn't revive my father like the father in the story, my father was still able to return and tell me not to be scared. He used the story to help me heal from the grief of his body's physical death.

Another time, I was on holidays on the Sunshine Coast in Queensland with Mick and our children, Kia and Orin. I took a moment to relax on a recliner in the sunshine to warm up after being in the pool. As we were enjoying looking at the flowering grasses swaying in the wind, I suddenly felt my Dad with me. I said to him, give me a sign that you are here. He showed me in my mind the image of a bird. Ok, I said, show me a bird, something significant and then I will know you are here. There weren't a lot of birds around; we were in suburbia, in a big hotel complex with a massive water park and lots of concrete. But I knew to look out for something special, not just a bird flying over -head but for something more substantial.

A few minutes later Mick and the kids came back. They were finished playing in the awesome hotel water playground, and Orin started yelling, "It's a bird, a bird!"

I turned to see Orin chasing after a black and white bird that was running on the ground! It was a funny sight and it was without a doubt my Dad's little message to me. I told Mick what had happened, that my Dad was going to give me a bird sign, and I felt teary and very happy at the same time. My Dad always did have the best sense of humour!

Listen to the Angels to Protect Others

Another big lesson for me is to listen and to follow through with what I am told. Sometimes however I don't seem to listen to the angels, I test what I am hearing – especially if I don't think there will be any dangerous consequences.

I was cleaning out the family car when I saw my son's bouncy ball and thought it would be nice for him to play with. As I threw it out of the car, I heard a female spirit tell me to leave the ball in the car. Instead I kicked it towards the garage.

Then the spirit told me to leave it in the garage.

I saw in my mind that Mick might kick a pretend goal with it for fun as he loves soccer and playing with our young son.

But when I went to kick it into the yard it fell by the side of the gate. She told me to leave it there. But I picked it up and put it in the yard. I remember staring at the ball and feeling energy around it but I decided to leave it there to see what happened. It certainly didn't feel like particularly bad energy to me at the time and by bad I mean that someone would die or anything tragic like that!

The woman stopped talking.

The next morning, I was in the kitchen when Mick jumped in on one foot, holding the other foot with his hands. He was moaning in obvious pain. I asked him what happened, I had just seen him a few minutes before walking out to the front of the house and he was fine!

He said he was daydreaming about kicking a winning goal for Ireland in the world cup (he's very cute my husband) and he kicked the ball, scored his goal and twisted his ankle as it came down on the uneven ground. He said he couldn't move for a few minutes because of the pain, but he managed to get up and make it to the kitchen for some treatment (and attention!).

His ankle was pretty sore for a few weeks, and black and blue for a few days. He is a musician who plays several instruments at once, including a foot stomp, but luckily he was still able to play so he could go to work, even though he was in a bit of pain.

I made a choice to bring that ball into the yard despite the voice telling me not to.

I am learning all the time about this psychic sense. Mick didn't blame me at all, but said he should have been more careful on such uneven ground. I do wish I had listened so that he didn't get hurt, but there is a part of me that is glad I tested the voice (hopefully Mick will forgive me for saying that!).

I learnt that I must listen in the future, and even though I might not ever be able to prove what has been avoided, I will always know in my heart that I prevented someone being hurt or something unfortunate happening. I will always be very grateful for the guidance those on the other side give us for the big AND the small things that happen in life.

Driving, Angels and Speeding Tickets!

I'm so happy when the angels can get through, but I

have to really be calm especially when I am out and about living my own life. Once my friend's deceased father got through to me when I was driving and I got a speeding fine! I stopped to send her a text about his message and I sped off doing 60km/hr. forgetting that the limit was 50km/hr. and the speed camera was just up ahead!

Another time a friend's mother got through to me with a health warning for him and I totally missed a change in speed sign. Again, I was only just over the limit but I got a ticket from a policeman who just happened to be close by!

It made me really aware of being in that mind space where the angels can get through easily, particularly while driving or doing things that are more automated for the mind and body. I am much more careful now.

I wasn't doing much over the speed limit or driving dangerously, however rules are rules. It's not a good excuse, "Sorry officer my friend's father who just passed away was telling me an important message - it won't happen again Sir."

"No worries Miss, great job you're doing there, go about your business then, I'll let you off today!"

No it's just not a good excuse at all!

The spirits get excited they can get through to us, just like we do, and it makes my physical system, particularly the area around my chest shake a little and I get nervous type sensations. My mind can race with all the thoughts and the things they want to say, so I have to be calm and for that reason I don't really drink alcohol or have too many stimulants in the way of caffeine (although I do love my Irish tea and a generous smacking of good chocolate!).

I believe the body is an important source of information and the barometer of our soul. If the body is clear, strong and healthy we are much better able to get good reception with those we love on other side.

An Angel Saves My Friend's Baby

I was heading towards my home in Dolphin's Barn, on the canal in Dublin City, Ireland. I heard a spiritual being telling me to turn around and visit my friend, and in my own body I felt that she was sick. When I got to her house she was indeed ill from the flu but there was something else also. She confided in me she had just found out she was pregnant. She already had several children and wasn't planning any more. She confessed that she was thinking of getting an abortion.

From the moment she said it, a male spirit came to me. He was so beautiful and gentle, the essence of pure love. It felt like he was meant to be here.

I saw how much he would add love and solidity to the family and how much my friend would adore him. He would complete her in a way she couldn't yet imagine. The spirits had sent me to her that day and then they spoke through me.

I told her about the beauty of her son's spirit and how I was sure he was meant to be here. I told her how he would complete the family and how incredibly beautiful inside and out this baby was and how much she would adore him. For a few days I kept in touch and I kept saying firmly what I believed and felt to be true. I am sure I was annoying. It was as if those on the other side were pushing me to do this.

I even went as far as saying that I would even raise him if she would just give birth to him. I actually felt at the time that she wouldn't really get an abortion, I had seen him playing with his siblings in my mind, but I had to speak up for him just in case, when he couldn't yet do so. My friend decided to keep the baby and he is a lot older now.

He is the most beautiful child, gentle, loving, intelligent and so happy. His family adores him and, just like I promised, he was the perfect addition to complete their beautiful family. He is the apple of her eye and he has made her the happiest woman, his smile just lights her up. When I hear of how he is going now I feel like a proud aunty and tears well in my eyes. I love this little boy very much and so do his family; they are so grateful that he came into their lives; just like a gift from the stars.

Donna

I had a dear friend named Donna. She lived in Drogheda in Ireland. She had the most beautiful philosophy on life. She loved children and angels. She used to say, "Follow the children, they lead you to the truth."

She once followed my little one-year-old girl around and around her house, countless times, while she pushed a little baby pram, giving Mick and I a well-deserved break. Donna was so full of love and acceptance of others. She read tarot and angel cards and worked in a gift shop.

She worked hard to pay her bills and didn't have a partner, though she had a daughter and grandchildren who she loved dearly. She rang me once and we had a long chat. During that chat she told me that she felt like something was wrong with her but she couldn't grasp what it was. A female spirit spoke to me in my mind and told me that Donna, my sweet friend, was very sick and that we didn't realise how sick she really was.

When Donna asked me if she was going to be rich, the spirit told me to tell her that she would be really rich, surrounded with such deep love and abundance within the year. She was very happy when told about the love and abundance, though I meant it was spiritual love and abundance, not earthly love or monetary gain.

Spirit showed me that her illness was too far

progressed to heal and that it was her time and not to interfere. I was told not to tell her about her impending death. To do so would have been like 'pointing a bone at her' and a very negative thing to do to her.

They showed me that this illness was Donna's porthole into the next life and while the earthly human side of her may have feared this, it was her soul's chosen journey. The spirit showed me that Donna, who believed very much in angels and God, would be completely surrounded by her angel brothers and sisters and experience deep love, healing and happiness on the other side.

This was a hard one for me, because I know of our human attachment to our physical life here, but I loved Donna so dearly and knew it was not my place to interfere with her soul's journey.

I grappled with my role, just as I had to with my friend Peter and his unborn baby, but I know I did the right thing by my friend when I gave her hope and filled her with the love of the angels that she adored so much. She has since confirmed this to me in spirit and helped me when I needed it by giving me advice at just the right time. I still have a beautiful scarf that she gave me as a birthday present and I will always treasure it with all my heart and I can still always feel her wisdom and her love shining through to me and to her family.

A Stranger Sends a Father's Love

I was walking along the River Liffey in the heart of Dublin. I walked past three people sitting on a bench overlooking the river when a male voice spoke clearly in my head, "Please tell them I am ok and I love them."

I turned around, even though I felt shy and a bit silly, walked up to them, and said something like, "I just have to say there is a man here and I can hear him, I think he is your husband and your Dad and he has just died. He told me to say that he is okay and that he loves you and not to worry please."

The three people, a woman in her fifties, and two teenagers just started crying and hugging and nodding at me. The woman, obviously their mother said thank you several times. I walked away leaving them knowing that their father and husband was actually right at their feet, trying to console them all and show them he was there. I can see him right now, where he was in my mind's eye, kneeling before them.

My Friend's Mother Visits Often From The Other Side

The mother of one of my best friend's passed away when we were in our early twenties. I loved this woman dearly; she was not just Despina's mum but my friend also and she had been my favourite teacher at high school for many years.

I had settled in Ireland by this stage and my friend, Despina, and I spoke every few months but we both had busy lives so we didn't speak often or regularly. One night her mother came to me in a dream and told me that I had to contact Despina as she and her partner were having issues and she needed my support. Sure enough when I contacted Despina the next day she said she had a fight with her partner and we had a big heart to heart that helped her immensely; knowing that her mother was looking out for her helped also.

Another time, again in a dream, her mother came to me and blew out candles on a cake. She said it was her birthday and that Despina was sad because her mother was not alive to celebrate it. I rang my friend and before I could say anything she blurted out that it was her mother's birthday and she was sad.

Another night I had a powerful dream that Despina

and her mother were shopping and hanging out together. I rang Despina to tell her and I never forgot it when Despina told me that this is what she had been dreaming of too!

Her mother hadn't left her at all! She was such a special woman here on this earth, a great teacher who treated her students and everyone around her with such respect and love. She instilled a passion for drama and English in her students and encouraged us and built up our self-esteem and sense of worth. She was everyone's favourite teacher and she is still guiding us now from the other side.

Our deceased loved ones are powerful spiritual beings now that they are on the 'other side'. They will come to help us when we ask them to. It's truly a beautiful and inspiring thing to see them and witness their continued existence and their love for us.

Jog

For some time, I kept hearing in my head and feeling in my body that I should jog. I had gotten out of the habit of regular exercise after my second pregnancy – I was so sick that I could hardly move for much of it. Several years on however I was feeling the urge to jog and I talked to my friends and family about my desire and explained how I was building up my jogging/walking a little bit at a time. I was occasionally going to the beach and alternating jogging and walking and sometimes if I didn't feel like driving anywhere I was jogging and walking down my long driveway. However, while I jogged a little here and there, I wasn't really committed, at least not until the moment where the angels definitely told me to jog!

This is how they did it.

I was driving home on the highway after dropping my husband off at the Gold Coast airport. I was thinking about how I really wanted to exercise but questioned whether jogging was the answer and I asked myself what I should do. At that precise moment a car passed in front of me, and the letters on the license plate said J.O.G! Wow! It was definitely a sign from my angels and I remember smiling non-stop and feeling so amazed and touched! I couldn't believe they had managed to pull off this scenario it was so amazing! Absolutely incredible!

CWA

Several weeks after the J.O.G. number plate incident, my family and I were driving on a busy stretch of highway into Brisbane. Mick was driving and I took the time to relax in the passenger seat. As I sat there staring out at the road, I heard a female spirit voice whisper in my left ear, "The answer to one of your issues." Before she had finished speaking I felt directed to look at the number plate of the car directly to the right of us. I turned my head just enough to read the letters CWA.

In Australia the initials CWA stands for Country Women's Association, which is a not for profit organization run by women in rural country towns. The women involved in a CWA often knit baby clothes and bake cakes to raise money for local charities. For the previous year I had been writing down ideas about creating a CWA in my local village! I would daydream about what we would call our CWA, and make lists of things we could do together – from sewing to baking, babysitting and so forth.

So once again, the angels were able to send me a powerful, tangible and much needed message to confirm I was on the right path. I must say that while I didn't formally start the CWA, I did make more of an attempt to be closer to my girlfriends and for us to support one other in our local area. Sometimes the angel's messages are not intended to be literal but rather, they are metaphoric or symbolic confirmations. At the time I felt that the term CWA was a message to band together with my fellow neighbourhood women because there's no doubt, we need each other to feel happy and supported in this life.

Amanda

I was driving around Byron Bay, thinking about a teenage novel I was writing about a psychic girl and her friends at school. I was actually thinking about whether I should name the psychic character, Amanda, after myself, since she was based on me, or whether I should name her something else. At this exact moment I slowed down for a pedestrian crossing and two girls yelled out from the footpath to their friend who was on the other side of the street.

I'm sure you can guess what the girls yelled out – remembering it was at the exact same time I had asked myself about the main character's name in my fiction novel.

They called out very loudly to their friend so they could be heard above the busy traffic, "AMANDA, AMANDA!"

As you can imagine, I looked at the girls in absolute astonishment! In order to be heard, the girls had to call out across the path of my car and the answer had traveled directly into my open car window as if they were directly responding to my thought! If the spirit world wants to get through to you, they will find a way!

This is the magic of the angelic realm; and an example of our angelic brothers and sisters on the 'other side' giving us direct answers to direct questions. They put us, the two young women and I, in the right place at the right time to fulfill two important roles – one to answer my question, the other to get their friend's attention.

Some people like to call such things coincidence but I have obviously experienced way too much to call this a simple coincidence. There is an amazing interplay between human and angelic beings and they can help us in incredible ways if we are just open to listening.

While it is my choice to decide whether or not to listen, I have decided that when I write the fictional version of my memoir, the main character's name will definitely be Amanda!

Angels Come Through When I Get Healing Therapy!

I love getting massages and healing work done on my body. When I relax the spirits can get through to me more easily and because I am not busy, my mind is in an altered relaxed state and I can hear them more clearly!

I was receiving a wonderful healing from an amazing practitioner, John Carty, based in Crumlin, Dublin. His Endorphin Release Therapy technique is somewhat revolutionising our approach to healing pain. His mother who had passed away only recently came through during the healing and was able to give him some comfort. She absolutely loved flowers and during the healing I was inundated by the scent and sight of flowers in my mind! I shared her visit with him and he then refused to charge me for the healing!

Another time I was in Lucan, Dublin receiving Amatsu, which is a Japanese art of body alignment and healing. During the treatment, the healer's grandfather came through to me and showed me a silver box. She told me that he used to carry that silver box everywhere with him and that it contained his tobacco. It was a very specific and recognisable personal object to show me to prove to his granddaughter that he was here.

In a beautiful state of trust and relaxation, the

communication with the other side is even clearer. So relaxation can really help us to tap into the other side, just a reminder if you want to improve your communication flow with those you love on the other side.

Chapter 3 Exercise:
Connecting with your loved ones in spirit.

- We ask the divine to bless us and allow only positive energy to come into our lives. We ask for protection and guidance at all times. Only positive spiritual energies are allowed into our energy sphere and lives.
- Take a few moments to relax your mind and body. Let yourself feel at one with everything and everyone, and feel safe, loved and calm. Just feel the breath going in and out of your body and feel grateful for being alive at this moment in time.
- Take a few beautiful, deep breaths in. Breathe in positivity and all things good from the universe and divine spirit. Breathe out anything that no longer serves you. Breathe in positivity and breathe out negativity. Do this several times until you feel relaxed and calm.
- After you feel peaceful, relaxed and calm, think of your loved one on the other side that you would like to connect with. Send them love and positive thoughts. Picture them in your mind; perhaps think of them sitting across the table from you or next to you. Then start a conversation with them, say something you want to tell them and pause for a moment. You may hear them respond in the form of a thought or a vision or even in the

form of a hug.

- Continue this as if you were having a conversation with them and they were responding to you just as they would if they were here. Let this free flow, don't try to control it or make anything happen. Just let it happen if it does. You might just see the person standing there with you or hugging you. They might say a word or two or just smile. They might show you something symbolic or you might sense or feel something.

- If you can't picture them at all, hold a photograph or envisage a past positive memory such as them smiling at you at your birthday party or something that you can remember clearly.

- Tell them you love them and hope they are happy and safe and if you want you can ask them a question and see how they answer – it might be in a thought, a word, a feeling, or afterwards in a dream or vision.

- Know that if it can't happen clearly right now that this is okay, say to them that you might see them in your dreams and then look out for them there.

- Sometimes they are present and you will feel them strongly or see them in your mind very clearly, other times you might just feel a sense of peace and calm, know that there is no right or wrong and that on some level, perhaps in your sleep and dreams you will have a visit with your loved one.

- Just let this unfold and relax within it. Nothing can happen that will hurt you. Know that God and the angels protect you at all times, see yourself as protected by their loving sacred light.

- Close your meditation with a grounding exercise like in Chapter 2: Peacefully ground to the earth that sustains us. In your mind's eye picture that you have beautiful tendrils or tree-like roots connecting you to the earth. These energizing tendrils can be any colour or form you wish; they could be green like tree roots or silver thread or red soil or even pretty ribbons. Whatever helps you to ground to the earth while you simultaneously feel the love and joy and energizing light of the angels is the right thing for you. We feel the breath as it slowly goes in and out of our body. We draw beautiful energy and breath from the earth up into our feet and into our bodies, it goes up through the top of our head to the divine, then the divine sends the healing breath and light back into our bodies and down into the earth. Do this several times and finish when you feel centred and calm, grounded and peaceful.

- Open your eyes and feeling grateful and calm, thank your loved one and the divine for this beautiful connection.

Know when you do this meditation that all life is sacred and special and beautiful. All of our lives are to be entwined and interconnected for a long time to come so there is no pressure or stress, we are eternal beings, we are playing and experiencing here, we will see each other again, now, in dreams, and in the future when we are in our own spirit form.

Know that there is no real divide, only the illusion of one. Remember our spirit family and friends want the best for us and to keep living so that we complete our life's journey to the best of our ability. They understand we grieve, but they don't want us to dwell in negative thoughts, emotions or behaviours. They want us to prosper and go into a future that is of our making, to help others and partake in the bigger plan of life.

Go back into your day, safely, calmly, feeling happy and at peace that you have connected in with your loved ones in the spiritual realm.

AMANDA McHUGH

CHAPTER 4

Examples Of Psychic Readings

SEVERAL YEARS AGO I WENT TO THE MELBOURNE COMEDY FESTIVAL to a show that I was particularly interested in because the comedian was also a psychic. Her show was one-part psychic readings for the audience and the other part comedy. She had an intriguing story to tell. She told us that she became psychic following surgery after a stroke. She said that she was not aware of a psychic gift before the stroke and surgery.

I was seated in the second row of the small theatre. From the outset the comedian was very funny, but there was also something about her, a certain vibration. I could feel with my own psychic gift that she was reading the energy around us all and of the spirit world. She was a very aware person. Furthermore, though I was trying to deny it because I didn't want to sound self-important or grandiose, I could actually feel her energy reading me specifically.

She started to get a bit nervous when speaking and then she stared right at me and said in front of everyone, "I can't do this in front of you. It is like I am a student in front of my college professor; you are an incredible psychic."

This was definitely not a part of the show!

Everyone turned to look at me and I confirmed that yes, I was a psychic. We spoke back and forth a bit and I said that I saw black rubbish bags that were somehow related to her deceased mother. The psychic comedian confirmed that black rubbish bags were important to her mother.

As you can appreciate seeing black rubbish bags is a 'unique' and very particular sort of thing to see and not something one normally says in a reading! This was very relevant as it was something her mother used to collect. I saw her mother's mental illness, which she also confirmed.

Towards the end of her comedy show she normally did a few readings for people through some funny tarot cards she had devised, however she said she couldn't do them that night because I was in the room. I told her not to worry but she was very affected by my presence. She was definitely a psychic, no doubt about it, and it was incredible how she managed to single me out from the eighty odd people in the room. She just knew that I had a powerful psychic gift.

We spent some time talking after the show and connected on a spiritual level. To me, this situation was astounding evidence that we are in connection with a higher source of information and with something innate and powerful.

Formal Readings

I have given professional readings to people who have questions about the past, present and future. Sometimes I help people understand energy in their life that has become stuck in the past and how that continues to affect them. They might want to communicate with their deceased loved ones and I am able to provide this link for them.

Sometimes readings are just accidental and they happen when I am out and about living my life. I could be just walking along and a deceased spirit person will speak to me and ask me to give a message to a stranger that is in my vicinity. I could be in my kitchen or in my car and I will see something that is going to happen to me or to someone I know or a person in spirit will contact me to give a message to their loved one.

Formal psychic readings, where someone sits across from me and asks for a reading to be done, are a snippet of energy and information for the person at that particular time. I do my best at each and every reading to be of service to that person and to the guides/angels/spirits who are trying to help us.

I've had funny things happen like the person coming for the reading really wants to get through to a particular person in the spirit world, but a different spirit person will come through to give a message to somebody else that the person getting the reading knows, like their friend or sister in law or something like that. The spirit world doesn't always present itself the way we are hoping it will.

The intention for the reading is usually set at the outset with the lighting of a candle, the holding of hands if appropriate, and a prayer to the God, Divine Source, angels, ancestors and our spirit family asking for information for the highest good of this person, to help them here in this physical world. I will often clang my Tibetan bell or cymbals to help me shift my gaze from this world to the next. I also like to hold crystals, particularly rose quartz, amethyst and clear quartz which have the effect of amplifying the spiritual connection also.

So, even before the person comes for the reading I set the scene in my home or workplace by bringing love into my heart through prayer and thanksgiving. As I have said before, a meditative, peaceful and loving mindset strengthens the gap between our world and the invisible spiritual world.

Before I do readings sometimes I also meditate on who might be coming in. A lot of the time I won't know a thing about the person I am about to read, however a psychic can still scan and find out a lot of information about and for that person. When I do this and get impressions about the people coming in, the impressions tend to be accurate. Their loved ones in spirit might even come to visit me before the person comes in for the reading. I will take notes if they do so I don't forget their messages. I have read that other psychic mediums sometimes do this also.

I am a trained psychologist as well as a psychic, so validity and professional, ethical practice are important to me. I will validate the reading, by making a mental or a physical checklist of accuracy when people confirm the information given in the reading. There is only one person in my whole seventeen years or so of doing these readings formally that complained, but it was funny because even before her reading, a spirit came and told me she wouldn't like anything I said and wouldn't be happy because that's how she was about everything!

I have seen firsthand the amazing natural and unfolding psychic events in real life, which to me are second to none. These incidents can be validated by the fact that I give people, often strangers, highly accurate information about themselves, their lives and loved ones, that by everyday 'normal' standards I should not have been able to give them.

Following are some other examples of readings that I have done. I've tried to stick to telling the bare bones of the reading or the main thing that stood out in the reading to me at the time. Readings often take an hour, but some can be much longer because I generally operate on divine timing and will let the session run its natural course when I have the time to do so.

In this category, I would also include the story about the twin girls that I told you about in the first chapter, as I saw them in a formal reading at their mother's house. I won't repeat the story here of course but it's an important one to keep in mind as we go about our daily lives, its irrefutable proof that there's so much more going on in the world at any one time than we are consciously aware of.

Books, Books and More Books!

I was doing psychic readings at a holistic fair in Ireland when a striking silver haired lady sat down for a reading. She looked to be at least in her seventies but she was very spritely and felt like she had the energy of pixies and fairies all around her. I immediately said to her, "Books, books and more books".

She smiled and said that she was a writer and she was writing a series that would be comprised of seven separate books! With a knowing smile she said to me, "I hope to be finished the series before I die!"

I felt like I was beside an Irish fairy woman who was a living national treasure!

What do a Baby, Singapore and a Pilot have in common?

Lydia came to my house for a reading and Osho immediately came through for her. Osho was a contemporary Indian mystic and philosopher who died in 1990, aged fifty-eight.

He was a controversial figure who espoused unconventional views; he was outspoken against socialism and established religion and was an advocate for meditation, love, creativity, dance and humour.

He had a group of followers who lived with him in communities for many years of his life and Lydia was one of them. He was so clear and strong in my mind. He told me to say that I could see the words baby, Singapore and pilot all together and to ask what that could possibly mean.

Lydia said that she was doing a project in Singapore with a pilot and that the project was in its infancy. She said she called the project her baby!

The Engagement

I was working at another holistic fair in Ireland when a beautiful young woman, Yvonne (pronounced 'Evon') sat down beside me. She had stunning bright blue eyes, a fantastic big smile, gorgeous skin and long blonde hair. She was really open and happy to be getting a reading. Yvonne sat down and it was like reading an open book. I immediately saw a stunning large shining engagement ring on her finger. To me it was so real I thought it was already on her finger and I asked her if I could look at it!

However, Yvonne was adamant that she and her boyfriend were not getting engaged and she said they had never even discussed it. I also told Yvonne that I could see tickets to Spain, which she also refuted. I saw some stuff at her workplace, things she was able to agree with, though unfortunately because she didn't believe that she was to be engaged shortly or that there was a Spain trip to follow, her energy started to close down on me. She didn't look at me with such love, respect or gratitude as she had when she had first sat down, when she had been initially open and excited.

At the end of the reading I told Yvonne that I knew she wasn't happy, but that I would charge her the full amount because I knew these things were going to happen. I then proceeded to apologise to her because I said I had ruined the biggest surprises of her life.

About a week or so later she rang me and said, "I don't know if you remember me?"

Even as the phone rang, I knew immediately who it would be, a picture of her face came distinctly into my mind and I told her so. She proceeded to tell me that everything I had seen had come true. Her boyfriend had the engagement ring and the tickets to Spain hiding in a cupboard at home, planning to surprise her with them!

This lovely young woman wanted to send all of her workmates and family to see me however I was moving to Australia and had pretty much packed up my house. I agreed to see her mother before I left though because I felt she really needed it.

Her mother was one of those examples of people where anxiety and fear and worry affected her ability to enjoy her life and her loved ones. She was so scared they were going to die or that something was wrong with them. Her reading was focused on this, on helping her to release her worry and live her life to the full.

This is what the angels wanted for her and what they want for all of us. When we live in constant fear and worry like this woman, we fail to enjoy what we have when we have it. We fail then to also hear our beloveds on the other side. We all must die and leave this particular incarnation at some time, there is nothing to fear, so why not enjoy our time here with our remaining loved ones? I know it's hard, we love our family members so much, but we will see them again I assure you!

Doing a Reading About the Readings

In Dublin city, I used to do readings in a trendy coffee shop in Rathmines. I loved doing the readings there, amongst the gorgeous smells and the great atmosphere of that cafe, which just happened to be my favourite hangout as I lived just around the corner. I had developed a bit of a party trick with these readings.

Before people would come in for readings I would sit and think about the evening ahead. I would do a reading before the readings and write down who was coming in. One afternoon I wrote a page of notes about three girlfriends who would be coming in that night.

When they sat down with me, I said, "Oh this is you three," and read from the notes I had made.

They looked stunned and amazed and couldn't believe what I had done. It was spot on for each of the three young women! There were others who I had done this for as well, but these three stood out to me because they came in as a group, yet each one had different energy, a different reading and completely different personalities and each one benefited in different ways from their reading that night.

Different Legs

A man came to my house for a reading and his mother instantly came through for him. She was able to tell him that she didn't show her emotions enough when she was alive, and she felt she didn't express the depth of her love for her family.   Unfortunately, I don't think that he fully grasped what she was trying to say. She was really pouring her heart out for healing, but he was saying that she wasn't too bad with expressing her emotions. Because she had been on the other side and knew the true meaning of openness of heart and love, she knew that she had been holding back emotionally when she was in her physical incarnation.

To make him more comfortable, I did a body scan and told him that there was a notably different feeling down one of his legs compared to the other. He said that he had trouble with one of his legs and was getting treatment for it, while the other leg was completely fine. Angels had told me that blood circulation around the body is very important and the issue with his leg was important information for his healing journey here and his ability to enjoy his life.

We spoke about financial issues and business dealings that he was involved in. He seemed much more comfortable with these issues than the issues of the heart and that is fair enough, sometimes to keep the energy flowing in a reading, we have to focus on what a person wants in a reading, not always what they need. I always hope that I plant a seed and that the healing will occur later or the information will make sense later when they have had time to process it.

Dirty Money

When I was doing readings in Dublin, at a healing space in Dublin, run by a Celtic Shaman, a notably rich woman, Anna, came in for a reading. I could feel that her money was actually not her own and that it was tying her to her rich ex-partner. Anna was still living in his mansion, under his rules although they were no longer together. He had promised to still give her access to a virtually unlimited credit card if she would stay living under his roof. They were worth millions, well at least he was. She did not have access to cash as such but she had a cheque-book and credit card at her disposal.

The only way to describe Anna's energy is to say that she felt dirty. For me, it oozed off her. Her soul felt sick with greed and she confirmed that she hated her situation.

Anna said she knew that being able to use his bottomless credit card at will as long as she stayed in his house was an awful situation because he could abuse her at will also! She said it was an awfully controlling situation as her ex was an alcoholic, who constantly verbally abused her.

I could feel all of this truth within her physical system; his abusive energy was very strong and could be felt all over her. The dirty feeling I was getting from her body was actually making me feel sick in the stomach and her greedy thoughts made my head spin.

On a positive note I told her that I saw her living on a beautiful green hill overlooking the sea, in a pretty little cottage. Anna confirmed that this was her dream; to live overlooking the sea in the West of Ireland, in a little cottage of her own, warmed by a small fire, doing her pottery and art. She said she daydreamed about this often. I had described her dream life precisely to her.

But, she said, the pull of the money was too strong and she just couldn't leave his mansion or the cheque book behind.

I could not seem to get through to her, though I hoped that for her soul's sake enough of a seed was planted, that perhaps in the near future she would uproot herself and go into the light-filled life that she dreamed of, away from the abusive relationship that she couldn't bring herself to leave.

I could literally feel the angels in the room urging me to encourage her to live an authentic pure life, not one based on greed, control and misuse of power. It was ironic that at the time she paid by cheque, as she didn't have cash of her own, and then she only gave me half of what she owed me, saying she didn't realise she had to pay by the hour.

I completely let go of it and prayed for her. I refused to feel out of control in the situation or take on her greed, negative energy or her abusive behaviours towards others when relating to them and money. I actually felt that although she had a fortune at her disposal she liked to cheat people or at least to get a bargain and I was not the only one that she underpaid in this life. Because truthfully, the money wasn't hers, she knew it wasn't really unlimited, therefore it didn't actually feel good to use it and she used it in the same vein that it was given to her in, without any heart.

It made me seriously wonder what her karma was going to be, how it was going to play out over the course of this life and the next to come. I sincerely hoped that she was able to negotiate a change in her life. I saw how beautiful her life would be if she made the choice to accept it and I sincerely prayed for her that she would.

Backpacking through California

Tom came in for a reading at my house and I saw him backpacking through California. Backpacking through California is something I had actually done and it was tempting to discount the vision as my own stuff coming through. Also, his health was quite poor and I could have discounted this vision on the account that his health would not be up to such a challenge.

However, I chose to trust the vision and tell him exactly what I saw. I also added that I saw that he was carrying a guitar or ukulele on his back. Tom confirmed that it was his utmost dream to backpack California with his guitar.

The Venue Is Not Right

I hope this story makes sense! Sometimes my dreams and my own thoughts get mixed up with other people's thoughts. For several weeks I had been daydreaming about doing readings to large groups of people however I knew that I wasn't ready to do this yet as my book was not yet finished to tour with.

I kept feeling that the venue I had chosen (in my

daydreams) in a small town not far from where I live was the wrong venue and I had to change it. I remember saying to my Mick that I hadn't even booked that venue let alone organised my large group readings/show yet, and yet I kept thinking to myself I needed to find another venue.

Pamela came for a reading and held the answer. Worrying about the venue had nothing to do with me!

In 'real life', Pamela had booked the exact venue from my daydreams and was questioning whether it was too big for the event she was holding! I was able to share my story with her and confirm that she should move her event to another smaller venue. She had already investigated a smaller venue that she wanted, but she just hadn't booked it yet as she wanted confirmation it was the right smaller venue to move to. I was able to confirm this for her; it was in the same location, that in my own visions in the previous weeks, I felt I had to move my group readings to as well!

The reason I may have linked in with Pamela before she came to see me is because her partner had been to me previously for readings. Pamela had been thinking about coming to ask for my advice for several weeks.

It may have been that because she was thinking of me in relation to this issue I had 'heard' her thoughts through my intuitive pathways and linked in with her energy and her needs. Just as I often feel the telephone a few seconds before it rings or texts, I picked up on her thoughts about contacting me through the 'airwaves'.

The Healing Power of Yoga

A gentle woman in her late thirties came to see me and I could immediately feel the practice of yoga all around her. She was a very feminine woman with a slim, slight, almost fragile looking build, and she quickly confirmed that she was a teacher of Dru Yoga (a particularly flowing, graceful and powerful form of mind-body-spirit yoga).

The young woman had experienced long-term health problems and counted Dru Yoga as her saving grace. As she spoke, I could feel the remnants of her past energy as if it was my own and I became aware of a great heaviness in my head and neck. I explained that all of her problems had started in the back of her head, down into her neck, when she was in her teens.

She confirmed that she had suffered from viral meningitis when she was sixteen years old, and that this was the beginning of her problems. She said it had mainly affected her head and neck and she couldn't go to school for a year afterwards. She got chronic fatigue shortly after and her whole life changed as a result. When she started Dru Yoga, she could hardly move and now she teaches it!

A Market Reading

I was doing readings at a market in Byron Bay when a lovely couple in their late 40s came up for a reading. They had a joint reading, which was very fitting as they were very close emotionally and it was a delight for me to see them together. Their combined energy was so full of love and they were enjoyable to be around.

I immediately explained that I was seeing old cars being fixed up and made beautiful again. The gentleman, Max, was very taken aback and his eyes widened with surprise. He had never had a reading before and I could sense his excitement and amazement. He said that he had just recently opened a custom car restoration business. He wanted to know if the business would be successful and I was able to confirm that it would continue to be.

His wife Pam was a very warm and open person and she had also just started a business teaching yoga. I was able to see a few things that might be relevant for her. I felt they'd had a child who died in the womb and Pam confirmed this to be true. This angel's energy was able to gently come through, and to assure them that what happened was meant to be. There were also some health issues, particularly liver issues for Max. I could feel that there was an issue with his blood and he confirmed that he was attempting to remedy this through juicing and dietary changes.

When they contacted me sometime later for another reading, I explained that I saw them going on an overseas holiday to Bali in the immediate future. They were able to confirm that they were actually booked to go to Bali in two weeks' time!

CHAPTER 5

Different Types Of Psychic Intuition

THERE ARE MANY OTHER TYPES OF SITUATIONS WHERE INTUITION KICKS IN. If we think of it as just another sense, it is always working in the background, and just like we often aren't aware of the other senses at work, so our psychic sense plays out and does its job naturally.

The following stories are varied psychic situations and I've put a heading at the top of these stories to help us categorise and understand all of these different possibilities for our intuitive sense.

THOUGHT COMMUNICATION WITH ANIMALS

Like many people I absolutely love animals. One interesting and very useful intuitive skill is empathic animal communication. The following stories about animals are important because they show that animals can communicate with us through our thoughts. They also show that animals have complex feelings, thoughts and desires just like humans. I hope that by sharing these stories people will have even more empathy for their animals and try to communicate with them more consciously in future.

Kess

When I was in my early twenties, I had a beautiful chocolate Burmese cat named Kess who I absolutely adored.

Because I lived on a busy street, Kess was an indoor cat with an outside cat run. She would most likely have been killed if I hadn't kept her inside as she had no road sense.

I know this sounds unusual, but one night while I was lying on the couch watching television, I suddenly became Kess. Although I was still technically sitting on the couch, I was breathing, sensing, seeing, and experiencing everything through her eyes, as if I was her.

One minute I was watching television, the next I was sniffing around the garden and roaming free outside. I knew that somehow Kess had gotten out of the house and was walking in the garden bed around the side of the house.

"Kess is outside," I said calmly, although I felt like I was panting.

When I got no response from my flat mate I remember saying it again, "Kess is outside."

I should not have been panting because I wasn't out of breath! I was just sitting down watching television!

"What are you talking about?" Replied my flat mate. "She's upstairs in the bedroom."

"No, I can feel her in the garden. Go have a look."

My flat mate raced upstairs and a few seconds later was back down the stairs, "She's jumped down from the second storey, from the air-conditioning window, the board blocking the window, it's open wide, and she must have climbed down the side of the house."

"I know," I said back, "We have to get her before she

goes onto the road."

Five minutes later, my flat mate walked in the front door with Kess in his arms. "She was in the garden bed," he said.

"Yes, I know," was my response.

I had felt her moment of freedom. I had seen the garden through her eyes.

I was breathing, smelling and seeing the ground as Kess! It was such a momentous moment and because we were so connected and very much devoted to one another, I was able to suddenly merge into her brain and feel everything she could feel.

She must have been experiencing such intense emotions and sensations and perhaps in that moment she thought of me and it formed a binding connection. Or perhaps her intense emotions were projected outwards and I was able to pick them up in the ether or the energy field because of my sensitivity.

Becoming Kess was an exhilarating feeling.

I remember feeling so intensely alive. I experienced her breath and her sight and her wonderment, intensified by her sensitive animal senses. I could see what she was seeing; the ground, the foliage and through her eyes in the dark it looked like a yellow/brown hue covered everything. Like the world was sepia coloured. Her/our breath was so strong, so powerful, intense and quick. She was panting with excitement and smelling everything around her/us.

I wondered if this was what the Native American Indian people were talking about when they chose their totem animals. In ceremony, for example, they actually become the animal and see through the animal's eyes. I once had the experience of being an Eagle also. However, it was many years ago and I forgot to write the experience down in its entirety so the exact details have escaped me. I do remember that I was soaring high in the sky above everything and everyone. The sense of power and wisdom and knowing and strength was immense. I remember seeing the ground and soaring so fast that things were a blur, yet I had precision eyesight and saw everything that I wanted to focus on perfectly. The wind felt so amazing under my wings and I soared with the current.

Several times since the Kess incident, I have heard the thoughts of animals and they have communicated with me.

The Dog Needs a Drink!

Several years after the incident with Kess, I was back in Australia again, after having lived overseas, marrying my Irishman and having had many angelic and psychic experiences. When we returned to Australia, Mick, Kia (who was three at the time) and I were on a journey travelling across Australia. We were in the wilderness somewhere in South Eastern Australia, our coaster bus parked on the side of the road and we had friends with us who had done a long walk that day with their dog. He was a beautiful, big, strong German Shephard named Rupie.

We were all settled down for a late lunch when from the other side of our friend's bus, I heard Rupie's thoughts! Although I couldn't see him, I distinctly heard him thinking, "I've got no water in my bowl!" and being extremely annoyed with his female owner who usually doted on him.

I got up from the picnic table and made my way around to see him. There he was staring up at me, standing above his empty water bowl. I told his owner what had occurred and she immediately got up from the table and got him a drink. She felt guilty because Rupie had walked a long way that day and she hadn't looked after his needs.

She was an attentive owner and she treated the dog like her equal. He slept in her bedroom with her and had the run of the house. He also protected her with his life. Once, when she was walking along a beach in Adelaide at sunrise, a vehicle started to follow her and it stopped someway in front of her and a menacing looking man got out. The man just stood there staring at her. She stopped and Rupie stood before her and started growling, staring intently at the man. Needless to say after a short time the man got back into his car and left.

When Rupie spoke to me in my mind, his voice suited the way he looked! It was the voice of a strong, old man, and a grumpy one at that!

Rosey

There was a lady I knew who had a lovely old dog named, Rosey. Rosey sauntered up to me one day and put her wet nose under my hand for a head pat. It was then that she told me in my mind about her ear being sore for a long time. I'm sorry, I said to her in our thoughts, I will tell your owner.

When I said something to the owner, she said that Rosey had been treated many times for that ear; it was a recurring problem for her. Rosey had let me know that it was still troubling her the poor darling.

Talking to Rosey reminded me of talking to an elderly woman about her illness; you know how an older person will be in pain and will express it clearly on their face and in their energy and appearance, talking to Rosey was exactly like that. She was just a little old lady telling me that life was okay, but that this ear was getting her down a little. God she was a beautiful old girl.

Our animals have a lot to say to us, if we only know how to listen, or perhaps if we just take the time to trust that we can hear them.

Blues, The Horse

We live in a beautiful old farmhouse in countryside near Byron Bay and our new landlord had been bringing horses onto the property. It was lovely having horses around, hearing the occasional whinny in the night or seeing them gallop freely in the open paddocks during the day. It's a beautiful sight to behold.

When we went overseas for a month, Ellen, a friend looked after our house for us. When we returned there was a new horse there that we hadn't met before. I went over to the horse and he told me in my mind that he missed Ellen because she used to bring him apples all the time. I went and got him apples regularly after that and patted him and told him it was okay to miss her and I would try do my best to visit him.

A week or so after our return, Ellen popped over to see me. She told me that she missed Blues and she used to give him apples all the time. I told her that he had told me that and I had been giving him apples in her absence! She was amazed that I had received that information from him! To show her I wasn't joking; I opened the fridge and showed her the apples that I had cut up and placed on a plate, all ready to give to him.

PRECOGNITION

Precognition is the ability to see an event or situation before it occurs. On an everyday basis it works to help me survive and look after my family and myself. There are many simple examples. Sometimes I can tell if a piece of fruit will be rotten before I pick it up or I can be shown something breaking like a toy, drinking glass or household appliance.

On a more serious note, I can sense an illness before it occurs or tune in about an upcoming monetary issue so that I can be more prepared when it actually does happen. I have been shown engine problems with my cars before they broke down so I didn't get a surprise when it actually happened!

White Eagle

My dear Irish friend Sean asked me to tell him whenever I had a premonition. I talk about him more in the memoir later on, but for now suffice it to say, he had seen me do and say many things and we were trying to see more of what I could do. In Chapter 3, you might recall Sean was the friend I told about the unborn baby who told me he would die before being born.

So, I said to Sean one day, "Tomorrow, watch for the white eagle."

To that, we laughed and laughed and laughed. We thought it was the funniest, hippiest, airy fairy, most hilarious thing I could have said.

The next day I went for a massage with my regular masseuse. After my massage I was about to leave, when the masseuse stopped me and said, "I have a gift for you!"

He went into his little office cubby and came out with a small blue box. He said something like, "I thought you would like these and get use out of them."

They had a picture of a white eagle on them and were 'Face The Sun: Sayings of White Eagle with Affirmations' cards. There was our white eagle and I have kept the cards to this day.

One of Those Times When I Wish I Had Listened - A 'Harmless' Cup of Tea

I really enjoy the experience of consuming hot drinks

from pretty floral cups. I love beautiful floral tea sets, modern or antique and the ritual of having the whole serving set in front of me, matching cups, teapot, sugar bowl, and milk jug/creamer.

On this particular afternoon I was enjoying a lovely cup of Rooibos tea with honey, I was drinking out of my favourite pottery mug at the time, a lovely large pear shaped piece, painted with a sweet pink flower and matching painted pink rim. Anyway, I was thoroughly immersed in this hot cup of tea, savoring every sip as though it was an elixir and wishing it would never end.

When I was about half way through, I saw a vision in my mind's eye of a dead brown moth at the bottom of the cup, over to one side. I ignored it and continued sipping my tea ignoring the vision, but I couldn't manage to shake the feeling.

I always test myself. And this was one of those times.

Even though with each sip I could see the brown shadow in my mind, I had no emotions attached to it. As I got to the bottom of the cup there it was - a large dead moth stuck to the side!

I nearly threw up the entire drink! Suddenly the emotions flooded me, I felt ill to my stomach and very annoyed with myself for not taking heed of the vision I had seen.

I have found this happen with other premonitions as well. Sometimes I can see an image in my mind but the emotions don't actually catch up and relate to the image until it becomes a physical reality, then the emotions prove to be really strong! Needless to say, it's quite funny but I wasn't able to drink out of that cup again, I had to give it away and I couldn't drink that particular type of tea for a long time afterwards!

Washing Machine

Our washing machine had broken down and as we live rurally the repairman only came to our region once a week on a Thursday. I had to wait a week for him to come and evaluate it. He came to inspect it and then he had to order the parts to fix it, which took another week. It was Wednesday and he was supposed to be coming the following day with the parts. I was walking through my house when I was suddenly stopped in my tracks.

In my mind I heard the house telephone ring, only it hadn't actually physically rung. I answered the phone in my mind and it was the lady from the washing machine repair business. She said to me that the parts that arrived were the wrong ones, they had to re-order the right ones and they would not be able to do the job until the following Thursday. I spoke to her in my mind and acknowledged the change and re-scheduled the appointment. I hung up the phone in my mind.

Instantly, the house telephone then actually rang for real, in the physical world. It buzzed to life and well, you know the rest… It was the same lady, with the same news, and I said the same things to her, all the while with a look of amazement on my face that thankfully she couldn't see!

After I hung up the phone, for real this time, I went immediately to tell Mick what happened. I asked him if he thought that everything in the world had already happened before and somehow I had access to this information? He wondered if the lady from the washing machine repair place had been thinking of ringing me and what she would say and I picked up on that – although that doesn't explain me having the exact word for word conversation with her on the phone that I had just had in my mind!

A Pregnancy

I have a very dear friend, Sofie, whom I felt was going to become pregnant by the end of the following February. I told her about this feeling approximately four months prior in November. Immediately she was adamant that she would not get pregnant and would take extra precautions as she was having difficulties in her relationship.

She knew that I had a strong gift and that there was every chance it could happen. One day I received a text from Sophie saying my prediction had come true.

My dear friend had some difficult choices to make regarding this pregnancy as the father was no longer with her and had been seeing somebody else behind her back. Sofie was already a single mother of one and couldn't afford to have another child by herself.

Despite warnings, foreseen things still happen. Perhaps the warning is too late, or perhaps the energy is just telling us that this event will happen for our learning and growth to occur. One thing for sure change is constant in this life and we adapt and cope with what comes our way, the best way we can.

I Couldn't Save My Dad

Another time I had a powerful vision that made me cry. In my mind's eye I saw an old black man whom I loved deeply. I saw him become very sick in his heart by overdoing it in the heat and ending up in hospital. The man was so weak.

Even though I couldn't see his face, just his dark skin, I knew that it was my Dad (his father was Malaysian and his mother from Java). I experienced such a great level of pain in my heart and fear for his life.

I rang my Dad to warn him. I told him about my

dream and that he must not over do it for he would end up in hospital. He appeared happy that I was thinking of him and looking out for him, but assured me he was really healthy and feeling good. He told me he would be careful. As usual he was jolly on the phone and chuckling away. I was living in Ireland at the time so I couldn't exactly keep a physical eye on him.

It was really hot where my parents lived in North Queensland with a tropical climate, he was seventy-six years old and still working full-time as a mechanic! He felt invincible. I tried to get him to understand but I didn't get through to him. Not long afterwards he was hospitalised with heat stroke. He had been working under a tractor in the blazing summer heat for too long without a break for water. He was never the same after that; not just because of the heat stroke, but a hospital blunder left him with a paralysed hand that never fully healed.

My heart was broken for him, but yet this was a time that was meant to be. Certainly it was the beginning of his transition from this existence. The destruction of his physical body had to begin somewhere so that he could move on. It was part of his development; his metamorphosis and the journey back to his original state of being.

For that reason, it was an unchangeable part of his destiny and no matter how hard I tried, or how painful it was for me, I was only a loving witness to it.

Grace & The Prediction of Her Death

The name Grace is such a beautiful one. I met Grace when I was living in Dublin city, Ireland. She was a young lady in her early twenties who was in a lot of emotional pain. Sadly, her grandfather had abused her for many years when she was younger and despite ongoing counselling she was not well. She had been having psychotic episodes and periods of depression. She had been undergoing psychiatric treatment but it was not enough.

I met her through a dear friend of mine, Anna. Anna introduced us both and we met a few times. I longed to do something for Grace but I knew that it was not for me to intervene. Grace only trusted a few people in her life and Anna was one of them. Anna had a small daughter, who was only eighteen months old and she was naturally very protective of her child. Grace had been having delusions, but was still coherent and had asked Anna if she could stay with her. Anna was feeling torn between helping her friend who really needed her and protecting her little girl.

I spoke to Anna at the time and warned her that I could see suicide and that Grace would most likely leave this world by her own hand soon, within the year. Anna chose to protect her daughter; she did what any mother would do I believe. Anna felt she could not expose her child to the negative thoughts, beliefs and delusions that Grace had created about herself and her world to help her cope with her grandfather's betrayal. She was concerned that Grace could turn on them one day and somehow put them into her delusion and perhaps hurt them.

About a year later Grace took an overdose that did not kill her immediately; the doctors thought she might survive. She was talking and sitting up in the hospital bed for a few days following the overdose. Anna visited her and vowed to help her friend from that moment on. Then without warning her liver shut down and Grace died. There was no way to save her.

I don't think there is anything anyone could have done to save Grace, apart from turning back time and protecting her from the abuse. She was in a lot of pain and I sincerely believe that the angels have helped her in the next life.

Anna and I were quite good friends. One day she was telling me about the house she was living in. Her partner's grandmother who had passed away owned it and she had left it to the family. I saw the grandmother in my mind and she said a boy's name to me several times, which I repeated to my friend. Anna looked at me with sadness. The name I had given her was the name of the grandmother's nephew who had suspected involvement in a robbery in this very house.

Though she never spoke of it to anyone when she was alive, it was believed that their beloved grandmother had seen his face during the robbery and died of a broken heart. I think that the grandmother wanted to tell her story and confirm the truth of her nephew's involvement in the robbery. His name was the only thing she gave me and only Anna could have known what it meant. The nephew was tied up in all sorts of illegal things from stealing to drugs and the family suspected that he was involved though when she was alive, the grandmother would never, or could never, confirm it.

From the other side, she got to have her say.

A Child in Need

I had a premonition where I saw one of my two children in my mind showing me their neck, as if something was wrong, but in my vision I couldn't see which child it was. At the time I thought it was my son because he was about to attend his afternoon circus class in Byron Bay and that I should remind him to tuck his neck in for the rolls and tumbles he would do.

After the circus class I took the children to a local restaurant for an early dinner. In my mind I then saw a little pack with scissors and tweezers and other things like that. I felt that I could buy this pack at the local grocery store if I needed it. I had no reason to need this little pack because I had one at home, but regardless I was aware it was in that shop if I needed it. The idea that I would need it literally just popped into my head.

As we finished dinner my daughter started crying, she realized she had a very sore neck and that it was probably a tick. As in my vision, she exposed her neck to me and there was the tick. As I had no tweezers with me to extract it, I knew exactly where I had to go to get the tweezers and I felt prepared and forewarned because I had seen that I needed them several hours before actually needing them.

Ultrasound is Incorrect

When my brother's girlfriend became pregnant, I felt strongly that their child would be a boy. I had moved overseas but I could still feel his energy all around me. They had an ultrasound and it had revealed that the baby was a girl, but I was adamant that it was a boy and I told everyone so. I already felt so connected to him.

I was in the bath one evening when I felt this massive surge of power. I felt the child's soul surge past me and then a candle blew out and shattered the glass on which it was sitting! I knew that my nephew was being born. I later found out that both mother and son were very strong and healthy and I was very proud to welcome my new nephew into the world. My nephew had visited me several times prior to his birth and even an ultrasound was not going to sway me from what I knew about him!

Playing Family Board Games

Many times I have spoilt a surprise by seeing it beforehand. For instance, when Mick would buy me a gift, I would often see what it was and where he had hidden it before he gave it to me or just before he would surprise me with something I would become aware of it.

When I am playing board games I often seem to know what the answer is in advance. My daughter complains and won't play with me anymore. I think it's because we are close and when she sees the answers in her mind, she projects out her thoughts and I see them.

Every once in a while I will still make a mistake because I have misinterpreted the energy she sends out or I'm tired or not concentrating properly.

Recently I had an appointment with someone who lived half an hour away. I had negative thoughts during the entire trip to her house. I felt I should have rung her beforehand to check if the appointment was still on. I had forgotten our previous appointment the week before so I told myself she wouldn't forget this week because she was adamant that we should keep it. I worked on my negativity, saying that I just didn't feel like leaving the house because I wanted to write.

But when I got there, my suspicions were confirmed! She actually had forgotten the appointment and I had wasted several hours of my day that could have been used so much more effectively. I was annoyed with myself for not making the phone call that I knew I should have made. I was annoyed for not listening to my gut when it was telling me I shouldn't be in the car.

So, sometimes, depending on the circumstances, I still don't listen to my gut instinct and I let my thoughts and emotions get in the way. In this instance, I let my guilt override my thoughts because I had forgotten our previous appointment the week before. I wanted to show her that our meeting was important to me. I let emotions and thoughts rule me, rather than trusting my gut. Luckily it was a simple lesson; no one was hurt and I made something positive come out of it. I went for a walk along a beautiful river and then to the library to make the most of my time out so no time was really 'wasted' at all.

I'm sure everyone can think of a situation where their gut instinct told them something and they didn't listen. Trusting this feeling and following through on it, is something we learn in life.

Car Accident

A week before I was involved in a car accident with Mick I had a vision that I would be in a car accident with him and we would be okay but that I couldn't stop it from happening. I didn't know when it would be so I just had to carry on regardless. The accident happened and we were relatively ok. It was a freak thing where a car ahead of us just stopped abruptly on a fast highway on a busy weekend morning. We were in the middle of a five car pile-up.

I did hurt my neck and back and needed some physical therapy for some months and some support for the shock, however what it did was shift a few things in my life that needed shifting, made me kick into gear with some changes that I needed to make.

I also felt very grateful to be alive and for the fact it wasn't worse and that we were in the best shape we could be in. Our car was covered by insurance, it could be repaired and no one was seriously injured. My back and neck would heal in time with proper treatment and tests also showed up past neck whiplash from when I was in a car accident as a child with my mum. It helped me to realise that I needed to ensure I kept exercising and stretching to keep my health and wellbeing up.

When we count our blessings like that, it always seems to be that more blessings come. I met some lovely new people after the accident, people involved in healing and I saw just how supported I was in life when several beautiful friends went out of their way to support me through it. The accident enabled me to access friendship and support that I didn't know I had before and let people show me how much they cared for me. I made the most out of a difficult situation and turned it into a positive.

Bargain Hunter!

On a lighter note, I love a good bargain and wonderfully, I can be shown an item that my family needs or wants and where it will be at a particular discount shop or inexpensive market stall. I daydreamed about a coral coloured dress for several weeks before I walked into a secondhand shop and there it was! I saw it instantly and knew it was the dress I had been dreaming about. It is so pretty on, funnily if I hadn't seen it in my visions I might not have tried it on, the label on the dress is several sizes below my size. But I knew I had been seeing it in my mind, so I tried it on despite the label and it fit beautifully.

Mick had torn his good jeans that he wears to work gigging as a musician. I saw a pair of jeans in my mind at a charity shop about half hour down the road from my house. I went there and found them for $4. They retail in the shops for about $100! Another time, Mick needed a matching pair of pants to go with a vest that he wore when he was performing on stage. In my mind's eye, I saw them in a different town, at a different opportunity shop. I went to this shop and there they were for only $5, a pittance of what they would have cost new!

There is a wonderful second-hand market that happens once a year in our little village and it's a great place to stack up on books and toys for the kids. This particular year Orin was two and a half years old and obsessed with the movie Toy Story and in particular the characters, Woody and Buzz.

The toys were expensive when purchased new,

retailing for between $50 and $60 and I was hoping to pick them up second-hand. On our way down to the market, I saw Woody in my mind's eye seated on a shelf at one of the stalls and I also saw a price tag of $2 attached to his leg.

At the market, I went directly to the particular stall that I had pictured in my mind and there was Woody for $2 much to the delight of my son! In my mind I had literally seen exactly where the toy would be, right down to where it was seated on the shelf. The market stalls are always different each year and never in the same position, so it was a precognitive insight.

My ability to hunt out a bargain psychically has been extremely useful in my life but I have also been shown physical, mental and social problems pertaining to people I have just met. For instance, I can often sense if someone is going to be in a bad mood prior to meeting them or I might be shown whether a person will say something mean or out of line in a social situation. Seeing these things in advance has helped me to deal with people and situations that could otherwise have been difficult for me to handle.

The Escalator

I had a slight falling out with a friend and we hadn't seen each other for some time. During that time, I kept having visions of her standing at the top of an escalator in a local shopping centre. This particular shopping centre is over an hour's drive from where my friend lives and she rarely goes there for this reason. However, my family goes there regularly as we live much closer to it.

For months I kept expecting to see my friend when I went to this shopping centre and I knew I would have to face her there one day. It's not that I didn't want to face her, I knew that it was just a matter of time.

Then one day, several months after first seeing the meeting in my mind, I saw her standing at the top of the escalator. I had to cope with the knowledge that this was not a vision and I also had to cope with knowing that we had some issues to sort out. She said she rarely came to the shopping centre but just decided to out of the blue (obviously it wasn't out of the blue for me!). Thankfully we spoke and sorted out our differences, several metres from the escalator.

We left with smiles on our faces and warm forgiving hearts. It was a powerful scene and one for which I am very grateful. I felt like the angels were there with us, helping us heal. Did spirit tell me beforehand that she would be there or was I accessing what some call the Akashic records (also called 'the book of life', a spiritual record of everything that has been and will be, a universal super computer storehouse if you like)? Have we all lived this before?

Regardless, what I do know is that healing such a rift is important, not just for our hearts and souls but for the soul of everyone. We all have way too many negative stories and experiences that we carry around with us and they often don't get resolved because we fear such emotional moments. If you both have love in your hearts, and a real genuine desire for peace in this world, you can come to an understanding and healing can occur despite the fact you might not understand or agree with what the other person is saying. This is exactly what happened for my friend and I. I could have avoided that shopping centre knowing what was coming, knowing the strong emotions I was about to face, but I chose not to. I chose to face it head on.

I am also coming to understand that sometimes things have to happen in order for us to grow. As hard as it is for us to understand or grasp, this does appear to be true. There is a bigger picture and though we might not fully understand it, we are all given glimpses into what is to come.

As I have said before, it doesn't mean I can stop what is coming or that I should stop it, but rather, it teaches me that some things must happen. I put my trust in our spiritual guides, knowing that if I am meant to stop something I will and if I am not then I will have to learn to accept and grow from each situation.

Learning to trust and accept takes time, but I approach this practice with love in my heart and a positive viewpoint in my mind. I love the Buddhist teachings where nothing is either good or bad, and everything is impermanent in the world. Choosing to see things as they are and not necessarily attaching labels of good or bad is empowering. This type of thinking is powerful. We all know that what can seem 'bad' can turn out to be good and what can seem 'good' can turn out to be bad! Many things can turn out to be however we perceive them! Perception is powerful.

The Fire Engine

This is an example of what you can do to access what might be coming the next day. Sometimes I lie in bed at night and calm myself completely. I say to myself I wonder what will come tomorrow. But I do not stress or attach any need or want to this. I just gently wonder and know that an image or perception will come through if it is meant to. I do gentle breathing exercises and become mindful and relaxed. Then sometimes an image will come to mind.

I did this one night and I saw a fire engine with its sirens going. As I live in the country I don't see this very often; it's quiet except for the occasional rooster crowing, dog barking, bird chirping or car going by. I quickly wrote down 'fire station' in my phone. I was tired by this stage and meant to write 'fire engine'. I did this so that if I saw a fire engine I could then show whoever I was with my prediction.

The next day I was in a Mullumbimby café with my daughter. We were enjoying our smoothie drinks, when out of the blue a fire engine started its siren and whizzed past us. I showed Kia the note I'd made the night before. I've never seen a fire truck in the town before let alone with its sirens blaring.

You might like to try this exercise for yourself, see what happens.

PROPHETIC DREAMS

Needing no introduction, prophetic dreams are just that, dreams that tell us something about what is going to happen in the future. Just like my friend in Chapter 2 who had the dream that she saved a baby from drowning in a bathtub and then the spirits asked me to give her a further message to help save her son from drowning in her in-ground pool, the spirits must be able to put messages into our dreams for our greater good.

We are being gently supported in this way from our spirit family, how lucky we are that all of this goes on without our conscious human knowledge! Although the cat is out of the bag now!

I Dream My Son Will Get Hurt Before He Does!

I had a dream that my children and I were high up in a moving carriage suspended by electrical cables. Kia who was seven-years old at the time leant over and started to fall into the water below. As she was falling through the air, she suddenly morphed into her two-year old brother who was bigger and older in the dream. Orin went in face down, stomach first and although I jumped in after him,

I felt frozen, like I couldn't move quickly enough. I swam around in the murky water and pulled him out with his bottom facing me. As I held him, I recall staring at his bottom, and saying, "Wow, you are older now because of this."

It was a very stressful, emotional dream and I knew that something was going to happen to him. I watched him closely for a week, especially around his older sister. In my dream, he had started out as her, and so I felt he was going to hurt himself by copying something she had done.

About two weeks later, Kia, Orin and one of Kia's school friends were outside our house, playing on their swing set. The girls were putting on a 'show' for Mick and I that involved jumping on and off the slide and climbing to the top of the swing set. It was around the time of a full moon and I was tired after a poor night's sleep with Orin. He always slept poorly around a full moon and my guard was down as a result. I had just removed his nappy and left him in a pair of a shorts so his bottom was not protected by the thick softness of a nappy. Sure enough, he jumped off the top of the slide from a height of 1.3 metres in an attempt to copy his big sister.

As he landed, his feet were suspended in the air and his bottom hit the bottom rung of the ladder, with a distinct and sickening crack.

During the hospital visit, it was confirmed that my son had broken his tailbone. The next day, Mick turned to me and said, "He seems so much older now."

Just like in my dream, he had in fact grown up very quickly. It had only been a day since the fall but somehow he seemed older, wiser and more mature. Within the next few weeks his language developed at an incredible speed, as did his capacity to comprehend what was going on around him. He took an interest in movies that previously held no interest, and his empathy for others was magnified.

Due to his own traumatic experience, he was no longer the same little baby who ran around the yard and pulled at his pet dog without any awareness of danger. Overnight, he had become a present, focused and empathetic little boy.

Orin came out of the incident extremely well and his injury healed quite quickly. Just like the dream had suggested, it felt like an important and necessary step for him to grow and learn.

I know some people will say it is disempowering to suggest that his accident 'was meant to be'. However, I want to reiterate that when I was watching the children, my ability to think and sense danger was impaired due to exhaustion. I actually became aware that I was forgetting something but the point is, I wasn't meant to remember. I was sitting there thinking 'I have forgotten something'!

Though the angels had showed me that my son would be better for the accident, I am still a mother with strong maternal instincts and I may have attempted to intervene had I remembered the dream. I believe the spirits helped to soften the edges of my memory so that I would forget and let things happen as they were meant to happen. Why else would I forget such an important dream, especially one that appeared in the form of a warning?

Again, I learnt a great lesson from this experience. I see things before they happen. I get warned. But that doesn't mean I am meant to intervene or stop things before they happen. We cannot control everything. There is a bigger plan at work behind the scenes and sometimes, even 'accidents' are meant to happen.

The Chemist and the Car

I had this very intense dream where I spent a very long time in a chemist shop. In the dream Mick was outside waiting with my uncle in a flashy gold car and he said something about women getting caught up in shopping.

The next day we were at a small shopping centre and Mick, Kia and Orin were waiting for me outside the supermarket. As I walked out of the supermarket, I noticed that the kids were playing in a little coin-operated car - the kind of ride that rocks back and forth for a few minutes. Situated in front of the ride was a chemist shop and as soon as I spotted it, Kia made a comment about how mother's shop for too long!

It was different, but also very similar to my dream. Often dreams contain elements of what will happen but the details are slightly skewed. Sometimes we are left to interpret the images, and other times they are close approximations to what happens in real life.

Daydreaming and Choices

I was in the kitchen cleaning up at the time when I had a daydream about my friend. In the daydream she asked me if I wanted to rent out her spacious home for $250 per week. Two days later I received a text message from my friend actually asking if I wanted to rent her place for $250 as she was relocating to the city for at least a year. This price was significantly cheaper than my rent so I would naturally want to jump at such an opportunity.

My daydream had given me a small head start to think about the offer. Around the same time, I received a text message from a relative of mine, questioning why life had to be so complicated.

This text made me realise that moving into my friend's house could perhaps invite complications into my life. For instance, if my friend's move did not work out, and she wished to return to her home, it could prove difficult for me to find another rental property in the area. Properties were very scarce in the area and it wasn't easy to find a place that would take all of our animals. Besides, we already had an existing long-term arrangement with our landlord (a gentlemanly farmer), which was actually more than adequate. Still, I was very grateful for the heads up about the offer a few days before, because then I was more prepared for it, and thus less likely to make any hasty decisions that could affect my family's lives.

Incidentally my dear friend did find someone else to rent out her house, but then at the last minute she couldn't actually leave her house because of personal reasons!

The messages we receive are not always direct and in this case, the spirit guides were working through my cousin to send me a message about complications, which in turn led me to see that the offer was not as stable as it appeared. My friend was really adamant she was moving, and she didn't know that she would renege on the offer, but the spirits knew and they made sure that I knew as well.

Rinpoche

I had a powerful dream where a kind-faced Buddhist monk came up to me and he bowed, with his hands in prayer position, and then looked at me and called me "Rinpoche." I woke up and looked up the word. Even though I have read a few books on Buddhism I didn't know what the word actually meant. I thought it was a teacher.

When I did a google search on the internet I found the following definition:

"Rinpoche: A Tibetan word which means "precious one." This title is applied at the end of the teacher's name. In most cases, the title is bestowed upon one who has been recognised as the reincarnation of a great teacher. "Rinpoche" is occasionally given as a title of respect to living teachers who were not formally recognised as reincarnate lamas while they were young but have demonstrated extraordinary qualities in this life." *

I thought to myself, wow this is me. I can do all these things, I've seen past lives of myself and others, I have a highly developed psychic sense and a wisdom able to help other people that was always beyond my years. The term made sense to me and I thought a beautiful way to describe people such as myself.

I have had so many other dreams, too many to count and too many to share, that have given me answers to questions I had. I will wake up, say at 3am with a voice distinctly telling me something I need to know or remember or that I need to deal with when I wake up such as something to do with my children or something else important to me.

Sometimes when I wake in the middle of the night or early morning, my mind is literally writing words for this book, or a song or poem. I grab my phone or my notepad by the bed and quickly copy those words down. Before bed you can ask spirit for answers to your questions and during your sleep they can get through to you. For example, recently before bed I asked for help with formatting this book. In my dream, as I was waking up so I could remember it well, I heard the name of a book. This particular book was just the perfect one to help me find the formatting I wanted for my own memoir.

The dream state is an important avenue for spirit to get through to us, and for our higher self to work through things that are important to us, but that can get put aside during our busy day time lives.

* *Quote from http://fpmt.org/mandala/archives/mandala-issues-for-2007/april/other-titles-in-tibetan-buddhism/*

REMOTE VIEWING

Remote viewing is the ability to receive information on a target that is unseen because of distance or time (past or present). I have some interesting examples around this skill that helps to explain what the term means. In addition, post-cognition or retro-cognition is a term used to describe psychic awareness of something that has happened in the past ('cognition' means 'knowing' and 'retro' means 'backwards, behind'). Precognition means the psychic ability to see into the future ('pre' meaning 'before').

Why Did You Do That?

When I was living in the quaint seaside village of Tramore, Ireland I started working in a lovely local café. The pocket money came in handy, but working there also helped me pass the time and meet people in the area. I quickly made friends with a customer named Sue, a local single mother who shared my deep sense of spirituality.

One day I was working at the café when I felt Sue go into the shop around the corner and start gossiping about me to the woman who owned the store. The shop owner was quite a nasty woman who liked to gossip and speak down to her customers and staff. One moment I was standing behind the café counter and the next moment I started crying. Though I hadn't physically seen this play out, my mind had witnessed both women speaking negatively about me and I knew Sue had betrayed my trust.

A few minutes later Sue came into my cafe. I knew she had entered the cafe before I saw her but that didn't stop me from getting upset again. Sue approached me, and I looked up at her, tears filling my eyes.

"Why did you just do that?" I asked.

Sue looked back at me confused. I explained what had happened, detailing exactly what I had been shown and she started to cry and apologise for what she had done. Sue said she felt terrible and she promised me that it would not happen again.

This form of remote viewing happens to me often. Sometimes I can feel when things are happening to close friends and family. For instance, though we were very far apart at the time, I could feel the moment my friend realised that her husband was having an affair. I recall sitting on my deck, when she came into my mind and suddenly I was experiencing her emotions. I then also felt her decide to leave town for a while. The emotions were so strong they traversed the distance between us and I felt them as they occurred. Later she actually physically told me what happened.

When I lived overseas in Ireland, I could sense that my mother was unwell and this was confirmed with a phone call home to my Dad. Remote viewing is a strong sense or intuition that you feel within your energy system. It can also be a very strong and powerful vision occurring in your mind's eye and it can often happen in real time.

Psychic Impression of a Friend in Danger

A person appears to transmit the energy that has been most around them during their life or that has left a strong impression or that is currently very powerful. For example, if they were in an abusive relationship, the person's energy would show this to me. It would show itself as a feeling of oppression, of being scared and hurt or guilt and embarrassment, and it would possibly appear as pictures or a brief movie clip in my mind. I might see the person being hit or being afraid of being hit.

I do not always know who is sending this information to me. Sometimes I can sense a distinctly male or female spirit, other times the information just appears in my mind.

Over thirteen years ago I was working with a young Indigenous Australian woman Kim (who later became a friend) and I visited her community. My friend Sean had also come to the community for the day to join in a nature excursion because it was in a beautiful part of the world and we both admired an amazing forest view, which literally shimmered with energy and light.

Sean and I were able to see the incredible energy shining up at us from this sacred place full of power, mystery, and abundant life-giving energy. The woman's partner and father of her children, John, also came along on the nature excursion. He was a lovely young Indigenous man. We really enjoyed his company, though I admit that even then I could feel something in him, a deep sense of unhappiness and anger, though it wasn't apparent from his easygoing manner. By outward appearances he was a semi-successful artist and a really nice young man, seemingly a gentleman.

I can't remember when it was exactly, but the workday had finished and we were back at home again, I had the feeling that he was hurting Kim. In my mind's eye I saw her scared and isolated, screamed at and physically hit. In my vision, I saw him put a knife put to Kim's throat. It was very terrifying.

I also saw that time and time again their two little girls were witness to John's anger and frustration. I told my friend Sean what I had seen. He did not and could not believe such a thing. He said John appeared really nice and there was no evidence whatsoever to suggest otherwise. I told him to wait and see, that I would approach her and make sure she was okay.

Kim was a very honest and lovely person. We got on extremely well. I rang her and very carefully and gently asked her what was happening in her life. I remember saying that I could see things in my mind and after assuring her that I liked her partner, I explained I could feel something going on that wasn't right. I said I was shown a vision of him backing her up against a wall and putting a knife to her throat in front of her little girls.

I don't think she even stopped to take a breath. She didn't hesitate to acknowledge that the knife scene had happened that morning, exactly as I described, just before we had arrived to work with them.

He had literally pushed her up against the wall and put a knife to her throat in front of their two young daughters. She spoke about his fury and his deep sense of worthlessness. He was a creative and proud man, but it was hard to make a living at that time from his creative pursuits. He was driven to despair and was very angry with himself and the world and sadly, it was the innocent people around him who were paying the price.

To make matters worse he was abusing alcohol and marijuana and of course these things were just fuelling his rage and his feelings of ineptness. He was also a very sensitive man and she said he had a lot of anger for what happened to Indigenous Australians and he was having trouble letting go of this anger and pain. There were a lot of serious social issues where they were living due to longstanding poverty and the effects of colonialism on their people.

Kim had a plan to get out of there with her girls. She feared for her life and for what her children had seen and how their experiences would shape them. She wanted to be a powerful role model for Aboriginal women. We lost contact after that because I moved overseas, but with all my heart I always hoped that she got herself and her girls out of there and John got help with his emotional pain.

My Mum

One day I remember thinking about my Mum and I just knew that she was in a really bad state of mind. I knew it was related to symptoms of menopause that were really affecting her mentally and emotionally, as well as physically with hot flushes and night sweats and insomnia. I was still in Dublin and my Mum was in the tropics with my Dad back in Australia. Mum and I sometimes wouldn't talk for a few weeks because we were all so busy with our lives and nothing much had changed for us to make contact.

I rang her one day and said I knew her head was really negative, that I could feel it and she became angry and asked me who had rung me and told me. I had to assure her that no one had told me, that I had gone into her and felt how much her hormones were affecting her moods. She was going through such a hard time. Now she is through it and is doing well which is great news.

She did accept what I told her at the time that no one had rung me.

I explained how I just thought of her and felt something was wrong. What I actually did do was remote view my consciousness into my mother's situation. I thought of her and my body told me what she was experiencing by allowing me to feel what she was feeling (this feeling then dissipated almost immediately afterwards). I saw and heard what was happening by seeing images and pictures in my mind that were related to her behaviour.

The Dentist

One day I was spending time with my friend Sean, when I was suddenly transported into a dentist's clinic. In my mind I could see Sean sitting in the dentist's chair and I could picture the room, the dentist and the dental assistant in perfect detail. I could also see that Sean and the dental assistant fancied one another but Sean appeared much younger and was too shy to ask the assistant out! I was then taken to another dentist's office and I could also describe this scene and the dentist in perfect detail.

Prior to this experience, Sean had been in a bicycle accident that cost him his two front teeth. I knew that he had been to see a dentist shortly after the accident, however he hadn't discussed the details and I didn't know he had seen a second dentist. This is an example of remote viewing a past event. I saw the situation as if it was happening in real time, but in fact, it had all happened many years before! I could not think of any reason as to why I had been taken into my friend's intense memories at the time, but he was certainly able to verify all the details!

The Dark House

I was attending a coaching workshop in Byron Bay when I started to get a strong feeling about one of the women in the group; a woman I had only just met. I suddenly felt that she needed to let light into her house and I could picture her drawing the curtains. I said, "I don't know you but I feel you need to open the curtains in your house and let light in - you need light."

The woman smiled and told the group that her house was very dark and that she was always opening her curtains and trying to get as much light as she could into it her little dark house. There were some other things that were accurate, but this simple example stood out to me.

Averted Car Accident

One day I stopped at roadworks on the outskirts of the town of Lismore, NSW. I was on my way home and had just left town after completing my shopping, when I suddenly saw, in my mind's eye, a car careening towards me. There was no way it could stop in time, it looked just about to hit into me. I braced myself and held my breath and felt a wave of anxiety hit my stomach, but just as suddenly as it appeared it was not there! I looked everywhere for the car but it had just disappeared. I swore it was there. Anyway I got home in one piece and confused still, I explained to Mick what happened. To me it was a mystery, however it was one he was able to solve!

He said, "I forgot to tell you but yesterday when I went to Lismore and I was at those roadworks traffic lights, a car came at me and I thought he was definitely going to hit me, there was no way he could stop in time, he was going too fast, when at the last second he pulled the car to the side and went over to the other side of the road and just missed me by a hair!"

We had been driving the same car, almost around the same time of day, but a day later, and I had experienced what he had experienced the day before! It had not happened to me at all, it had happened to Mick. Yet somehow I saw it and felt it as if it had happened to me.

Linking in with Other People's Energy

Once I do a reading for a person, I can usually link in with them again when I least expect it. When they come into my mind, or when I actively think about them later, I can see other relevant and important things. A woman I had done readings for mainly through email had moved overseas. I was just thinking about her one day and suddenly in my mind I saw her walking in an area cold with snow and I sensed that she was scared of wolves living in the woods nearby. I had no idea of the sort of place she was going but I emailed her anyway to tell her what I saw. She confirmed that she was living in a cold part of the United States, where there was snow.

She explained that she often went walking but was terrified by the wolves! She said most people in the area were scared of the wolves and for protection they carried weapons, particularly when they went walking near the woods. I had done a lot of email readings for this lady after she first contacted me for help. And although we had never met in person, she said I was spot on every time. I don't know if she was easy to read because she believed in me, but reading her energy and future was so easy. I recall she was a sensitive, intuitive, caring person who worked as a nurse and I think this also helped me to read her energy.

I did finally meet her once and it was very significant because in our emails I had felt there was something very powerful and noteworthy about her eyes. When I met her this feeling was confirmed for me, she had these incredible light hazel eyes that sparkled and seemed to look right into your soul! She said that people had trouble looking at her because of the way her eyes were. It is very thought-provoking how these certain things of significance or uniqueness stand out to our perception, without us even having to see such a thing with our own eyes; somehow the mind just knows.

Seeing My Daughter for a Very Long Time

I had been seeing Kia ever since I was a teenager. I mean really seeing her. I would go for a shower and hold my belly and chat to her in my mind. I was only young, but I knew she would come from my tummy and I knew she would have beautiful dark hair and dark Asian eyes.

In my visions, we would walk on the beach together talking and holding hands, which is something we love doing now. I could feel that while she was my daughter, she was also one of my dearest friends.

A few months after I met Mick I told him that a baby was coming for us in the near future. We weren't pregnant but I sensed that we would be shortly. I saw that she would be a beautiful girl with jet-black hair, tanned skin, and dark, almost black, slanting Asian eyes. I have auburn hair and Mick's hair is brown and we both have eyes with a mix of brown and green. Therefore, my description of Kia meant that she would be a throwback to my Asian heritage. Kia was born the following year and she was exactly as I had described!

Kia is intelligent, sweet and wise, but also very strong and powerful, just as I had envisaged her to be. Like me, she has a psychic gift and it shows itself in the most natural way at the most unexpected times. For instance, I can remember when Kia was still quite small and she said the word chocolate out loud just after I thought to myself that I felt like eating chocolate!

When I first started seeing our little boy, Orin, several years before he was born, he had blonde hair in my vision. When he was born, and for the first few years of his life he did indeed have fair hair, and his personality is exactly the way I had envisaged. Orin is a loving and caring person, and he says the most interesting and pertinent things! He's also got the most hilarious sense of humour and he loves teasing his family members!

When he was two and three quarters years old, we were in the kitchen and I was suddenly struck by how much I loved him and how happy I was to have him with me. In that precise moment, he stopped what he was doing, looked up at me with serious, wide eyes and said, "You are feeling very happy aren't you?" He used the exact word that had just flashed in my mind. There is another amazing story about his mind reading abilities in Chapter 7.

Our children are so much more than they appear! We have so much to learn from them. They can help us remember who we are at our core, how natural intuition is and just what we can actually do with it.

MEDICAL INTUITION

'Medical Intuition' is a term that has taken on much interest in the last decade or so. It is a process whereby a person can read the energy of another person and sense an illness, injury or disease in a certain part of the body. Among other things, medical intuition has been used to detect cancer and heart disease, broken bones, anxiety and depression. It is also something that is natural to the shamans and healers in Indigenous cultures around the world. Whenever I do a reading or meet someone for the first time, I find that I am naturally able to use medical intuition. I have included several interesting examples below.

Arm Pain

I was backpacking in San Diego, California in 2000, when I felt drawn to go for a walk towards the beach. On the way I found a lovely arcade, filled with enchanting small stores including a crystal shop, and a bohemian gift shop that I was drawn into first. Upon entering the little hippy shop, my right arm immediately became painful. I struck up a conversation with the woman behind the counter and I asked her if she had a problem with her arm, because the longer I stood there, the more intense the pain became.

She acknowledged that her right arm and shoulder was indeed wracked with pain and she prayed to the angels right there and then to remove the pain from my arm. It helped, but it would be some time before the intensity of the pain dissipated. The woman had severe arthritis, which particularly affected her right arm. She was on anti-inflammatory medication but some days it was just so bad, nothing would help, and this was one of those days.

Despite the shared pain, or perhaps because of it, we shared a lovely interaction - deeply spiritual, deeply connected and full of love.

Through medical intuition we can see into each other's bodies, hearts, souls and minds because we are in essence so much more than just the physical, so much more than what we appear to be.

Incidentally, I also went into the crystal shop, which was owned by friends of this lady, and I purchased the most stunning rose quartz crystal ring. That ring was so powerful and meaningful to me that I wore it for a very long time thereafter. It was a precious reminder to me of the power of the angels and of the transfer of love and energy that surrounds us on so many levels in our everyday lives. I felt led into that shop that day, like the two of us needed or were destined to meet. The fact that we had never met before (at least not in these bodies) meant absolutely nothing to us. We were like dear long lost friends meeting by chance while on holidays somewhere remote and out of the way.

This is a fantastic reminder of how we are all connected, spiritually to one another. We can meet people for the first time but feel like we've known them forever. Time does not exist in the spirit world and there is no separation between souls, not in the way that we often feel separate from things here. We follow time so we can organize our lives but time is really an illusion that makes things appear permanent and binds us to the physical world.

In death, we experience this impermanence when the physical body dies and life renews itself again. Death is just the body shedding old clothes to the soul.

Sensing Cancer

Sally was a lovely lady who worked in a little bookshop in Waterford City, Ireland. She appeared to be a very kind person who emanated this special feeling of love and peace. The problem was, I knew she was sick, and each time I visited the shop, I could sense that she had cancer. You couldn't tell from looking at Sally that anything was wrong and I never said anything, as it just didn't feel right to me.

One day I went in to see her but as I got closer, I already knew she wasn't going to be there. I felt she was getting cancer treatment. Although I thought I knew already, I approached the new lady behind the desk and asked her where Sally was. She explained that Sally was getting treatment for cancer, which had only just been discovered. I prayed that she would get through her ordeal and I asked the angels to help her through it.

Painful Periods

I was looking at doing readings in a new office space and I arranged a meeting to look at the room. The woman showing me the room was very professional and friendly but I felt as though her womb was literally screaming at me! We were in the kitchen making tea when I told her what I felt.

She explained that she had just gotten her periods that day and she was in pain as it was her heaviest day. Even though I was talking to her at a normal distance away, I could literally feel the buildup of energy in her womb pushing at me. It felt explosive and very powerful. The woman was wearing light coloured blue jeans, that were almost white, and they were quite tight fitting. There was no physical way to tell what she was feeling. She was hiding it well, but nonetheless the feeling of dense, red, painful energy was strong.

Another time I was doing a reading for a young woman and I could feel something foreign in her uterus. I told her I could feel something embedded in there and asked her what it was. She told me she was fitted with a contraceptive coil.

A Blood Clot

My friend Jim was a masseuse in Townsville and I gave him a very serious warning about an impending blood clot. I advised him that there was a blockage in the artery in his neck; I could feel it, and I knew that it signified a stroke. I urged him to go to the doctor, as it was extremely serious.

In his younger years, he had been a soldier in UK Special Forces and they had eaten a lot of salty preserved products. He knew that his body had been affected in a negative way and he explained that he had developed a white salt ring around his eyes as a result of poor diet and lifestyle choices.

I left for overseas not long after his reading, however a mutual friend told me by phone that Jim had suffered a stroke just after I went travelling. My heart went out to him because he was left paralysed entirely down one side of his body. I spoke about him previously and how every time I met his wife I felt something wrong with her tongue. Later I found out she had cancer of the tongue. I now know this energy when I sense it in someone else because it was verified in her situation.

The Photo Tells It All

A newly made friend, Angie, showed me a photo of her teenage daughter. The daughter's eyes in the photo spoke to me, although she was smiling, I touched her eyes in the photo, and the pain behind them reached my heart. I said 'Oh no' and the tears in my eyes immediately conveyed to Angie that I sensed her daughter had been sexually abused when she was a little girl. Angie then confirmed that her daughter's grandfather had abused her.

It was so sad; I could feel this beautiful young girl's anguish pouring forth from the seemingly happy photograph. I wonder if this is one reason Aboriginal people do not like to be photographed and do not like to see photographs of deceased Aboriginal people – the photo comes to life for us, shows us energy and we can 'see' so much more than what is just printed on the paper.

PSYCHOMETRY

Psychometry is a natural intuitive gift but it is also something that can be easily taught or learnt. It involves holding a personal item or belonging in your hands and feeling or intuiting something about the person's life (or a situation).

It is a fascinating and fun activity that can be taught in a few minutes and anyone can give it a go. It can be surprisingly accurate and also very useful. For instance, it can help shed understanding about a person or an event and it can help the person unlock and understand areas that need to be worked on, healed or at least acknowledged as being important in their lives.

It can also be used in important situations such as in police crime scenes and I have read about situations where psychics have held items, received impressions and given important clues to police.

Psychometry at a Writer's Retreat

When I was twenty-six, I attended a weekend writer's retreat in the mountain range just north of Townsville. I had been to a few of the writer's group meetings in Townsville and I had previously met a few of the attendees but I didn't know them very well.

This particular retreat was held in the rainforest and before we started writing, we were all asked to share something that we could each do. One person shared their knowledge of energy work and Chinese medicine, and I shared the gift of psychometry.

I explained that psychometry was a practice of clairsentience (psychic knowing through feeling/touch) that involved reading personal items. I gave the group a brief demonstration and then we broke into pairs to practice. I was paired off with a young man, Andrew, and he gave me his watch to hold. I closed my eyes and the first thing I saw in my mind was a mathematics graph.

It was just a basic graph with a vertical line on the left hand side and a horizontal one on the bottom. I couldn't see any labels on the graph telling me what it was about, however I could feel that it was about personality. On that graph his father's curve was almost off the graph, and I could feel he was a strong, arrogant, overpowering and controlling man.

In my mind, the mother's curve looked small and gently flowing. I felt that she was a very quiet person. Andrew was a very timid person and it was evident that he had been very affected by his Dad's overpowering nature. We had a talk about it and he was able to confirm that this was correct and the 'personality' graphs I saw in my mind made total sense to him. We even looked briefly at the influence of his father on his life; I was of course hoping that it would help him find strength to be a happy, strong person in the future.

Another lady, Margaret, gave me her ring and I saw that she had fallen out with her granddaughter and that this needed to be healed for both their sakes. The granddaughter really needed the wisdom and love of her elder but both were being too stubborn to make up. Margaret said she didn't even remember why they had fought and that she would make more of an attempt to connect with her granddaughter. I recall there were issues with Margaret's daughter also not being there for her granddaughter, making Margaret's relationship with her granddaughter even more important.

It's interesting what psychometry can reveal for a person. It might be something upsetting or traumatic they have unconsciously forgotten or it might be something attached to them that they are not even aware of.

Once I had highlighted the relationship between Margaret and her granddaughter it was like she was pulled out of a dream and she remembered how important the relationship was to her.

As I said above, psychometry can be a really fun exercise and can also be a wonderful way to test and awaken the psychic sense. Many people don't realise that they can do it and it's delightful to see their faces when they get a correct impression.

Psychometry can be a very powerful tool in our lives if we decide to use it. Of course if we do this exercise with someone, we have to remember to be respectful and caring with the words we choose to share our impressions. We can accidentally hurt or trigger people with words and intentions that are not thought out, so we should always be aware of this and choose our words carefully (and with loving intentions).

Psychometry Workshop

Many years ago, I was giving a psychometry workshop at a mind, body and spirit festival when a spirit whispered in my ear. We were all sitting outside under trees on mats and the spirit directed my attention to a young man at the back of the group who I had not seen before. They told me he was a beautiful soul, inside and out, and they told me to ask him to take off his sunglasses.

The young man nervously agreed to remove his glasses and everyone gasped in amazement. He was a stunning man with the most incredible blue eyes like shining crystal water. I had never seen eyes that shade of blue before or ever since. The spirits told me to tell him not to be afraid to show himself, he was important, like a sign that the divine existed on earth.

He came to me after the workshop and hugged and thanked me for the acknowledgement that he received that day from the spirits. He was so grateful that they had recognised his inner beauty as he was often judged on the beauty of his physical appearance. His eyes were amazingly beautiful and bright blue but he was absolutely beautiful inside as well as out.

PRAYING FOR HELP

They say that you can pray to the angels for help and they will help you. We like to pray in our family and talk to the angels and spirits all the time for guidance, support, and assistance for ourselves, for others and for the world.

Seeing Where We Will Live
Before We Know We Will Live There!

Mick and I have moved around quite a bit. We moved around in Dublin a few times before we ultimately came to live in Australia twelve years ago. Before we had to move out of a house, we would hold hands and pray that the perfect place would come to us. It always would and each place would be better than the last.

In Australia, we travelled around in a coaster bus that was given to us by the owner, Frank, because we had helped fulfill his dream to walk across Australia. We gave everything to help make his dream happen and we were rewarded with a portable house! Before we had even met Frank, I was planning the advertising campaign for Mick's music career and I came up with the slogan "Who is Mick McHugh?" When we met our friend Frank, the quirky slogan for his walk was "Who is Harvey?" and I just knew we were connected somehow and had to help him.

After travelling for almost two years around Australia, we settled in the hinterland of Byron Bay. The house we rented was a charming little cottage right in the centre of the community. We loved it and we seemed to fit right in but I had a feeling that the house would be put up for sale by the landlady. We had been living there for about a year when the niggling feeling got stronger and it just wouldn't go away.

One day while I was playing with my daughter Kia, she started tapping the walls of the house, saying, "This house is for sale. This house is for sale."

I looked at Mick and we both knew that Kia was right and that it would soon be confirmed. Sure enough, within less than an hour, the telephone rang and it was our landlady telling us she was sorry but she had to put the house on the market.

Even though I had prior warning through my own intuition and then Kia's natural psychic ability, I was still sad. Before the real estate agent had a chance to tell me what the offering price was for the house, the amount just appeared in my head. Several days later, a new adjusted price popped into my head. Then a phone call from the owner confirmed that the price had been dropped to this new amount. I don't know how I see the amounts, they just pop into my head.

It's interesting to consider – do I pick up on the thoughts of the real estate agent or the owner or does spirit place the monetary amounts into my mind and to what end? Are they thinking of telling me and so I hear their messages via the thought airways prior to their physically picking up the phone to ring me? Or was I just clued into them because their energy and my energy was attached to the house and important to all of us?

I saw that we would move to a large house with an amazing view of pastures and hills, with a lot of natural light streaming in. I saw that our two dogs would run free around a large space. The house that we were offered next was extremely large, and in fact, one entire side was made of glass panels, instead of solid walls, letting maximum sunlight stream into the entire house. There was no fence and it was situated well off the road, which allowed our dogs to roam free through fields, creeks and farming property just as I had seen.

The view from the house was magnificent, with beautiful green rolling pastures and a direct view of the sunset over the hills; every day the sky was magical and clearly visible through the glass walls, overlooking the view. When this house too went on the market a year later, we had to move again.

I had also seen this coming and I was actually grateful too because despite its beauty, the house didn't suit our needs. Mick and I held hands and prayed and asked the angels to send us the best place possible for our family. We'd had our second child by now, Orin, and we needed something spacious, but ideally something that had a fence for the dogs and our active little baby boy (Orin was literally running at 9 months old!). We held hands and prayed for a nice honourable gentleman farmer to rent to us, with rent at $250 a week, with a fence for the dogs, an office space, a good paved driveway and three bedrooms for our growing family and for guests.

We put a sign up at the local shop and the next day a lovely gentlemanly farmer offered us his three-bedroom house for $250 a week! Amazingly, it was fully fenced, had a lovely straight, un-potholed driveway, an office space, a two car shed with extra storage space and a lovely deep bathtub. Not only did he agree to let us have the dogs but he also said that we could get a cat, which was a dream of ours. We got everything we asked for plus more!

I don't know if we manifested this lovely farmhouse or if we saw it because it was coming! Either way, the universe provided exactly what our family needed, and we have lived here ever since. This quaint little farmhouse has been the perfect space to finally write the book that I had been dreaming of for so very long.

If you know what you want or need and you ask for it, I believe that the angels will try hard to support you in your quest. Though if we had not put the sign up at the shop the farmer would never have known we needed the house. We followed through with action after we asked the angels for help, after we said exactly what we wanted, and this enabled everything to come together for us.

Sometimes it can take some time before what you need comes to you, but I always trust that I receive what is in my best interests and that the angels and our spirit loved ones always hear our prayers.

Praying for My Daughter's Little Toy Car

This is a sweet little story set when we were living in Dublin, when Kia was about 18 months old. We were on a tight family budget at the time, with both of us working several jobs each to pay the bills. I saw these little toy ride-on-cars for toddlers and really wanted one for Kia, however at around 50 euro each I couldn't spare the money at the time. So one day I decided to pray to the angels for a little toy ride-on-car for her.

Lo and behold, on that very same day I prayed, three different people offered us toy ride on cars for Kia! Out of the blue, without us asking! Two work colleagues of Micks and our neighbour all said they were cleaning out their attics or garages and wondered if Kia would like a little toy ride on! We ended up with three to choose from!

Amazing isn't it? You get what you ask for and more when it's something the spirits can do just like that!

SEEING AURAS

There are some people who say that they can see auras around living people, animals and plants. I never realised that I could do it until I was travelling America and met some very religious people. I saw their auras and I was mesmerised! Since then I never doubt people who say they see things like auras, in the right conditions I've learnt that it can happen so I say never discount a thing!

Seeing Auras of Devout People

When I was travelling America, I was fortunate enough to stay with some Seventh Day Adventists and spend an interesting Christmas with them. I don't always see auras; I have to concentrate to see them but during this time my diet was completely vegetarian and I believe this may have enhanced my ability to see auras.

We went to visit a devout family who were puritans in both their diet and lifestyle. The woman of the house, an attractive, slim woman in her early forties and her son, a teenager of about thirteen, both glowed. From their heads I could see the soft colour of yellow light being emitted; a solid block of yellow light that wisped out at least forty centimetres from their heads. It was beautiful and I couldn't stop staring at them. I recall they were intelligent, academic people and I always wondered if that is why their auras were bright yellow; a colour strongly associated with intelligence and thinking.

A Beautiful Purple Aura

When I was pregnant with my daughter, I was sitting on a bus in Dublin city, travelling to the Rotunda, which happens to be Europe's oldest continuously operating maternity hospital, for a check-up. As I looked around at the people on O'Connell Street, people's heads started to glow with soft lavender light. It was such a beautiful sight to behold that it took my breath away. It was also powerful and slightly strange and I remember distinctly feeling like I was in a Star Trek episode!

One particular woman stood out. She was a beautiful, powerful-looking African woman and her purple glow was significantly stronger than the rest. I do not know why. Perhaps she was a very spiritual or devout person but either way, her aura was stunning and I found myself turning in my seat to keep her in my view. I felt exhilarated seeing her and the feeling remained with me for a long time afterwards.

Auras in Nature

Every living thing in nature has an auric light that shines several metres above and around it. Whether it is the golden glow above a large oak tree or a pristine stretch of rainforest or even a waterfall; the auras in nature are so beautiful that they can often overcome me. I often see a golden auric arc that branches out across roads connecting trees to one other. I have also seen this arc of light around flocks of birds in flight and it is a powerful sight to behold. I have been mesmerised by the aura surrounding waterfalls and the foliage growing around them. The energy shimmers and shines so beautifully I have been reduced to tears of joy and wonderment.

There are places on earth that are extremely important for their strong energetic centres. These places, such as beaches, rainforests and waterfalls, lift the positive energy of the world and help to keep our energetic vibration high and we must respect and protect them at all costs. This is important for our long-term health, survival and overall general healing, positivity and strength of mind, body and soul and the soul of the planet.

WEATHER

They say that animals can predict the weather. Indigenous people have also shown that they can do this. Also there are many people in the world that say they can feel rain coming in their joints or other body parts. We are physical beings and our bodies are comprised of a lot of water and we are thus connected closely to moisture and weather conditions. It makes perfect sense that we would be natural barometers.

The Sky is Cut in Half!

My Irish friend Sean and I were driving between Waterford City and the little beachside town of Tramore in Ireland. I was seated on the passenger side when quite suddenly and for no apparent reason I clasped my hands together and lifted them in the air, using a vertical sweeping motion. I raised my hands and arms up and down several times in front of me as if I was motioning to cut the sky in half.

As I stared up at the sky beyond the windscreen, I told

Sean that the sky would be cut in half tomorrow, and one side would appear entirely different to the other. I didn't exactly know how or what this meant, just that it would be extremely obvious tomorrow.

The next day Sean and I were driving around again, when I looked up in surprise and saw the sky. I called out to Sean and pointed up, and we both stared up in sheer amazement - the Irish sky appeared to be cut in half! Literally one half of the sky was the brightest blue and the other half was the purest white. It was as if a line had been drawn down the middle of the sky and painted blue on one side and white on the other!

It was an astounding sight and one I have never seen since and most likely won't see again - at least not in this particular lifetime anyway. We were listening to the radio in the car that day when the news came on and mentioned the sky formation. The reporter stated that it was a freak phenomenon, one that occurs only once in a million years or something as far-out as that! An incredible occurrence, made more incredible by the fact that I saw it the day before it happened!

Tsunamis

I was looking at a world-map when I saw a natural disaster coming to the Asian continent. I told Mick that something was coming to the Japanese coastline and I also mentioned it to a good friend. I said I could feel the energy building along the coastline of Japan. Then a day later on the 11th March 2011, a massive tsunami hit Japan and three nuclear reactors there were damaged causing horrific nuclear leaks.

Following this tragic event, I made a vow to check the world map for energy build up more often.

I scanned the map and saw strong energy down the centre of the USA. I wondered if it was tornadoes and the next day tornadoes hit.

I don't just make global predictions like this all the time; so far they have only happened a handful of times just before a major event or natural disaster. Although I am still learning more about my own sensitive abilities, I have heard stories of animals and deeply spiritual people, particularly Indigenous Australians and Native American Indians, who have similar warning systems.

The other major event I predicted was the 2004 Boxing Day Tsunami in Sumatra. I felt energy rising in the area around Indonesia and I told Mick something was coming to that area in a day or two. I didn't really know much about tsunamis at that time so I don't recall describing it by name. I could just feel this intense buildup of something ready to explode and I remember thinking that there was going to be a natural disaster.

Though my experience with predicting global events is fairly rare, I can automatically tell the difference between a natural disaster and the chaos caused by terrorism, bombs or explosives. The energy is entirely different. The energy of a weather event feels grounded to the earth; I can picture an area on a map or in my mind and the energy builds and swells in the ocean around it. With a bomb, or terrorist attack my chest shakes and instead of feeling grounded, it makes me feel scattered and anxious. I can feel a buildup of negativity in human thoughts and emotions. With bombs, the energy is dark and ominous; a feeling that something is not right with certain people in that place and time.

I also once sensed that flooding was about to occur off the Chinese coastline a day before it actually happened. I also sensed very bad weather coming for Germany the day before they had severe storms and weather damage. I rarely watch the news or television in general, so I am rarely aware of what is going on in the wider world (though I do see things reported on social media). I can just suddenly get prompted to think of a world map, then think about a specific place and then I feel energy build up around that area. Generally, within a day or two a natural disaster will strike.

The Little White Car & Hail

One day I woke with the biggest tension headache. I knew that something was coming and I felt strongly that we shouldn't leave the house. I shared this feeling with Mick and Kia, and told them we should stay home but they had other plans. Mick had an appointment with someone in Byron Bay regarding a gig and Kia wanted to go to the beach.

We had not long purchased a little white car to run around in. The car was in pretty good condition, and after driving a long, heavy coaster bus for a year and a half there was a great sense of freedom driving something compact that we could zip around in. I reluctantly climbed into the car and we took off down the road. I recall feeling very annoyed with them and with myself for being in that car and my head felt like it was going to explode!

On the way into Byron Bay we were caught in an intense hailstorm. Golf ball sized hailstones were pelting down on our new car and our windshield was broken. As soon as the hailstorm was over, my headache disappeared. We still went into Byron Bay but the man Mick was supposed to meet never showed up and it was too cold to go to the beach. We had only owned the car for only a few weeks and it wasn't yet insured. In fact, the insurance papers were sitting on the computer at home, ready to be completed. For about three days before the hailstorm I kept saying, this car has to be insured as soon as possible. I just knew something was coming! The car wasn't an expensive one, but it was dear enough and we had spent a good chunk of our savings on it. However, in order to fix all the dents and the windscreen, we would need to spend a good chunk more!

Needless to say, I learnt to listen to myself that day. Now, whenever the overwhelming feeling to stay home is accompanied with intense physical pain, I know it is a big sign to listen! I've actually started to notice that hailstorms give me a headache, as do some types of thunderstorms. The pressure really builds in my forehead and temples in particular.

If I keep listening to the warning signs in my physical and emotional body, I can be much more prepared and potentially avoid a similar disaster in future!

Just when I think I have told most of my stories, I remember more. There are many intuitive events that happen in our lives - we just need to pay attention. In my own experience, I always feel an intense knowing and a subtle vibration that lets me know my intuition is at work. Learning to trust my intuition is an ongoing learning exercise every single day.

AMANDA McHUGH

CHAPTER 6

Everyday Intuition

IN OUR WESTERN CULTURE, INTUITIVE EXPERIENCES ARE OFTEN NOT TALKED ABOUT. They are generally reserved for 'special' occasions, like after someone dies or has been saved by a strange 'coincidence' or they become campfire ghost stories. Many people don't seek me out until the loss of a loved one, then my gifts become a very real and integral part of their life and very important.

But if you decide to, you concentrate on intuitive gifts and enhance them so that intuition is an everyday occurrence and extremely useful to everyday life. Here is a simple example.

One day my children and I had fish and chips for lunch. We were meeting some friends at the beach afterwards. I had some leftover hot chips from our lunch, which normally I would throw because in the heat in Australia food goes off quickly and could make you sick. However, in my mind I saw that my friend's seven-year-old daughter was very hungry and would need to eat. I knew they were eating at home beforehand and she was bringing a picnic so there was no reason to see this.

Sure enough out of all the children present (seven in all) the girl in my vision was the hungry one and ate all of the leftovers that I kept for her. Her mother had accidentally left her picnic basket filled with food on her kitchen table and was running late and they hadn't eaten a proper lunch.

It's simple, I know. But it's just an example of how my mind sees the specific details or energy of things before they happen. This sort of example might not seem that important but it is if you consider how my friend's daughter would have been hungry and complaining and it might have ruined our wonderful time on the beach – it was important to our day!

I can often be prepared for things like this that happen. I can deal with things before they come up, like not being disappointed when a friend arrives late, because I have seen it beforehand and have already accepted it will happen. I can be shown what a person's mood will be like before I meet them, so I can be prepared for meeting with them.

I can often have something calming and reassuring planned to say to someone because I have already thought of what to say to help them, based on what I have already seen in my mind occurring for them. So instead of being angry or frustrated, I can diffuse a situation by being prepared and ready for it. People often say I appear very calm and peaceful, I think it is because I tune in regularly for meditation, mindfulness and positive affirmations and this helps me to remain centered. Sometimes I can also be ready with a good comeback if that's what the situation calls for!

I was minding my own business one day when a man started to have a go at my beliefs in God, spirits and continuing life after death. I answered him quickly, firmly and wisely. His partner said to me that I knew just what to say. I said yes I did, but I didn't explain to her that the day before spirit had spoken to me and told me to be ready for the negative people, the naysayers who don't believe in what I do because they choose not to. They choose to ignore all of the signs and messages.

This particular man called himself an atheist and he said when we die we go to nothing. I explained to him that the two of us had had very different life experiences, I had lived a rich psychic life full of messages from deceased people for their loved ones, such as the twins at the start of the memoir coming to visit their mother in person. He was quite rude to me so I ended up telling him he didn't know me at all and to leave me alone. He ended up apologizing to me and saying he offended me, I told him that he didn't offend me, he was just wrong, which promptly ended the conversation!

Sometimes we have to stand up for what we believe in. My experience was so different to his and I would never go around trying to make someone believe what I believed, but I will never stop telling my stories about my spiritual life journey because I think some people might want to benefit from this knowledge. People can choose to listen or not, that's their spirit life journey here, their free will to choose.

Everyday Intuition is Common Place

Many people have experienced everyday intuition. You might get a feeling that the telephone is about to ring and you know who it is before you pick up the phone. Or you might feel certain that something is wrong with one of your children and then you discover they are sick or have fallen at school. You might be out shopping when someone unexpectedly pops into your mind and then minutes later you run into them.

At work you might feel someone is backstabbing you, talking behind your back or making trouble for you and then you find out that this is true. Other times you might feel that someone likes you and has a crush on you and then you get confirmation when the person asks you out!

We can often have a strong gut feeling about someone

or something that just comes true. We can get a warning not to do something, like travel that day, and find out we avoided a major accident on the route we would have taken. We might have a dream about someone that then comes true or they unexpectedly pop up in our lives when we haven't seen them or had anything to do with them for a long time.

Learning to listen to your spiritual side is no different to developing any other natural skill. The more you use it, the more it will develop and the more often you will start to notice it in your everyday life. You can keep a diary or a journal about your intuitive experiences, because sometimes it can be hard to remember later, even though you think you will!

Once you start to use your intuition, you will also start to notice subtle messages or 'coincidences' in your life. Sometimes you are shown symbols or pictures that you need to decode or expand upon by using words. Or you might sense an angelic type presence or hear the gentle voices in your ear of those who have passed over.

You really have to trust that you are receiving information from the other side. The more vivid the images appear in your mind, the more likely you will be able to understand them. If you are going to share these images with people, I suggest describing what you see as neutrally as possible. For example, a couple in their 60's came for a reading. Two spirits visited, an older man and an older woman. I called them "grandparents" at the time because that is what they looked like to me. The couple who I was doing the reading for were looking for their parents, and it was them I could see, but because I had interpreted their images using my own words, said the word 'grandparents' rather than describing what I saw, they were finding it hard to believe that the spirit people that came were actually their 'parents'.

Recently I felt that a friend was going to an Asian

country. However, instead of asking my friend if she was going to Asia, I used the word Bali without thinking. It turned out that she was actually going to Thailand in two weeks' time. In this instance, I could feel the sense of an Asian country, but not the exact location.

We should never assume anything when speaking to the spirits. If we are shown an image or we sense something strongly in our visual or auditory cortex (related to sight and hearing), then we must pay attention to relay these sensations as accurately as possible.

I met a teacher who was extremely sad because one of her much-loved female high-school students had been hit by a car. The girl was on life support and whether she would live was touch and go. Some young spritely, energetic female spirits came into my head and said clearly, "She will live. She will live!"

I was happy and I imparted the information to the teacher.

Unfortunately, the girl's body died.

I later realised that where the spirits were concerned, the teenager was actually alive. I learnt a valuable lesson, yet again, about treading carefully when relaying the spiritual meaning. Yes, she did live on, but not here in our physical dimension, not in the body that the teacher knew and loved. I vowed to be much more careful with words in the future and to make sure I did not venture into my own interpretations.

I'm trying my best to do this work but I am a fallible messenger. I can never assume to fully understand the spirit realm, but I always try to be willing and open to do my best to impart what they say, without my own biased interpretations as much as possible. I try to come from a place of love for all beings, I think this love makes us better messengers and listeners.

Recently when we were on holiday, I felt that something was going to happen to my son while he was in the water on a surfboard/boogie board. On the Monday I told Mick that on Wednesday afternoon I wouldn't be in the water but our son would be on the board and there was some strong energy, I didn't know what it was, but something would happen.

Well on Wednesday afternoon we were at a river inlet and after my swim I was lying on the beach with our friends watching the children continue to play in the water, my son was on a boogie board. My friend sitting next to me, said, out of the blue, "A very large bull shark was spotted in this inlet one evening around dusk." There was the energy surge!

I was trying to get the kids out of the water because I sensed it was coming into that dusk time when it can be dinnertime for most animals, and then she said that in a matter of fact sort of way. But my inner response and my husband's was one of protection for our children, who were still in the water by themselves. Needless to say they were out of the water a minute later and we were on our way home safe and sound!

But that is what I am talking about when I say that I can feel strong energetic changes coming or hear a warning in my mind. I might not be able to tell you the exact thing that will happen but I can sense when and where the energy will change and a highly emotive response will be elicited.

Here are some other simple examples where I have been helped by hearing a spiritual voice in everyday situations.

Buying Just The Right Baby Gift

Some years ago now, I bought a gift for a friend who had just had a baby. Standing there in the shopping aisle I had to choose between many beautiful newborn outfits. The one that stood out to me was a bright green and pink polka dot, full length, winter outfit, buttoned up the front.

On the upper chest section of the outfit was a lovely embroidered ladybird. I had chosen from at least twenty or more designs, but that one stood out to me and I heard a female spirit in my left ear saying, "This is the right one for the mother."

When I gave the outfit to my friend, she immediately asked, "Did you know that ladybird bugs are our thing for the baby?"

I said, "No, but I felt this was right because its energy jumped out at me for you." I then told her about the female spirit in my ear.

She took me to the bedroom and showed me that they had decorated the baby's bed in ladybirds. They were on the sheets and the blankets and quilt. The ladybird was the parent's chosen animal symbol/totem for their baby girl. The woman in spirit clearly managed to tell me this as I chose the gift.

Buying Just the Right Parting Gift

On behalf of a group of people, I had to buy a parting gift and card for a woman who was leaving her place of employment. Though I didn't know her very well personally, we got on really well in a work capacity.

I looked around at all the different cards, but the only one that stood out to me had a picture of hot pink lily on the front. As I looked at the card, I could picture the lady and hear her saying, "Those are my favourite flowers."

So I purchased that card and as she opened the card she excitedly exclaimed, "Those are my favourite flowers!"

I had also been asked to purchase flowers but I didn't feel that flowers were a suitable gift on this occasion, even though I didn't know why. I decided to have a chat with her about it because I wanted her to get something she actually wanted and not something that would be wasted.

As we spoke, she told me that she was going away for a few days and although she adored fresh flowers, she wouldn't be home to appreciate them.

In my mind I kept seeing a gift voucher from a particular store in a town close by. I mentioned getting her a gift voucher and when I asked her if she had a favourite store, she picked that particular store that I was thinking of.

Now someone might say 'who cares'. But I do. I think many others would too. I was able to use my intuitive gift to thank this lovely woman in a way that was appropriate and personal to her. I was able to get her favourite flowers by buying her a card with their picture on it and get her a present from a store she loved. How much money do we waste on unwanted presents?

Another time I was buying a birthday gift for a friend's child when suddenly this mug just jumped out at me for my friend. I purchased a present for her child but also bought the mug for my friend, though I had no reason to. There were lots of different patterned mugs on the stand, however this one had definite strong energy around it and I felt almost pushed to buy it for her. When I gave it to her, her eyes lit up! She couldn't believe it, it was her favourite design, and one that she had bought many times for others in the past as presents! I didn't know any of this at the time, but something inside me told me so strongly that it was important to get it for her.

Living authentically like this means that we can make informed choices so that we all benefit.

Carrot and Cheese

One night my family and I were having dinner at a friend's house. My friend was busy preparing some food for the children, and normally I would have been helping but she had it under control and so I was relaxing. As I reclined on the most comfortable day bed, soaking up the last rays of the warm setting sun streaming through the house, I kept hearing the words carrot and cheese, carrot and cheese.

I was going to say them out loud but I stopped myself because it just didn't make sense. Of course I knew that I would eventually learn why the words carrot and cheese were significant and low and behold a few minutes later my friend piped up and said, "My daughter loves eating carrot and cheese together!"

Sometimes we are shown things that are not so important, like 'carrot and cheese', and other times we are shown things of greater importance such as to give a special message to someone or to contact someone - to ring, email or visit. When this happens I know I must follow through as it might be something really important for that person or our relationship. There have been several times when I have saved people's lives by following through on this information, and at the very least helped myself or other people who needed help.

Helping a Friend in Need

One day when I was doing my grocery shopping I heard an angel tell me to buy three days' worth of groceries for a friend, who, as a single mother was facing challenging times. She never asked for help, but the angel told me she needed groceries this week. So I did an extra shop, with enough meals for breakfast, lunch and dinner for three days for a family of four. I was also told not to take the groceries over to her because it would make her not feel as empowered - we all deserve to feel respected and powerful, we humans are proud and humble beings. She popped over to my house and I was able to say, "Oh

I got you something." I came back from my pantry with several full shopping bags and my friend couldn't believe it.

She was teary as she said, "Just last night I said this is the last of our food, I don't know how we will get any more, I don't get paid for three days."

Well she didn't need to worry because the angels were looking out for her and they made sure I heard that she needed help and that she'd have enough basic food for her family for the next three days until she got paid again. What's really beautiful now is that my friend has really fallen on her feet and she worked hard to get a fantastic full time job where she helps people who are in desperate need of it. We can all be earth angels here; we can act as messengers or as active participants, doing the angels work here, and looking out for each other.

Angels Can Protect Us from Bullies

I had a friend who had low self-esteem and to make herself feel better, she would sometimes say things that were not very nice about you. She was due to visit when a female spirit came and spoke to me in my mind. She told me to trim the ends of my long hair before my friend's visit the next day because she was going to have a go at my split ends or the unruly state of my hair.

I was also shown that I would feel bad about myself if she did this.

So I cut the ends of my hair like spirit said to and there was not one split end to be found! The next day, as warned, my visiting friend said that my hair was really split, damaged and unhealthy and that I should cut it. I defiantly and strongly was able to say, "You can look in my hair, and you won't be able to find one split end!"

She did too! My friend actually picked up a clump of my hair in her fingers, and carefully examined it and couldn't believe her eyes. She appeared dumbfounded. Sounding surprised she said, "You're right."

I didn't want to hurt her, but I did want to avoid an uncomfortable situation where I felt devalued. It's a sad fact that people put other people down to make themselves feel better, we are probably all guilty of it at one time or another. Well I suppose we can take from this that spirit sees all and that we don't need to do this to others. We just need to love ourselves and be loving and have good intentions for all, and it is this that makes us so absolutely beautiful inside and out that we never feel the need to put anyone else down ever again.

We are Loved and Beautiful No Matter What They Say

I took Kia to get her ears pierced as she had been begging me to do for many months. As she was getting seated, the word 'dirty' came into my mind and I thought that the woman doing her ears might think she was dirty because she was barefoot and her hair was unkempt and her dress wasn't exactly clean (we lived in the country on a farm!). I didn't think so though as the lady was very nice to Kia.

Kia was a wonderful active eight-year old at the time and still young enough not to care about her appearance. She loved dressing up and using make up and all that sort of stuff, but she also loved her dolls, and little toys and running around barefoot on the farm and getting into mischief with her little brother and her friends.

As I looked at Kia sitting there, I was overcome with love for her. In fact, my entire being filled with maternal love. At that moment she became even more beautiful to me and I didn't care what anyone thought of us at all. My friend Lisa worked in the same shopping complex and we went to visit her after Kia's ears were pierced.

As I was sitting there with Kia and Orin, I looked at

Lisa behind the serving counter of the café and in my mind heard the word 'dirty' again. Lisa has the most beautiful long blonde dreads to her bottom. She is a stunning woman to look at and her essence is just as beautiful. Again I was overcome with maternal love but this time for Lisa. I experienced an absolute love and acceptance of her, and I felt that her deceased mother might have been coming through to send love to my dear friend.

After Lisa finished work about twenty minutes later, we all went outside and she said something that made me realise spirit had been trying to get through to me for Lisa that afternoon. She said that at the start of her shift some people had mentioned to Lisa's boss that they wouldn't eat at the cafe because Lisa's hair was "dirty."

Lisa was very sad and I felt it wasn't time to share my story about the spirit voice telling me that word or detract from what she was feeling. I hugged her and supported her as best I could.

Lisa didn't deserve to be called 'dirty' and she was anything but dirty. Some people can be so cruel and yet WE ARE ALL ACCEPTED IN THE EYES OF THE ANGELS!

This message of love and acceptance from the angels and our loved ones in spirit is for us all. They don't discriminate on our skin colour, how we wear our hair, whether we have money or whether we don't or what religion we choose to follow or anything like that. We are all their beloved brothers and sisters on earth.

Angels and our spirit family can provide very valuable information, which in turn can protect, empower and enable us to feel prepared for the things that come into our physical lives. We always have a choice to listen or follow through on their advice. There are many things that can be seen if our eyes are open and if our minds are ready to receive the information. Sometimes the information is symbolic or coded like in a dream and will be relevant to our understanding of them and what we see and feel in our mind's eye. Other times it will be as clear as spirit saying the word 'dirty' to me and then patience as you wait to find out what the word is in relation to.

Powerful Aboriginal Encounter

In my mid-twenties I was waiting outside a small store for an ex-boyfriend, when an Aboriginal man, also in his twenties, struck up a conversation with me. He stared me up and down; he was really taking me in. He asked me how old I was and I told him I was twenty-five. He told me he was ageless, timeless.

When he was staring at me, he said "I staring at you, looking at you, not in that way, I just looking." I told him I understood that he was reading me and looking into me, my spirit.

He said, "We are all brothers and sisters." We were speaking of spiritual matters.

I was able to see his home in the bush and I told him to go back there and tell the Elders there that I was coming, that I see things and can speak white man and black man language.

An Aboriginal Ancestor came into my mind and told me to tell him to stop the drinking and go back to the bush for his health and long-term for the good of his people. I told him that my ex wouldn't understand what we were talking about and that he would be coming back any minute.

It was so funny because when my ex came out, immediately, the beautiful, wise Aboriginal man knew that what I said was true and he pretended to be really drunk and mutter some silly stuff and walk away. He looked behind and we linked eyes knowingly and with such deep profound knowing and consciousness and love.

My ex was freaked out about it, scared by the Aboriginal man's mannerisms. He said some derogatory things and asked me what I was doing talking to that man. He thought I was crazy and had put myself in danger. I stared at him and laughed and told him that the Aboriginal man was pretending to be drunk because we knew that he wouldn't get what we were talking about.

He stared at me in disbelief.

My ex was a staunch atheist, who didn't believe in other worldly things at all – although he once told me that he would probably accept God on his death bed, just in case! I believe he was in my life to teach me about people like himself, people that didn't believe in anything and just experienced things here in a very linear, very tangible sort of way. His God was money and his religion was the accumulation of it.

Although he and I were so different, I did love him and wanted the best for him. But after nine years together I realised that love wasn't enough, that we didn't make each other shine and weren't the 'ones' for each other. I realised our paths had to part, because I had to go and find my prince and he had to find his princess.

Love for another can make you stay in a situation for a long time, but love isn't meant to hurt or change you into something you aren't comfortable with or make you feel wrong or bad. I learnt that sometimes love just isn't enough to stay around, that there needs to be so much more - shared spirituality, shared creativity, positivity, life goals, real joy and companionship and true sight and acceptance of each other. We can all have this, sometimes we have to go through some searching to find it and the people that we resonate best with (which I discuss in Chapter 9)!

A Powerful Aboriginal Angel Dream

While writing this book, a powerful visitation occurred while I was sleeping though it was more a spiritual experience than a dream.

I was in a house and I saw a man I knew in the garden; I can't remember who it was but I knew he was trustworthy. I walked out into the garden, which was more like a small grassy clearing with some trees. I noticed a shadow and immediately saw that it was a young Australian Aboriginal man in a small leather lap-lap putting what appeared to be soil or sand onto a fire that was almost out. It was as if he was hiding the last of the sacred ceremonial evidence.

It was very dark, but I made him out and saw his essence as he jumped towards me. I was not scared. I stood and in greeting I said, "Hi brother." Simultaneously, he placed his hand over my mouth but not so it was closed over it, so it was open and allowing maximum air, only his fingertips touched the skin around my mouth.

I breathed in and immediately started talking in tongues. He sent energy into my mouth and I was completely stopped. No breathe, no voice. I felt this burst of energy completely stop me. But I was quickly able to speak in tongues again and breathing in such a way that was like the hiss of a snake and the sounds of animals and wild things came from me. He understood and then as he took his hand off my mouth he reached up and my left hand and his right hand clenched in solidarity together and he smiled at me. I was able to say, "Bye."

Then the others became visible and they, the Aboriginal children that had been hidden in the dark, ran off following their brother, looking into my eyes, smiling at me and laughing with sheer delight.

There were small ones, some little girls, curly haired,

tight curls around their beautiful little heads and big dark eyes staring at me with such love and knowing. Then another very tall Aboriginal boy who was smiling at me came out of the shadows, and I heard in my mind that he wanted to touch my hand too. He quickly jumped to me and our hands clenched in the same way and I said, "Bye."

It was sort of a weak 'bye' because I had been speaking in tongues up until that time but our hands were strong and I felt his love and connection through our hands. He smiled so brightly at me as he almost flew away to the left and beyond to where the others were going. In the dark they disappeared and I woke up just as the young Aboriginal faces disappeared into the darkness taking with them the most incredible smiles and their boundless exuberant energy.

What was relevant to me was that I had felt their blessing. I knew that they were saying it was my time to talk, to share my angel/spirit talk and to not fear for they are with me. I know that the Aboriginal Ancestors will stand beside me as I talk of the spirits. They are my dear brothers and sisters.

The Aboriginal people are an ancient race who are very connected to the angelic/spirit/ancestor world. Their link with this world and the next is so natural, innate, and their language so different to the general society that it can be difficult for them to portray what they experience and difficult for people outside of their culture to grasp. Although their culture and their Kanyini (spirit, land, trees, animals and their families) was forever changed with the arrival of the colonists, there are many still living the old way and the way of the land, albeit in a different way now. They can sense people coming to visit them even though they weren't formally told of that visit. They know when rain or a storm is coming. They know about sickness of mind and spirit and how this affects the whole person and the clan itself.

It can be difficult to explain how one just knows something before it has happened by thinking or dreaming about it, such as the coming of the rain or a storm or how they know that a person is coming to visit them and when, even though they have received no formal news of such a visit.

At times in the past I found it challenging to express my experiences and I am a university educated English-speaking Western and Eastern raised woman. My father is of Asian descent and my mother's family were English/Irish convicts and English emigrants. I have many Aboriginal relatives because members of my family married Aboriginal people, so I have a very special connection and love for my Aboriginal cousins and relatives and communities in general.

If I find it hard to explain my psychic gifts sometimes then spare a thought for the Aboriginal people who have entirely different languages and traditions, and English is often their second, third or even fourth language. Aboriginal healers and wise ones were connected to all things and we would call them psychic. Their people call them the 'Clever Men'. These Clever Men lived in both dimensions, spirit and earth, simultaneously. There is some fascinating writing about them in historical books and journals. Just more evidence that we have so much to learn about what we can do as psychic beings!

Chapter 6 Exercise:
Relaxing visualisation for a peaceful state of mind

This exercise entails sitting quietly for a few minutes of relaxing mindfulness of your body and then visualization. Do this lying down or sitting in a comfortable chair. Read through this once and then close your eyes to help focus your visualization.

- Feel calm and centred, breathing gently in and out of your nose. Continue to breathe deeply and gently for a few breaths. Feel the breath go in and out of your nostrils. Feel your chest and stomach rise as the air enters your lungs. Feel your chest and stomach lower as you exhale. Be conscious of your breath leaving and entering your body.

- Next take your mind to each part of your body, starting at your feet moving slowly up your body. If you have an injury in any part of your body you can bypass it or just send it love as you do this. Feel your feet and relax them.

- Next move your mind slowly up to your calves, then your thighs. Notice any tension in your legs and consciously relax that part of your body. You might need to tense that particular muscle for a second and then let it go, feeling the relaxation enter that muscle.

- Let each part of your body relax. Feel relaxed and calm, peaceful and present. Move up to your groin, stomach, chest, throat, arms and face and head. Each section might feel different, there can be all sorts of sensations from heat to heaviness, don't worry about judging or understanding, just let it be the way it is and think about relaxing and letting go.

- Feel that every part of you has been scanned and relaxed.

- Go back to your breath. Feel the breath go in and out. When you are ready try the following visualization.

- Picture yourself in the middle of a nature

scene. This scene can be anything you would like it to be, you can try different ones at different times depending on your preference and mood. It could be a beach scene, a forest scene, a farm scene, a field of wildflowers and trees and birds, lying lazily by a pond or a rainforest or a waterfall or a beach. You might be in a twinkling crystal cave, or under a full moon in a garden. You might be sitting on a rock overlooking an ocean inlet, dolphins may jump out of the water frolicking happily or a turtle might swim by.

- Let it be whatever your imagination wants it to be. It is completely under your control. You can change the scene whenever you like.

- For two to five minutes just imagine that you are there, really there. Breathe in and out, feeling happy, peaceful and truly relaxed. See everything, feel everything, sense, smell, taste, enjoy delight, wonder. You are fully mindful of your beautiful, safe, surroundings.

- You are safe here and there is nothing that can harm you. There is only goodness and sheer enjoyment and peace and calm. Nature and fresh air beckon and invite you to enjoy the life and joy that surrounds us at all times. You can feel this beautiful, peaceful energy fill your body with energy and sustenance.

- You can come to this space any time you want night or day to help calm you and bring you into alignment with your peaceful core self.

- Come back to the focus on your breath. In and out gently and calmly, you become aware and conscious. Open your eyes and continue with your day, feeling grounded, centred, calm, focused and peaceful, full of energy with a positive, present and aware mindset.

It is through these mindful and meditative states of mind that we improve our ability to reach the other side. These states of awareness open the door, bridge the gap between our side and 'their' side, and we are able to communicate with our spiritual brothers and sisters clearly. Feeling present, grounded and calm, we can hear their guidance and what is best for our highest good.

CHAPTER 7

Child Psychics

I WAS A PSYCHIC CHILD. I felt scared and I had no idea what was happening to me. My mum didn't know how to respond to my requests for help with it. She told me it was my imagination or that things weren't real. She told me not to tell anyone what I could see.

So I learnt to quietly listen to the spirits. I would sit for hours sometimes in my room looking out of the window playing with a ball between my feet, talking to my spirit guides. There was a grandfather Native American Indian elder who was my favourite for a long time. He was so caring, gentle and soft. He taught me to listen to the wind in the trees.

There were others such as the Japanese samurai who came through when I did martial arts classes. When I was 18 years old, my martial arts instructor actually asked me if I knew I was bringing something through when I was training. I would let the samurai take over my body and I would simultaneously feel his power and knowledge surging through me. I felt invincible when we trained together in this way and had done so since I was about twelve years old.

There was the Socrates type man with the white beard and toga type dress who would come when I was at school, particularly in mathematics. There was the caring, gentle woman who since childhood would whisper in my ear to help me get through emotional situations.

Children have a depth to their experience that is powerful, profound and beyond their earthly years. They are deeply connected to their spirit and to their spiritual journey/purpose here. We would be wise to guide them carefully and to listen to them. They say the most incredibly profound things and can see spirits and past lives and might say things that frighten or alarm adults around them.

We don't have to be alarmed; we just have to acknowledge their gifts and teach them clarity, insight and how to use their gifts wisely. They can also get scared or uncertain of what they are seeing so we need to help them know that it is very normal what they are going through. We can teach them that many children are psychic, it's just that some seem to lose or forget their ability because they aren't encouraged to use it or it's just lost in the everyday busy life of school curriculums, after school activities and electronic screen usage!

We need to listen to these gifted children because they can tell us things that we need to know or remember. They can use their psychic sense to help themselves and their families and friends.

There are some amazing stories around psychic children and I love reading them - you can find them in the spiritual section of your local library, bookstore or online.

I also think we should learn to let go and relax a little more and have fun with children! They laugh with such honest delight and they have so much fun; this might prove to be the wisest teaching on earth yet.

The following stories are some examples from my own life. When you read them you really get the sense that there is such a thing as an 'old soul'.

My Son Orin

This is a powerful little story about the natural psychic ability of children. I was in the kitchen contemplating which shoes to wear for my walk up our long country driveway. No words had been uttered from my mouth. I was merely standing in my kitchen thinking of my sandshoes with the flowers and sparkles on them. I had many types of shoes that I could have chosen - sandshoes, sandals etc. I also did not tell anyone I was thinking of walking to the end of our long driveway.

Out of nowhere, just as I was thinking about my sparkly sandshoes, my three-year-old son, Orin walked into the kitchen with those exact shoes! He walked over, handed them to me and went to walk out again, giving me a beautiful smile.

Just before he left through the door, I said, "Did you hear mummy thinking about going for a walk in those shoes?"

Orin didn't answer but he just had this interesting kind of smile on his face, a knowing smile. He then nodded and left the room.

Before that, when he was only about two and a half years old he was shopping with me. I picked up a cheap bottle of generic home brand milk. He said, "No Mum not that one, this one is better." He had picked up a bottle of 'special' A2 milk that was a few dollars more expensive and that actually is purported to have better nutritional properties. He was right. Like him, I actually felt that the energy of the milk I picked up was not as good as the other, but I ignored my feeling at the time because of the cheaper price.

Before Orin was born, a spirit person told me that he would teach us to speak through our third eye, I remember pointing to my forehead. Time and time again he has proved this to me. Orin is very sensitive to energy and words. If I have to say something to him about his behaviour, I have to be careful not to send too much in the way of reprimanding or powerful energy because it will upset him so much. If I stay calm and keep those emotions out of it he will get the message and take it in and listen, but otherwise he can get very upset.

He's not trying to control me in those moments, you can actually see him physically recoil and feel the immensity of the energy as it reaches him. I know other people feel their children's sensitivity like this also, as I've got many friends who say the same about their little ones. I've also read a lot of stories about similar children. We really need to be 'sensitive' around their 'sensitivity'.

When Orin was four I tried to send him to preschool with lots of other children under the age of five years. He just couldn't attend and would cry and sob and refuse to go into the centre. My friend asked him why he couldn't go in and he said "there were too many" in there. I think that all of the energies, thoughts and feelings of the other children in there overwhelmed him and I felt such compassion and empathy for him. I think this happens to all of us at times, we just pick up on so much from people in a setting and we feel like we have to run or shut down before we explode with all of what we feel and sense!

When he was seven and a half years old he said to me that he felt really sorry for people; he pointed to his heart as he said it. Our children are truly so beautiful; beautiful, beautiful souls here on this journey with us.

My Daughter Kia

The year before Kia was born, before I was even pregnant with her, she visited me and showed me what she looked like and told me her name. However, this was not the first time I had met my daughter. When I was 15 years old, I felt her for the first time. I was in the shower and I was rubbing my stomach as if I was pregnant. I felt her and saw a vision of a black haired beauty. She was taller than me and I was older than I am now, and we were walking on a beach. In the vision we were so close, we loved each other dearly, and I felt that I missed her terribly.

Then, for about a year before I was pregnant with Kia, I could feel that she was coming soon. I would rub my tummy and see this dark haired beauty. I would say the word key to myself, that she was my key. When she was born I knew her name was Kia. When Mick and I looked up her name it meant ancient one.

Indeed, a lady in spirit told me and sent me the feelings and knowledge that Kia would know even more than me. She told me that Kia would never forget herself and her natural intuitive abilities the way I did, nor would she have to work through all the societal upbringing stuff I had with my mixed-race family (my parents were not accepted by everyone in Australia in the 1960's - my father being a dark skinned Asian Australian, divorced, Muslim and many years older than my Caucasian, Catholic, younger mother).

I shared in the previous chapter, how a day before Kia was born I was able to see auras everywhere. Especially, on the beautifully dressed African lady with the big bright purple aura walking on O'Connell Street around the corner from the Rotunda hospital in Dublin, Ireland.

I felt it was because Kia was close to being born and I had this knowing that my labour was going to start the next evening, which it did.

Several months later, when Kia was a wee baby, only a few weeks old, I was trying to catch a few minutes sleep upstairs in my bedroom and Mick was caring for her downstairs in the living room. In my sleep, a second before she screamed for her breast milk, I saw in my mind's eye a cork that flew out of a bottle! I felt her literally explode with hunger and I was instantly awake a second before she screamed the house down!

Kia made sure that she was heard!

Sometimes I do little natural psychic experiments to see if there is any effect. I have obviously a very flourishing psychic field around me with which to play and other natural psychics like my children and my husband to examine and learn from. I am an avid researcher and much like the wonderful David Attenborough is with animals and nature, I am with psychic events and people!

I think Kia was about eighteen months old when I did the following little experiment. It was a spur of the moment thing; Mick was driving, I was in the front passenger seat and Kia was in a deep sleep in her car seat in the back. As I was watching her I wondered what would happen if I 'went' into her mind by just thinking of being in there. I didn't think much about it, I just concentrated on being in her mind. Suddenly, at the second I did, Kia abruptly woke up, stared at me and screamed at me! She then instantly went back to sleep but she didn't seem as settled after that.

It was an important moment because I realized just how powerful both the intention to send and receive a thought could be.

I felt awful for doing that to her though and I decided never to do that experiment again; I felt it was rude and intrusive of me! I did it once when I was naive to its effects, but to do it again would be very insensitive. It was as if her scream was telling me to get out, she was so young she couldn't articulate to me what had happened in her dream state, but it did certainly appear that I influenced her consciousness somehow.

The intention of my test was to see if Kia would become consciously aware of me when I concentrated on moving my consciousness into her thoughts while she was in a dream state. This proved to be much more powerful than I anticipated. I would have been much more careful had I realised its effects. So I feel that if this was investigated further, it would need to be done ethically and with great consideration because it would most likely be quite an intrusive exercise for a sensitive person.

After this time, several other 'accidental' thought experiments occurred in the car with Kia. She was about two years old and I was driving and wondering to myself if we should make a visit to my mother's house or go to visit my friend to see her dog Woofy for a play. I hadn't spoken aloud but Kia, from the back seat, called out, "Woofy!", as if I'd asked for her opinion!

A day or two later I was driving again, with Kia in the back and I was thinking of chocolate! I tried not to think of it because by this stage I realised she would probably pick up on my thought and then she would want junk food and this wasn't a good thing because she went hyperactive and it meant I would have to run around after her!

Out of nowhere, a second after I thought of it, Kia called out, "Chocolate!"

There were no verbal cues sent to her, nothing to indicate that I was thinking of chocolate but she 'heard' it nonetheless.

Years later, Kia was between three and four years of age when she desperately wanted us to buy her a crystal pendulum from The Crystal Castle, a lovely tourist location in the hinterlands of Byron Bay. It was quite an expensive gift for a child, but at the time it felt right that she should have it. When we got home, I was sitting by an open window with her, and we were playing with the beautiful rose-quartz pendulum.

Suddenly the atmosphere changed. And so did Kia.

Sitting before me was no longer my child, but what can only be described as an ancient being. She still looked like herself, but her energy changed and her tone of voice and the look in her eyes became completely different.

Her voice became much deeper and older, with a strange mystical quality to it. Really, the situation was pretty intense but I wasn't scared, because I recognised instantly that she was a spiritual medium, the same as me. It was actually a beautiful and incredible moment to be a part of, the natural unfolding of a psychic gift, she was truly in her power as a spirit-human being.

The power of the spiritual realm emanating from her was palpable. The pendulum was swinging back and forth, she was holding it up high in the air, her head was slightly cocked to the side and her eyes were glazed over. In that ancient voice she said, "The rainbow is in my mind, my mind is in the rainbow. Do you see your son?"

Holy cow was I crying! My eyes were tearing up without any ability whatsoever to control them.

Immediately following this channeled moment, she became herself again, a sweet little girl, and with her normal high-pitched 3 year-olds Dora-the-Explorer-like voice she said, "Can we play now?"

I had been seeing our son-to-be Orin in my mind for some time, several years, and had just been thinking of him in the days before she said this. I knew he was coming and my daughter had my gift of sight, she was a natural; spirits were able to get through her to confirm that Orin was coming. I had told Mick that I felt Orin coming but I hadn't told Kia. About a week after the pendulum incident, I fell pregnant with him!

I knew that things would never be the same after Kia's vision, and also that I was not alone in my gift in my family. This made me feel the love from the other side even more and made me feel happy. It is wonderful when spiritual occurrences like this happen because they are a reminder of the connection that we have to spirit, to our own spiritual nature, to each other. It reminds me of where we come from and that there is a bigger picture for us all. I find this comforting, I don't know if everyone else feels the same way, but that's how I feel about such things. I see them as very positive and healing experiences.

Around the same time that Kia was channeling with the pendulum, she started crying one day in front of her father and myself. Kia was always an articulate and absolutely beautiful child inside and out. Her personality was usually bubbly, bright, positive and playful, so when she started crying for no reason, both Mick and I were surprised and immediately asked her what was wrong.

Kia replied, "I was just remembering my other mummy. We were on a beach; and I was playing with my brother. They had dark skin. A big wave came and when I woke up you were my Mummy."

Mick and I nearly swallowed our tongues. We didn't know what to say. We reassured her that all was okay now, acknowledged that she was sad over that loss, and that we were happy she was with us and that I was her mummy now. She said that she was happy that I was her Mummy now, she was just sad about the others, and then she said, "I don't want to talk about it anymore."

She was very serious and obviously sad about it. We didn't want to press the issue and we left it there.

A year later, we were living in a lovely old Queenslander cottage in the hinterlands of Byron Bay. The cottage was old and had been relocated from Queensland many years before.

One morning I saw and felt two little boys, dressed in early 20th century clothing. The little spirit boys were playing down the side of the house happily. They weren't disturbing me or trying to make contact, they were merely playing, but I was aware of them.

I told Mick about them but of course he couldn't see, sense or hear them. Kia was at preschool when I told Mick that the boys were there, so she didn't hear me tell him about the spirit boys playing.

That night she was very restless and she said she couldn't sleep because there were two boys playing loudly down the side of the house. She said they were wearing funny clothes. She had her fingers over her ears trying to block out the sound of their play.

I couldn't hear the boys playing like she could. I could sense their presence at the time and picture them in my mind but that was all. I knew they were playing but they weren't loud in my mind the way they were in hers. There were no outward physical signs that the boys were there but to Kia and I they were present nonetheless. I told Kia that we should have a chat to the boys in our minds and ask them to be quiet as they were disturbing our sleep at night. We did this and that was the last we heard of them. They never bothered us again.

I went to the library to get some children's movies for my kids during one lot of school holidays. When I was there I saw a movie, "The Tale of Despereax", on the shelf. I picked it up and thought, she's seen this and put it back down. But the energy of it jumped back at me and I saw Kia in my mind and felt something really strong about the movie. I decided she needed it for some reason though I didn't know why. I felt a very strong urge that I had to get it and that didn't happen with the other movies I picked up that day.

When I got home with the movies, Kia picked that particular movie out and exclaimed excitedly, "I have been dreaming of this movie the last few weeks, I couldn't get it out of my head! Thank God you got it."

She said, "Remember I told you I had a dream about my birthday, well this was one of my birthday presents!"

I felt I had to go to the library that day before it closed

and get those movies. Kia had seen it in her mind for a few days before receiving the movie. Her intuitive gift is opening up and strong. It might not seem like a very significant example, but it is.

Whatever is relevant to her is coming through for her just prior to it happening. With support and nurturing she is going to be a gifted intuitive, and better still she'll understand her gift and be calm and knowing. She doesn't need to have the difficult journey that I had, and that other intuitives often have with being psychic in our culture. I want my children to shine in their own right. I want them to develop their natural power/knowing not be scared of it or confused by it.

My mum used to tell me that my brother and I used to say things just like Kia, unusual things that we shouldn't know or couldn't know or things about past lives. Unfortunately, she couldn't remember the specifics of what we said, just that we said them and it freaked her out at the time!

Do I know you?

I remember meeting a lovely little girl named Sunny, when she was aged about six. Sunny was introduced to a Native American Indian Chief who had come from America to Ireland and upon meeting him she asked, "Why didn't you tell me you were coming? I would have met you at the airport."

In this particular lifetime, Sunny had never met this man before, but she greeted him as if she remembered him from another time or place. The chief was really taken aback because she also kissed the ground, and expected him to also, and it was some sort of ancient Native American Indian ritual that he knew of and was surprised that she knew of it too.

Her mother told me that Sunny was always doing

intuitive things with people. When you met her, there was this feeling around her that she was an old soul and very wise. You know that feeling that the child has been here before? Well that was what Sunny was like.

Teaching Our Psychic Children

It is important with children and people in general who start to show their psychic sense, to be calm and to see the skill as a natural gift, an intuitive sense that we all have in varying degrees and forms. It is not hocus-pocus or magic. Listening to them and validating their experiences, providing a balanced and well-rounded childhood is, in my opinion, essential to their growth and wellbeing.

If they feel safe and have a fun, happy life then their intuition will develop nicely in line with their development. You can help them by keeping a journal or keeping note of things that they say/do that are intuitive so that you can see what skills they have and how their skills are developing or if there are themes or areas you can work on with them as they get older/grow.

For instance, if psychometry is a strong skill for them you could get them to practice it and feel confident in its usage. If they are strong mediums then you could work on reassuring them of their safety, teach them psychic protection, prayers and calming meditative skills, and keep an open mind yourself so that you can support them wholeheartedly.

You can teach psychic children to invite their angels, guides, fairies or animal totem to protect them. They can also be given a statue, loving picture or a soft toy to represent the spiritual realm and protection. If they are mediums, the children can call on their spirit guides and protectors to help the spirits that they see. These protectors can help spirits to leave the child's house and help cross them over to the other side. This can ease the child's mind and emotions around seeing spirits. It helps the child as they have something to help them cope with what they see. My friend's daughter uses a unicorn statue that I bought her and an angel statue near her bed. When she needs them she visualises them in her mind helping her to get a ghost to move on and leave her alone. She's a very psychic little girl. We taught her that the angels and unicorns and God always protect her in a divine light and they help her at all times, especially to move spirits on that come to see her.

We can teach these psychic children prayer, meditation, mindfulness and visualization to help them remain positive, grounded and calm. They will feel safe knowing that they have help and can call on helpful angels or guardians to assist them whenever they need. They need to know they are not alone in this, that there are many others of us like them and that there are others that we can't always see helping us too. In my experience pretending that they don't have a psychic gift is often more damaging. It leads to anxiety and worry and fear and also confusion because you know you sense something but are being told it's not real. Then you start or learn to doubt yourself and your own instincts and intuition which is never a good thing.

As I have said before, intuitive gifts are as natural to us as breathing. Feeling what others feel, seeing things before they happen, talking to our deceased loved ones, and hearing other people's thoughts are all within our psychic spectrum. Some of us have stronger abilities and we can improve our psychic ability through practice, testing, experimentation and use. I believe teaching our children to use their intuition wisely and consciously and lovingly is the next step in our education and in our evolution as spiritual beings having a human experience.

One of the most important things we can do for

psychic children is to normalise this ability and these experiences. So far in our society we haven't being doing this, but it needs to change because we are highly intuitive beings living in a multidimensional spiritual realm. One day this will all be apparent, however until then, there are steps we can take to help our path along the way.

A Note About Negative Energy and
Children's Sensitivity

I have two main situations to share where my children and I felt a negative spirit or energy come into our spheres and where we dealt with them by calling on the protection of God and our Guardian Angels. I want you to know you can do this at any time if you or your child feel something like this, it doesn't happen often, but I can't pretend that it doesn't exist because it does. In fact, I will share with you that I did try to leave these stories out of the memoir. I thought they might be a bit too negative. However, my intuitive friend, whose daughter I gave the unicorn to in a story you read in this chapter, received a psychic message for me that I should include some darker stories in this memoir. She didn't know I'd made a conscious decision to leave them out that same week she received the message. So I decided that it was a sign that I should include them.

When my daughter Kia was only about one and a half years old we lived in Ireland, along the Grand Canal on Parnell Road in Dublin city centre. We lived in one of several stand-alone houses in a row, that although had been refurbished and made modern, the original buildings were very old. One day Kia and I were in our upstairs bedroom when at the exact same moment, the two of us felt a negative masculine energy literally swoosh into a corner of the bedroom. We both spun around, stared into the corner and Kia let out a cry. I gasped. Our eyes were wide with, and I won't lie, instant fear. Our bodies were rigid against each other and we clung to each other for life. She couldn't explain it of course; she was too young.

But to me, I will say it was like a terrifyingly, negative energy, a dark soul or personality. Like when you meet a person with really negative thoughts and negative history and you think, oh I better not make eye contact and in fact I had better get out of their way! Someone very angry, with extremely bad intentions. Well it was like that and it was the meanest energy I'd ever felt, living or dead. It was definitely masculine.

His dark mass clung to the corner of the bedroom and we could feel him watching us. Kia stared into my face, with those terrified eyes and then she would look back into the corner. I told her it was alright and I prayed to my big massive female guardian angel, she's massive, so tall, like a building, she's strong and she's got the biggest wings you've ever seen. I sent the light from the universe, the God light, and I saw him recoil from the light and he literally swooshed away and disappeared back through the wall in the direction from which he had come, which was back into the house of our ninety-three-year-old, blind, deaf widowed neighbour.

I never thought I'd have to face that again. It just never occurred to me I suppose. Then a few years ago, in the house that we live in now, we were in the children's bedroom, myself, Kia and Orin, while Mick was at work. It was a Saturday night and that day Mick and I had had a couple's tiff. We don't have them often, but we were under financial pressure at the time and just totally exhausted with two little kids and him having to go away for work all the time. At one point during the tiff, Mick slammed a door in anger. We were both upset in the moment but managed to resolve it and apologised to each other pretty much straight away. However, as I can sometimes see things before they happen, I had this niggly feeling that it would invite 'something' into the house. I had a psychic moment and foresaw a dark energy travelling down the road past our house and I saw it sense the energy of our argument.

That same night, as I said, the kids and I were in the bedroom. We were reading on the bed and having a lovely time together. I had realised that I had really vented to Mick that afternoon and probably blamed him for my feelings at the time, I realised we were in it together and that we loved each other so much, we'd get through the financial strain, we always did. He is such a hard worker for his family, just as I worked hard in the home with the children and my work, so we are a wonderful team, but even the most wonderful team has to let off some steam sometimes!

Suddenly, out of nowhere, I saw the negative energy flying down the country road past our house, I literally felt it stop and I felt it feel the resonance of the door slamming. Yet again it had a strong and angry masculine essence like the first time I'd experienced such a thing. It came onto the deck of our house in a swoosh and was coming into the room. At that point, Orin swung his head to the closed French doors and yelled out, "It's the woodsman." His eyes were wide and glassy; he looked terrified. The woodsman was a bad man, a children's character from a Scooby Doo episode that was way too scary for a little one to watch but because he had a big sister he had watched it. Interestingly Kia did not seem to sense the energy at the time, she didn't say anything about it. She would have been maybe about nine then.

I said, "Yes it is but don't worry honey, he can't get us, God protects us." And I said an instant prayer and called on the power and light of God to protect us. Now I need to make a confession that I had been finding it hard to use the word God for some time because it had so many human connotations, war in the name of religions, priests hurting children in churches, all sorts of awful things like that. I also live in quite a hippy area near Byron Bay so it's not really trendy to say the word God, people are very spiritual, but tend to be new age spiritual, so it's more acceptable to say source, divine, creator or light or even Goddess.

From that moment I understood that God was none of those human things and God was the highest light, the source of all the goodness and that we can use whatever name we feel comfortable with, Allah, God, Jesus, Buddha, the light, the source, it honestly doesn't matter, because God is God and God is pure love and light!

The bad presence tried to come into the room, there was a slight sense of its presence at the foot of the bed but it couldn't fully get in because God was called and then it went back down the driveway as fast as it had come in. It couldn't enter and it was disappointed. It sensed the small amount of anger in the doorway and then the rest was pure light and the light was just so beautiful and powerful, nothing could penetrate our light, our souls, or our space. That night I had an amazing dream and in it was this very mean little man and he said his name was Rumpelstiltskin and there was a doorway of light beside us.

The light spoke and said, "I am God and all you have to do is call on God and nothing can ever harm you."

With that Rumpelstiltskin disappeared into the light doorway and I was left basking in the glow of the light and this amazing feeling of God's love and protection all around me. I knew then that was all that we had to do if we felt that negative energy - call on God's light and love energy, God does the rest.

These negative energies feed on our negativity and our anger, violence or fear. They can influence us if we are unaware and trapped in a cycle of negativity and violence.

However, we can easily avoid their influence if we pray, have loving support around us, are looked after by loved ones, change our lives for the better and just pretty much ignore and negate their existence. They have to move on because there is just nothing for them, they only want or feed on negativity, and often negativity is a choice so we can lift ourselves out of it using our will and strength and supportive networks. They can't do anything to us when we are light and the light surrounds us. Prayer, positive thoughts, intentions, affirmations and behaviours (such as acts of kindness), can help any people we see in negative states or situations.

God and the spirits/angels/guides etc. intervene when we ask them to and they do what can be done. Sometimes what appears to be a negative outcome can still occur, but that outcome is for reasons we don't understand and can have incredibly positive consequences that make a big difference to many other human lives. For example, a person dies from a drug overdose and the family raise awareness and money and start a foundation to help young people on drugs overcome their addiction and get them back on their feet; there is a massive flood and much is lost, however the wider community band together and find something special together that their community just didn't have before.

We don't always know why these things occur, but by God we can pull together and move mountains and help each other when we realise that God is on our side and goodness is inside each and every one of us, sometimes a catalyst is needed to bring it out into the light of day. And so we do our best in this life and we trust in the powers that be that we are on the right path at all times. I need to say, 'Amen' to that, I just can't help myself.

A Powerful Example of Intuition

The following example is a potent reminder of why it is important to listen to our inner voice/intuition. It could also be seen as perhaps showing that despite a feeling or a knowing, things are meant to happen. This is a spiritual philosophical debate into fate and predetermined destiny that I am constantly reminded of because of my precognitive ability.

I rarely watch television, but one night in March 2011, I felt compelled to watch and I 'happened' to catch this short but powerful story on the nightly news.

The presenter reported that a young teenage surfer was killed in a freak accident in a surfing competition just an hour north of where I live. He then went on to say that the young surfer told his friends beforehand that he felt he shouldn't compete that day, that he had a strange feeling just before competing that he shouldn't go into the water. He felt something bad was going to happen to him, but he dismissed it, competed anyway and died in a freak collision with a rogue jet ski.

This young person's death was not in vain. We can all learn from this. We can cultivate our listening; develop our psychic gift. Your body will let you know because it will know without actually knowing! You will have a feeling, a knowing, a hunch something is about to happen.

It does take some learning to listen to the signs within the body-mind system. It takes patience, and inner strength and calmness also. You will usually know if it's life threatening because you will react automatically if you are meant to stop something from happening. You might hear a clear voice or see a clear image. You might cry or shake uncontrollably. You will just know and have a 'feeling' just like our young man here in this example.

I know the more I write this book and concentrate on

my intuition, the stronger my intuition is and the easier it is for the beings, images and messages to get through to me. A few years ago I had a strong feeling to go to a café and saw myself sitting there with my friend. I didn't go however because she was supposed to be meeting me at a park. Then, she text messaged to tell me she went to that particular café first so she was running late.

I didn't know at the time but she always went to that cafe. If I had have listened to my gut feeling I could have gone to the café first with her, then to the park, but our children were really happy at the park while we waited for her to come. So sometimes, even though you see something, it doesn't mean you have to follow it, you always have a choice.

The important thing is to trust and act upon your intuition when you feel it's really important. When you listen to yourself and do what feels right for you, others will benefit also.

Do not for example compete in that surfing competition. Do not get in that car with the drunk driver, especially if you feel really nervous in your tummy or just 'not right' about that person or the situation. Do not eat the last muffin or drink one more alcoholic drink when you know it will make you feel ill. Sometimes we do make the mistake because we have not listened to our intuition. If this happens use it as a learning experience and try not to repeat those same mistakes again if you find yourself in a similar situation. Also these mistakes can be useful to help you understand and learn what an intuitive feeling actually is.

When you feel the urge, do pick up the phone and make that phone call that is niggling at you. Do drive to your friend's house to check she is okay if you get a funny feeling that she needs help. Do take the right turn and not the left turn when you feel it is right to avoid a particular route, thereby avoiding an accident that has just happened. Drive carefully, slowing down when you feel that niggle inside, and thereby avoiding the toddler that just ran out onto the road (this happened to me!). I heard a male voice in my mind tell me to slow down because a little one was going to run out in front of me and then I actually saw the toddler in my mind as I approached the section of road, with a car park across the road and a shop on the other side. I slowed right down, almost to a crawl and the toddler ran out so fast into the middle of the road. He came out of now where. His father ran after him and looked at me with absolute terror! Had I been driving the normal speed of 50 km/hr that is allowed through that area, it might have been a different story.

Once I felt strongly that I should leave a party but didn't listen to that strong voice inside and an intoxicated person hurt my daughter's ankle. At the party I kept feeling I had to go. So did Mick. We tried to leave but just kept getting caught up in conversations or the kids would be busy doing something. We left it so late and then it was too late and our daughter was hurt.

Not too badly but enough that she was sore for a few days and it was a scary situation and we could have avoided it if we would have listened to the voice inside ourselves. On the other hand, she wasn't seriously hurt and we then learnt that this person wasn't to be trusted around children and were able to make a clear decision not to continue our friendship with this person.

Other times I will shake in my chest or cry incessantly and know that I shouldn't do something or that someone is in trouble. The body really has a strong reaction that is separate to the conscious awareness of knowledge. The body will know even before the conscious mind has caught up. Current computer research is backing this up - showing that the body and brain know what is coming in a computer test even before the computer has randomly selected either a positive or negative image to show people. Unfortunately, I lost the reference for this research but it was fascinating at the time and I never forgot the results!

The young surfer could have listened to his intuition and not competed however for whatever reasons unbeknown to us, he was not meant to. The lesson I received is to listen to our intuition, but to know that when things do happen they are for a purpose. It was his porthole out of here and he may have been so in tune with his life journey that he may have remembered that it was his porthole. I have learnt, as difficult as life can be sometimes, we must learn to trust in the flow of events.

His soul's journey is not for us to evaluate but to learn from. It might just help us to make the right choices that we need to make to survive or to accept when things happen to our loved ones.

Instead of running blindly through life, we can pause and reflect and obtain guidance to help us along the way. We can take our time and listen to our innate knowing because it just might save someone's life or our own. We have choices to make and we just have to make them based on everything we can establish as fact, as well as everything we feel or intuit. What never ceases to amaze me, is that at times, the intuitive or 'other' voice we hear can be so clear and so strong that it cannot be denied!

I also feel that the young surfer's life reminds us to live life to the full, at any time, the calling to return to spiritual form might be there, so make your time here count.

Relish it here. Enjoy it. Feel every moment. Enjoy every sunset and sunrise. Notice every beautiful and interesting cloud formation or the way the energy field surrounds a flock of birds as they soar overhead in the sky. Smell the croissants heating up in the oven, allow yourself to enjoy the tang of the raw, dark, organic, market-fresh chocolate as it melts on your tongue.

Live life without regret by being grateful, loving, thoughtful and peaceful. Do what you love. Live without harming others. Do not use others for monetary gain or your own physical pleasure. In fact, help other people when you can.

From what I understand, karma catches up with us, those moments of hurting others will be something we will work through on the other side and perhaps in a future life if we don't work through them while we are in our current human forms.

This emotional work on the other side can be avoided if we listen to that voice inside that tells us to stop or that something is inappropriate or wrong. We can learn the lesson just by feeling that it is wrong, not by having to hurt others and ultimately ourselves in the process. (We know that spirit sees all – I have a spirit voice that tells me to stop and think about what I am telling people now and I have found the times that I have ignored her warnings I have regretted what I have said).

Some people think of our earthly life as a game or as a type of school/learning centre for our souls. Regardless if it is a game or a centre of learning or both, I know that it is an important place for our soul development. What happens here does matter, to both our eternal existence as spiritual beings and in the overall bigger scheme of things that we cannot yet fathom.

Thus it is important to be present while we are here and we too could be as conscious and aware as our young surfer. We have nothing to fear, but much to look forward to, grow from and learn, both here and now, and when we return to our state of spirit.

Putting it into perspective

I have learnt that there are often reasons behind things that we just cannot understand or know at the present time, and these reasons may be just outside of our awareness. I try not to take things so personally, to see the bigger picture and to develop a spiritual perspective as the meaning of life. Of course, there are things that will challenge that perspective, such as the death of a loved one. But it will also help you see clearly as well.

When my father was dying, both he and I were so tuned in to the other side that his deceased family members were visiting us and preparing us for his departure in our dreams. Still when he physically left, it hurt so much. For despite being able to communicate with those on the other side, I was still a little girl who had lost her much-loved father.

CHAPTER 8

Psychic Sight &
The Prediction Of 9/11

MUCH LIKE MANY PEOPLE IN THE WESTERN WORLD, THE YEAR OF SEPTEMBER 11, 2001, is a year I will never forget. I had been on holiday in America at the start of the year and I felt very connected to the place and the people. I did encounter some negativity. Some people on a train tried to distract me while another man tried to get into my bag. I also saw a lot of poverty and what appeared to be mental health issues, people living on the streets and pushing shopping carts like in the movies, especially in San Diego. I remember thinking about these people and wondering about their stories.

I had never really encountered such things in real life, only on television. I had seen people on drugs in Sydney when I was there on holidays and some women who were selling themselves, and there was a lot of marijuana going around when I was growing up, but other than that my life had been sheltered to real homelessness and poverty, growing up in a small farming town in Far North Queensland, Australia.

There were issues in my country hometown of course, but with less people, a relatively easy-going lifestyle and an established social welfare system, the issues were easier to conceal, not entirely hidden away, but definitely not as apparent or prevalent as they were in the large cities in America.

In January 2001, I had been staying with a friend, Peter in the Florida Keys. I said to him one day, "Your people have opened themselves up to terrorism, it is coming soon."

He looked at me and said, "If you are saying that, then it is coming." He had seen me do readings for people and he knew my psychic ability was strong.

I had never felt anything like this ever before. But because I was in America the year that 9/11 occurred, I think I was able to connect in with the powerful energy of what was coming.

I didn't have much more information; just a strong knowing that terrorism would happen on American shores in the latter half of the year.

Several months later I was back in Australia. I was at a creek south of Townsville when a man, whom I can only describe as an old American hippy, caught my attention. He was wearing what appeared to be a leather lap-lap around his waist, and he sat playing a didgeridoo at a picnic table by the creek. I went over to him and listened to his playing, I had a friend with me but he didn't come over to the man. The man told me his name was Kao Windsong (definitely a hippy!). There was an amazing energy between us and I opened up my psychic channel.

I told him that the world as we knew it was going to change by the latter half of that year, that it started in America and that it would swoosh across the entire world. I saw this big bomb type cloud; like the ones you see when you envisage Hiroshima. As strange as he looked, playing a didgeridoo in the middle of nowhere, wearing next to nothing, he must have thought I was one of those kooky doomsday people, and he replied in the negative, stating that he didn't think so, that nothing like that would happen, that things would stay the same.

He said to me, "No, it's what we do on an individual level that counts." He said that he was going to keep walking the main road between the Australian towns of Cairns and Rockhampton so that people would keep seeing him and wake up (by which I think he meant that they would see that there are many ways to exist on this planet and it might just get them to think a little about their own existence).

I have always remembered his name and the email address he gave me. I tried to email him after 9/11 to point out to him that my prediction came true, but he never responded.

So, after his negative words, I didn't tell anyone else. I thought that it did sound a little strange what I was saying, and besides, I couldn't verify it. I had no reason to know or think that this big 'swoosh' would happen - that the Western world as we knew it would change forever. I couldn't prove anything and I certainly felt silly afterwards, after mentioning it to him, so I decided not to mention it to anyone else.

I was only twenty-six at the time and I didn't yet know how strong my gift was. It was so natural to me, it just always happened when it happened and I suppose I didn't know that others weren't like me (which my husband reminds me every so often when I wonder why he can't see what I am seeing in my mind's eye just before it happens in the physical world!).

Therefore, because I thought I sounded like a bit of a loon, I stopped talking about it and thus thinking about it. I was like a child in a way, very innocent, trusting and still very much in the beginning stages of learning about what I could do. I was making baby steps and my confidence in my abilities had not yet developed either. I still didn't really trust myself. Apart from Kao Windsong,

I didn't meet any more American people once I had returned to Australia. If I had perhaps the premonition would have arisen again.

It wasn't until three days before 9/11 that I started shaking. I had no idea why. I felt anxious in my chest, though my life was very comfortable and I had no reason to be nervous. It was the weirdest sensation and, being a trained psychologist, I remember that I questioned myself to find reasons for this anxious-type, shaking sensation, but there were none.

My chest felt like someone or something was physically shaking it or like I had just drunk a pitcher of coffee and was palpitating from a caffeine overdose. I felt that if you looked at it, you would see my chest shaking it was that bad.

By this stage, I was living in a little seaside flat in Tramore, County Waterford, Ireland. A lot had happened since my trip to America. I had returned home to Australia and been joined by my friend, a young Irish man, Sean, whom I had met while travelling.

We became great friends and formed a band together. Music was our passion and we wrote a lot of songs together. I loved travelling so it was only perfect that I should take up the opportunity and go to Ireland with him. Amazingly Sean's mother had a dream I should be at his brother's wedding and she paid for me to go to the Emerald Isle! I was surely on a magical spiritual path – wonderful things like this would happen to me all the time, coincidences, prophetic dreams, and people around me would be as much a part of this incredible magic as I was.

I was alone at home, as Sean had gone to work. I had told him that my chest was shaking and that I didn't know why. He also knew I wasn't anxious. I had been committed to changing my life from one of stress and hard work as a psychologist, to one where I was living a creative, healthy, music-filled happy life. I was really enjoying my freedom from not working long hours counselling people or doing any more laborious postgraduate study; I was dancing, reading, going for beach walks and writing songs at my leisure. I was eating well, had gone gluten free and pretty much dairy free for some time and I felt so energetic.

I was always aware that I had a destiny, books to write and a certain type of life to live, and I would practice working towards this by writing a document about living sacredly in tune with the spirits and angels, my own spirit and nature while on earth. I knew it wasn't the final book but I was writing it in preparation for when I was ready to write it in the future. As my muse, I concentrated on my beautiful young Godson Jake and thought of the important things that I wanted him to know so that he could go out into the world strong, intuitive, wise and prepared.

So there I was, in our apartment by the sea, Sean was at work and it was early morning about 9am. I had been dancing in the lounge room, trying to help shake the anxious feeling in my chest, when I heard a voice in my left ear tell me to turn the television on.

This was very significant because although we had a television I never watched it. I mean never! Sean and I played musical instruments and wrote songs together. We prepared food and ate together. We sat and read together. We went for beach walks and visited family and friends. We did everything else but watch television.

I turned it on and there was Oprah Winfrey verifying that the twin towers had just been hit only a few minutes before. I watched the scene unfold live. As I did so, the uncontrollable shaking in my chest abruptly just stopped. I was extremely aware and alert. It might sound strange to other people, but it was obvious to me that my chest shaking had been connected to the bombing and that I had been given three days warning prior to the event.

My chest completely ceased shaking at the exact moment I found out about the bomb. A strange calmness came over me. This was the thing that had been making me shake. I was very sad, and of course in shock, as I watched the scenes unfolding on the TV, as were so many other human beings that day and in the days and weeks afterwards.

As I had said to Kao Windsong, this was something that you just knew would change things forever. I was so distraught at the loss of all of those innocent people just living their lives. It broke my heart to think of those people and to feel the pain of their families - the loss was just astronomical.

Despite the horror and the awful sense of loss, I was putting some pieces of the puzzle together; I knew I was connected to this global occurrence. I knew I had predicted it, warned two Americans about it that year (having never ever said anything in my life previously about America or anywhere else being bombed), and I had physically felt it for three days prior to its occurrence.

I knew then that if I were meant to, I would see other bombs prior to their detonation as well. I knew that there were many more things I was going to see and do and that I really had to somehow apply myself so that I didn't miss the messages when they came. I had to learn to trust what I could see in my mind.

I wish so much that I could have done something about 9/11, and other things that I have felt and seen but I couldn't. I think, although we don't understand the evolution of things, the greater plan if you like, there are some things that happen and are meant to happen for our growth, development, change, evolution, whatever you like to call it.

Such bombings and terrible acts like this wake high numbers of people up on a global scale in a quick way.

We become aware of the suffering of others, we feel the horror of it, something in us awakens to loving compassion for our fellow human beings. There's a very sad beauty in this. These are higher order events that we don't understand. But every soul lives on, every soul is vital and important to the physical and the spiritual world. No one lives and dies in vain. We are all here for the love, learning and advancement of each other.

I would also like to briefly say that I don't mean to just tell the Western side of the terrorism tale. Many countries say that other countries have bombed them and have interfered with their politics for their own political gain. I don't want to get political here, but for some reason, I suppose because I have been brought up in the Western world, I am very attuned to the bombing that affected the West. That is not to say that I don't feel greatly for people in other nations and territories who have been in war and been bombed also. And having said this, at the end of 2016 I could feel that something awful related to terrorism would happen in Quebec, Canada. Sadly, I believe this was to be the horrific attack on a mosque in Quebec City that occurred at 8pm January 29, 2017. A man open fire on Moslems who were praying, killing 6 people and wounding 18 others. I can't think of anything more related to terror than killing innocent people engaging in prayers to Allah or God.

Predicting The Bombing of Madrid
By Waving My Hand Over A World Map

I did a lot of praying during the immediate aftermath of 9/11 and in the weeks and months that followed. I prayed for the souls of those in the buildings and the planes, I imagined that they were taken into the light and that beautiful loving angels and spiritual guides and loving, departed relatives were there to greet and support them. I imagined that they were told of the higher order of things and that they understood the parts that they played here.

While imagining the buildings and the people in them, I could almost smell the smoke; I could definitely feel the stifled air and claustrophobic feelings of being in a crumbling, enclosed place, darkened, smoky, and trapped. I could feel their terror, but then I perceived that I could sense their amazement as they were alive and walking through rubble and seeing themselves for the first time as spiritual beings, still alive, being supported by other spiritual persons who were gently leading them, helping them to come to terms with what had happened to them.

They took them somewhere else where I didn't go, but I knew that place was full of love and healing. I felt with all my being that they were part of a bigger picture going on to change our world, to awaken many souls. It still didn't stop me from crying though because so many people had suffered and were continuing to suffer because of that fateful day. That intense shared suffering does seem to be a part of our growth, enabling multitudes of people to expand their consciousness at the same time.

After my 9/11 experiences I knew that for some unknown reason I had a connection with terrorism, the terrorists and the bombs. I also knew that I wasn't crazy or making it up. After experiencing some prolonged soul searching (for at least a year I pondered the event and my part in it) and utter amazement at the connection between my predictions, the bombings and my bodily experiences, I finally realised that I might be able to become more consciously aware of this connection. So I did a little experiment.

As a trained psychologist - a 'behavioural scientist' - I was supposed to be very knowledgeable in human behaviour, but I had never been taught anything about intuitive behaviour in university. In fact, my main specialty was neuropsychology! I tested and wrote complex neuro-medical reports on people's cognitive (mental) abilities after stroke or car accidents or illness or to show cognitive decline during dementia.

But I always had an interest in alternative and paranormal psychology and I loved psychic and supernatural phenomena from reading popular fiction and watching movies. But I didn't know that people like me, with such a strong psychic gift, really and truly existed. I hadn't really met anyone like me in person. I had read a few spiritual new age books especially about natural healing but hadn't read books about angels or memoirs written by psychics yet.

As a psychologist, I also knew that even one example of a behaviour that discounted a rule or a popular idea, meant that there was something more to be learnt about a particular theory/idea/rule relating to human behaviour.

I remember clearly one of my psychology lecturers pointing out once that there is research that has been published where the subject studied is only one person, i.e. $N=1$, and that this can be just as powerful as an experiment where there are 50 subjects, i.e. $N=50$.

I realised that in this case something had been awoken in me and I was able to predict certain things of which my body and mind held the answers. My consciousness, the part of me that asks the questions, knew I could test the body and the mind because they create tangible physical results that can be measured and observed.

All those years learning about statistics and experimentation and questioning were important. One day, it all came together for me, in the quickest, easiest experiment I have probably ever done and I didn't have to write a paper and get graded for it which was even better!

I grabbed a large map of the world and scanned it. By this I mean I put my two hands, side by side, and scanned on top of the map, my hands were ten centimetres from the map, scanning from top to bottom, to see what energy I would feel. The impression that I received was that the city of Madrid in Spain was going to be next place to be bombed.

It was shimmering in this section of the map, sort of a gentle shaky feeling in my hands. A spiritual person came into my mind and told me that the terrorists thought that bombing Madrid would really shake up the Westerners' confidence and morale, because it was generally considered a safe, tourist destination that many people from the UK and Europe visited yearly.

I saw it about a year before it was to happen.

By this time, I was married to Mick and I told him that Madrid was to be bombed next. I also told my dear friend Paddy because his father had a holiday home in Madrid and they spent holiday time there regularly. I trusted my friend Paddy and knew he would believe me. He had seen me do readings before and knew I would not say such a thing without really knowing it to be true.

Sadly, and in all honesty, I didn't tell anyone else for fear of being wrong and looking like an idiot. I was still very unsure of myself.

I felt like one of those characters from the X Men movies, I knew that what I was doing defied normal, human explanation. Besides, hearing voices can be classed as a sign of insanity and I was worried that I might be seen as mentally ill. I didn't know who to contact and I didn't know exactly when or where it would take place, just that it would happen in Madrid in about a year.

Based on my previous experience with 9/11, I just assumed that I would start to shake three days before the bombing and this would be my signal. But I didn't have a plan of action or anything else yet. I was again a child without a roadmap, without any prior experience, without teaching or support in anything like this. I really felt that if I contacted authorities I would be ridiculed or worse, they might think I was involved somehow!

It didn't help that my Mum had always said not to tell anyone about my visions because they might put me away. It also didn't help that my dad had big issues with looking stupid and being wrong. He lost his foot in a motorbike accident at only twenty years old and then lost the court case for compensation. My grandmother told my dad to say that he was going to her place that day, rather than to his girlfriend's because she didn't want the people in the courtroom to think he was promiscuous. However, this made it look like he was lying in relation to the direction of the other (out-of-control) car and therefore he lost the case and the compensation money that might have set him up for life. So you can see, my trust in myself and in my abilities wasn't exactly that strong yet. I had a lot to learn.

I told Paddy that I would know when the time came and I also somehow knew that his family wouldn't be in Madrid when the bombs went off.

Then one day, out of nowhere I started shaking profusely and feeling extremely uncomfortable in my own skin. My chest felt like it was violently being shaken and I felt extremely nauseated. My chest felt the same way it had with 9/11 and I said to Mick, "I am shaking, I'm not anxious, I think the bomb in Madrid is going off in the next three days." We just looked at each other. There was not much else we could do. That's how it felt anyway.

In fact, I felt sort of in a daze, like even if I had a number to ring I just couldn't. I can't explain it, I felt confused. Scared. I wished that I had devised a plan of action beforehand so I would have known what to do. But I didn't know what to do. I only had my gut reaction and my intuition to go on and the not so confident voice in my head questioning if I was 'right' or not.

So, I did nothing.

Perhaps it was my fear about being wrong or looking stupid but I only told Mick. I didn't even warn my friend Paddy who had the house in Madrid (though I must say I felt he was safe).

I just didn't believe in myself, I still lacked the confidence. I certainly was never taught what to do in a situation like this.

It was a normal morning and I was at home. We lived in a two-storey house in the centre of Dublin along the canal on Parnell Road in Dolphin's Barn. Just down the end of the road were massive grey concrete flats with painted slogans on the side like NO DRUGS in big white letters. Sometimes local boys would hang out outside the shops at the corner at the intersection of Parnell and Crumlin Road and throw eggs at people as they were walking or driving past. It was a pretty rough area in some respects, but it was also comprised of good, honest, hard-working people as well.

On 11 March 2004, three days after I told Mick that Madrid would be bombed in three days' time, I was at home, looking after Kia who was a little baby at the time. Mick had gone to work as usual and later that morning I received a text from him telling me that Madrid had just been bombed.

I was speechless. Mortified. Guilty. Angry. Upset in every possible way. I felt the world had been ripped out from under me. I turned the television on. I saw people writhing in pain, confused, and in anguish. Although I was far from the fire, smoke and panic, I felt suffocated and sick to my stomach.

I felt that if I had the intelligence and the guts I could have stopped this from happening or at least tried. I was so very angry with myself for not trusting myself, not believing that I knew on some very deep level that this was going to happen.

I felt I should have faced looking like a fool so that this did not have to occur. I felt such a deep regret, a deep remorse; I cannot describe the pain that was in my heart, mind and stomach.

I vowed that I would never let this happen again. I vowed that if I saw another bomb I would let the police know. I would do something. Anything would have been better than what I did, which was nothing. I learnt a valuable, sad lesson. I felt responsible for not trying to stop a global atrocity. I know that might sound so silly to some. But it was so real to me. I did see it. I did feel it. I could have at least tried to warn someone, anyone.

In the aftermath of Madrid, I worked on myself on a deeply spiritual level. Through mediation and deep reflection, I came to an understanding where I understood that I wasn't meant to stop the bombs. I realised that for my part, and for all of us, the attacks were meant to teach us something and wake us up.

I could only believe that everything was happening for our higher learning, and that there were higher order things going on beyond our comprehension and our awareness. On a massive scale people were waking up, seeing things differently... social movements such as the 'We are the 99%' arose, where people were protesting and demanding their civil liberties and the rights of human beings all across the world.

Stopping a Bomb on a Train
in the Centre of Ireland

Like most people, I am not so good with dates, but better with certain details and feelings and meanings surrounding an event. So while I cannot recall the exact date when I felt that there was a bomb on a train in the centre of Ireland, I can tell you that it was shortly after

Madrid and that I rang the Dublin Garda (police) to warn them.

I couldn't explain exactly where it was but that it was in the centre of Ireland and that there were people in a farmhouse that were creating this bomb. I was able to say they were in the barn and there was something underground like a bunker. I could see the train travelling up through the centre of Ireland, but at this time I was no sleuth and had done no research whatsoever to find out the routes or anything.

Mick had confirmed that there was an internal train like I was describing so this time I didn't hold back and I rang the Irish Garda. A few days after ringing the Garda, I had the feeling to turn on the television, and the news was on (remembering that I still only ever turn it on so rarely!).

Mick and I were both watching when the newsreader said, "A bomb has been intercepted on a train in the centre of Ireland." They did not say much more at all, but they had used the exact words that I had spoken to the police.

Mick and I just looked at each other and we wondered if it was my phone call that led them to it. We had both heard the news report and we both knew that it was regarding the bomb I had phoned the police about. They did not contact me to discuss it at all, did not acknowledge or commend me, but still, I felt slightly redeemed.

I knew I had broken through a barrier, a blockage within me. I had done the 'right' thing and spoke out about my visions. I don't know what that bomb was intended to be used for but I do know that it was for no good. I'm glad I might have helped stop it; hopefully innocent people's deaths were prevented because of my actions.

London and Charles de Menzes

When London was first under terrorist attack in July 2005, I initially didn't feel it. My chest did not shake physically for three days before it like I did with 9/11 and Madrid. I don't know if it is because I was busy with work and looking after my baby daughter or just because I wasn't meant to be warned, but I didn't have a conscious awareness of it prior to it happening. I remember being very aware that London was in danger because I knew the same terrorist group had wanted to scare the British people with the Madrid bombing.

However, after the London bombs went off I could feel that it wasn't finished, and I felt it would continue in London for a few weeks. I also sensed that they were going to catch the people responsible. At the time I felt connected to the intense feelings of excitement and movement of the men who were responsible and I felt that I could also feel the police honing in on them.

Something that happened in relation to the London bombings proved to me that higher spiritual matters were at work. I feel there is so much to learn here – as I always say, spiritual lessons to help us grow but also the fact that there is a bigger plan. This particular incident that I am about to describe shows that we learn the hard way that we must protect human life at all costs and not let 'terrorist' fervor drive us to hurt innocent people.

It was two weeks after fifty- two people were killed in a London terrorist attack, and a day before another failed suicide bombing attempt. I was working at a charity in the centre of Dublin, on High Street at the time, when I just knew I had to make another phone call of warning. I was at work, but my mind was on other matters.

Without a doubt I felt that on Friday, the 22nd July, which was two days away, an innocent man was going to be killed in London related to terrorism. On the

Wednesday, I told my colleague about my vision, and she encouraged me to make the call. Although I didn't have specific information as to where, when or who, I rang the Dublin Garda. I told the officer that I had phoned in before about the bomb on the train in the centre of Ireland and that I had felt the Madrid and American bombings previously. I told her that a young man would die on Friday in London and that he was innocent and that it shouldn't happen. I said it could be in the subway.

I could hear her wondering in her mind if it was connected to the Prime Minister and I told her I didn't think it was. The vision first came to me on Sunday that this innocent man was going to be killed and I remember that my heart ached and grieved for him. However, I was not given the details of this young man's death in my vision, but I was shown the pain that his death would cause our world. She said she would pass the information on to her friend in Scotland Yard, but really without any more to go on, there was not much she could do.

At least I had made a phone call, although it wasn't much. On the Friday morning, my colleague and friend, Ann, looked up from her computer screen, her face was white and she was in shock. She sounded so sad as she said, "Here it is, it's happened, they have killed an innocent tourist in the Subway, mistook him for a terrorist." That was it. There was nothing that could stop it.

Jean Charles de Menzes was a twenty-seven-year-old Brazilian electrician and specialist forces had mistaken him for a suspected terrorist who lived in the same apartment block. Ann and I were crestfallen that police had killed Jean, a young man who had his whole life ahead of him.

We both knew that this was the innocent man I had felt was going to die and we had not been able to stop it. It was also a sad day because I think everyone knew that it was going to be hard to get justice for this. He was shot seven times in the head, as officers were told to shoot for the head as there could be bombs taped to a terrorist's chest. It was so horrific because it was so wrong. This beautiful young innocent life was taken in such a violent way and nothing could ever justify or right this horrible mistake.

The weeks around Jean's death were a massive emotional psychic rollercoaster for me. I was intensely tuned into things going on in London but there was nothing I seemed to be able to do. I didn't have enough information to help, but I had enough that it was painful for me; I kept feeling the energy of what was happening in London, the hatred and calculation of the terrorists, and the high intensity of emotions within the city itself. That might not sound like much, but to a psychic like myself, the terror was as real for me as if I were living in the heart of London. At times I felt so close to the terrorists I thought they would be able to feel me as much as I could feel them!

Leaving Ireland

Although I loved Ireland and the Irish people with all my heart, I was happy to be leaving in 2005.

I thought if I moved back to Australia, further away from all the terrorism action in Europe and the UK, I would not be as connected. I would be able to stand down and not feel all the stress of it in my system and maybe see things more clearly when I wasn't so close to it. Irish Garda were regularly having bomb raid practice in our neighbourhood and I felt great pressure to make sure I followed through if I felt any bombs again.

But even though I was living on the other side of the world, I was still deeply connected to the terrorist energy in London. I awoke one night in 2009 with the date 21

October 2010 in my head. I was told that terrorists would hit the yellow line, the inner circle of the subway, and then Big Ben. I have never been to London before, except the airport to exchange flights to Dublin. I had no idea of the names of the underground and all that sort of thing. Perhaps I have heard it in a movie, but at the time I didn't recall that at all. There was a distinct strong voice in my head telling me this information. It felt very much given to me, like someone reading important lines.

Upon waking up that night with all that information I checked it on the Internet and there it was right in front of me the yellow line, inner circle. I immediately sent off emails to the Irish Garda and Scotland Yard and the London Subway. I contacted an anti-terrorist specialist now living and teaching in Australia. His number was given to me through spiritual means.

I was staying in a hotel attending a women's conference in Brisbane and one of my friends was reading a newspaper. A spirit person whispered in my ear and told me to ask my friend whom she thought I should contact to tell them about this and on the next page of her newspaper was an article about this specialist who was now teaching terrorism studies at an Australian university!

I emailed this specialist and I also rang him. He said he had a direct line to a Captain in Scotland Yard and was going to advise him of the date etc. I was not advised if anything was done with this information, but this time I didn't stop until I was heard.

Regardless the event did not happen. I believe it might well have happened had I not made contact so much earlier in the year. We will never know now and that's how I like it. What I did note is that in the weeks and months even leading up to the date, there was a massive crackdown on the terrorists and many of them were actually caught in that time period and others were being closely monitored.

I could feel the energy changing and I knew that the event wasn't going to happen because of this. I told the anti-terrorist specialist this when I rang him the day before the possible date, and also told him that while I felt the energy had changed now and the event wouldn't happen, I still had to follow through, and give him a call to let him know this.

I will always try and do something about terrorism or other acts of violence, regardless of how I look or if I am wrong. I don't care anymore if I look like a fool, I haven't been wrong about it in the past and I think I owe it to everyone to listen if my heart and mind and the spiritual people tell me to act on such vital information.

Perhaps it is time to change things, the way we do things on an everyday basis in the world. Imagine if I had been encouraged to develop my talent, been supported and guided. I can only imagine how the world would be if we all had this support. Perhaps, in time, we can make this happen for ourselves and for the generations to come - the acceptance and enhancement of our intuition and strengthened links with our spiritual brothers and sisters - surely this would change our world for the better.

I don't think I necessarily see things beforehand to stop them. Sometimes I just feel them and I have to put up with it. I can't get much information or stop things even if I wanted to. One time I shook for a full day and talked to Mick about it. He thought it was anxiety. I said no this is something more. The only thing I said was, "America".

He said, "What?"

To which I replied, "Nothing, don't worry about it." I knew something was about to happen. I hadn't had that feeling so intense for some time but I also knew I couldn't see any information, just that something was coming to America again and going by my shaking I thought it would be in the next day or so.

The next day the Boston marathon bombings occurred and I could only say prayers and cry. I hadn't had any bombing feelings or talked about any such types of things for ages, and within a day of my chest violently shaking, there were bombs. I had to ask myself why couldn't I be told more, be shown more, be able to warn authorities, but I just have to accept it doesn't work like that. So most of the time, I'm a normal mum, and then suddenly my essence is alive with information, communication, knowing, strong sensing, and needing to keep calm and keep my head on my shoulders, though everything in me tells me a storm is coming.

In October 2014 I told Mick that I could feel a terrorist plot against the English Royal Family. I thought of letting authorities know but something stopped me, as if it was okay and there was no need. Two weeks later the newspaper reported that four terrorists had been charged with an attempted plot against the Queen of England.

Towards the end of 2015 I had a voice say to me that France was next. However, I didn't realise that the bomb would be at around the same time as I heard the voice. Generally, I'd hear about a bomb months or years before. But I shook for a day and when the shaking stopped after the day and didn't go for 3 days I didn't know what that meant. The next week, after this day long shaking, I was at an open air concert and as I was sitting in the crowd enjoying the vibe, I said to myself, "They are going to bomb a music concert. They will get them where it most hurts, at something so positive and innocent."

Then I was in a car accident and because I was dealing with the aftermath of that, I completely forgot to email anyone about my impressions. I have been emailing certain hotlines when I get impressions in the hope that they might take the information and use it. I felt so annoyed with myself when I didn't contact about that impression for France and the concert, I didn't realise it was so urgent. Then terrorist attacks occurred in November 2015 in France, including a music concert. I was mortified as I had sensed the attacks in France coming and preoccupied with my own troubles, I hadn't emailed any hotlines.

It is said that governments have been using remote viewing practices for decades to help them uncover the secrets of other countries, particularly during wartime. When you think about what's happening in the world, that information, energy, words and images can be picked up by the psyche, this makes sense.

I want to study this ability in much more detail in the future, because what we learn from it could help the world enormously. How can we help others see that killing each other isn't the answer? That we are in this life journey together and all our differences are only illusions?

At the end of the day we are all spiritual beings and we've come here to learn and learn we are doing.

AMANDA McHUGH

CHAPTER 9

The Search For True Love

OFTEN IT APPEARS THAT WE ARE LED TO CIRCUMSTANCES or people in our lives in what appears to be a series of well-fated decisions or spur of the moment acts. However, in this case, the spirit people told me where to go and who to look for! I was aware of exactly what they were telling me to do each step of the way, which is what makes this love story so unique.

It's now been over fifteen years since I met and fell in love with the love of my life. We have a love story that is magical and written in the stars. It is too important not to share with the world.

I feel that our story can offer hope to many people because it shows that if you follow a conscious path in your life and try to live life true to your highest and most creative self you can find love. If you consider how, when I was a teenager I went through a difficult stage and felt very much alone and suffered emotional pain, I think the story has even more power.

There is always hope for love, and there is great possibility in love, for healing and for a wonderful life. Mick and I discovered that when we decided to do what we loved in this life, the right person came along. We had both changed our lives and our careers and had decided to focus on music, dance, healing and creative endeavours. We both decided to be the best we could be and to follow our hearts! I didn't want to be a full-time, hard-working psychologist, always listening to how other people were living their lives, while I wasn't living my own! Mick had achieved a first class honour's degree in polymer (plastics) engineering, but after only a short time working in the industry, he knew he wanted something more for his life.

I understand that not everyone can hear the whispers of our spirit relatives as clearly as I do, but believe me they are whispering, and some part of us does hear it. They will help us find love, passion, meaning and happiness, as that is their higher calling to support us and we can support this process, for example, by making better choices for ourselves.

If you have always dreamed of doing pottery, music, dance, cooking lessons, travelling, changing jobs, running a marathon or helping others through charity, or something else, just do it, because you just never know where those things are going to lead you. They may help you find your joy, and, you just never know... I went to a three-day dance workshop and found the father of my children and my true love and soul mate.

A Female Spirit Leads Me to My Mick

It was in the Northern Hemisphere, in the summer of 2002, that I was led to that most wondrous piece of the life puzzle, true love.

I had just returned to Australia with my Irish friend Sean after a Christmas/New Year's holiday in America. Sean and I wrote music together and had a great friendship. I wanted to go to Ireland and do some travelling around Europe but needed to save up more money. As I said previously in the memoir, in an amazing twist, Sean's mother had a dream that I should be in

Ireland and she paid for me to go there! Sometimes spiritual events can accelerate your life, and this period in my life was one of those times. Coincidences, dreams, and readings were happening all the time.

I went to Ireland for what was supposed to be a three-month holiday, and ended up being there for nearly five years! I came back home to Australia with the man of my dreams and the most beautiful little daughter who was like a dream-come true child.

When I first went to Ireland in 2001 I lived in a quaint beachside town called Tramore in the Southwest of Ireland. It was there that I met a young woman named Sue. The moment I met Sue, a female spirit told me that Sue was going to a dance workshop and said I must go with her. When I asked Sue if she was going to a dance workshop she looked at me with a perplexed look on her face and replied that she was going to one in Dublin in two weekend's time.

I told her I was supposed to go with her and while she registered a look of surprise at my words, she was quite an alternative and highly spiritual person, she accepted both my psychic ability and my request.

We got to know each other pretty quickly and after telling her some of my stories she readily accepted that I spoke to the spiritual and angelic realm. I rang the workshop facilitator and booked in. I just knew I had to be there. Sue and I travelled together to the workshop by train. Her sister was away at the time and we stayed at her house in Dublin. On the Thursday night, which was the night before the three-day dance workshop started, the female spirit whispered to me again, this time saying, "Watch for the two boys."

I knew I was looking for these two 'boys', although I didn't even try to imagine who they could be. I felt like I was aware that love was coming, but I was also not aware, this is hard to explain but I will try.

Just previous to this meeting with Sue, Sean and I had travelled to Spain on holidays. We were having dinner one night in a gorgeous coastal cafe, and the waiter, who had little English connected deeply with me. We could hardly understand each other but somehow managed to have the deepest conversation about life. He ended it with the most powerful statement, which when said in his Spanish accent sounded even more divine, he said, "You are looking for love." Although I didn't know it at the time, the Spanish waiter was right.

I had told Sean previously that 'The One' was coming soon. It's weird but sometimes words just come out of my mouth, they are my own words, but they come from a place of deep knowing that I don't fully understand. Sometime before meeting Mick I also wrote an amazing love song called 'Forever'. When I was writing this song, it felt channelled from a higher source. Sean played some chords on the guitar and I started singing the song and it pretty much came out as a full, almost completely written song! I could actually feel that true love was coming as I wrote the song, that we had known each other forever and would keep loving each other and knowing each other for all time. It was the most amazing feeling and within the year of writing the song I found him.

The waiter's sentence was to be prophetic for me. I am often the link to spirits/angels for other people, telling them what is to come for them, but I rarely receive it myself from other human beings, more so from the spirit people themselves who speak directly to me, through me. So it was a very special message indeed. As I had been so happily occupied with the joy of travelling, discovering music and songwriting, and doing readings, that I didn't realise I was looking for love. But that waiter was right, I was looking for true love and that is why I went to the dance workshop.

It was held at the large RDS hall in Dublin city, with

about 90 people in attendance. I noticed the man of my dreams almost immediately and my life would never ever be the same.

The Dance

It was an incredible weekend of dancing where our bodies, minds and spirits were immersed in a spiritual healing dance process called 5 Rhythms, a movement created by a Californian woman named Gabrielle Roth.

It felt like I had prepared for this weekend when I was a teenager as I used to dance for hours most nights in my bedroom in front of the mirror of my white dressing table. I found this very healing and invigorating, it helped me get in touch with myself, which I now know is a type of movement meditation.

Friday night, Saturday and Sunday morning of the dance workshop were comprised of dancing in different styles, including flowing/staccato modalities. It was a sacred and positive healing space.

While I had seen him on the Friday, from across the room, it was on the Saturday that I became very aware of this particular young man and his friend. This young man literally took my breath away.

He looked so handsome to me, tanned, full of muscles, with beautiful dark curly hair and eyes with just the slightest exotic slant. I remember thinking he was so handsome that he was out of my league entirely and truthfully I remember having a quick thought that he was probably up himself for being so handsome (I was only 27 at the time)!

I had not yet realised that he had noticed me in the same way I had noticed him. I remember I was wearing a little white sports bra top for dancing and soft red chords. My flat, tanned stomach was exposed (I hadn't had children yet!) and apparently the instant he saw me, he too was very taken aback!

In the most amazing moment that I can never forget, this beautiful man and I were passing each other, in our individual dances, and just for a brief moment we locked eyes and my hand brushed his chest while his brushed my arm. I felt the most intense electric shock coursing through my entire being; it was so powerful, real and unexpected. The intense shock spread from the tips of my fingers to my toes, but mainly centred in my heart area and my head.

I was reeling from the encounter inside my body but I kept dancing, as we so often joke now, we were there to heal not to pick up! That evening the two boys asked me and my friend to join them and some others from the dance for dinner but both Sue and I knew we needed a sacred night to heal from the powerful day and we watched the boys drive away in a cab with some other people. Something was going on between the four of us that you couldn't put into words but there was something in the air. We were somehow connected - although we had barely spoken.

The next day we danced and there was a tinge of grief in the air that this amazing weekend was ending but also gratitude for having had such a sacred space to dance in, in the heart of Dublin city.

The dance workshop ended about 5pm on the Sunday, and we tidied up, then sat around and chatted. I longed for the young man to come and talk to me. His friend was a lovely handsome young man too and he was very confident, he had come to sit and talk with Sue and myself. I was thoroughly enjoying his company but I was literally praying, begging in my mind, that the other young man would talk to me. He came over and I remember feeling like the sunshine had just opened up a little path directly onto my heart and mind. Like a light was literally switched on inside of me!

It's hard to explain but anyone who has known an energetic connection with someone will understand, there is an attraction that makes your heart sing and makes you excited all over. This is what was happening to me. He talked to me. He was delightful. He was funny, charming and not pretentious at all. He was handsome yes, a city boy, but more like a country gentleman. There was something so honest in him that I felt myself being absolutely bedazzled. I felt like I could trust him completely and utterly. I just knew he wasn't one of those 'players' that went out with lots of different girls. He was too much of a gentleman and seemed like the sweetest, gentlest, genuine young man I had ever met.

His name was Michael. It was like music to my ears. It was a name I had never had much to do with. A few classmates were named Michael when I was growing up, but no one close – in fact I could never remember how to spell the name Michael, whether the a was before the e or vice versa - but now that he had this name, it would never be an ordinary name for me again!

Michael went by the name Mick to his friends or so I later found out. The two 'boys', Mick and his best friend, said they would walk us to the train station, and Sue and I eagerly agreed. I remember feelings of such excitement and joy and connection with these two boys. I never wanted to leave them but we all promised to meet again. We got to the train station and sat for a cup of green tea while we waited for the train. We had only talked for a small amount of time, maybe ten or fifteen minutes. Mick was to my right and there was something incredible between us. We were obviously 'into' each other.

He said to me, "Something's happening, it's like I've found you after looking for you for the last twenty-three years." And then prophetically he said, "I am going to marry you!"

"Yes," I said, "You are."

Prior to this Mick had always travelled Europe and beyond, and wasn't thinking at all of settling down, least of all having children! He had never spoken to anyone the way he spoke to me that day. It felt like spirit had spoken through him the way it usually did through me.

In a fateful twist, we lost track of time and of course we missed the train! It was the last one to Tramore that day so we couldn't leave until the next morning! The boys said we could stay at their apartment in the IFSC on the Dublin Quay. As we left the train station, in a moment of pure happiness Mick lifted me high into the air as if we were long lost lovers reunited and said my name aloud with such profound love.

Staring deep into my eyes and with such joy on his face, he said, "Remember this moment and bring me back to this again and again, should I ever forget."

David and Sue watched on, without really knowing just how profound it was for us that we had met. There was more here than a simple attraction and we both knew it. The magic of true love was in the air.

That night we only kissed briefly and lightly on the lips. We held each other and hugged. We had the smallest kiss and I was in heaven. I was home like I had never been before. This beautiful young man did not abuse my trust, did not do anything that was inappropriate. He was such a gentleman.

I said to him, "You are just pure love", and he cried because he said he longed to be seen by another, especially by girls who just didn't seem to understand or see him at all. He was only twenty-three at the time and I was about to turn twenty-eight. I always looked younger than my age, and back then people thought I was about twenty-one.

He later told me that he had seen me almost immediately at the dance workshop and pointed me out to his friend. He was taken with me from this moment.

He's very old fashioned sometimes and he told me he "fancied" me. It's actually an endearing word they still use in Ireland, and I was completely love-struck!

It was physical yes, immediately for the both of us, because we were attractive and in the prime of our lives, but within such a short space of time, became something so huge, so connected that it was outside of our realm of understanding in human terms. It was so powerful it had a life of its own! When I look back now our love was like a runaway steam train - nothing could stop it!

What is astonishing (and herein lies more angelic magic) is that for the two weeks prior to meeting Mick, I had been singing the song 'Michael Row the Boat Ashore' constantly! Then the week before we met, Sean's Aunt had given me a sample CD with a modern version of that very same song and I couldn't get it out of my head. If I needed any more proof that he was special for me, it was this. It was like the spirits were saying, this is your Michael/Mick - this is the one. It wasn't like I needed any more evidence – my heart and mind told me so clearly, but the song was a nice touch!

Amazing things happened to us on this first night when we 'missed' the train. Mick played the guitar and sang for me. He was just learning guitar and so had never sung for anyone else, but that night he sang for me. I told him he had a special timbre to his voice and should continue singing. The next day he wrote his first song, and it was his first love song for me, a very complicated poetic song called Adam and Eve. It was and felt very inspired not just from love but also from the spiritual realm.

I had been writing songs for the year or so before and poetry for my whole life so I knew just how complex and beautiful this song was. I used to write songs as a child but just sing them in the car and never kept them or recorded them. Mick didn't stop there with his first song,

I was to be his muse from that moment on, and then in the future, our children and his love for them would prove to be as well.

Now, many years on, Mick is a successful, full-time, touring professional singer-songwriter and musician! It is amazing what support and love can do for a person – a previous girlfriend heard him play the guitar and told him he was no good and to put it away!

That night something amazing happened to Mick, even beyond our meeting. The three of us, David, Sue and I witnessed him awakening to the energy of his deepest spiritual self. He was on the floor and he couldn't stop moving, he is a man who has a lot of energy generally anyway, so with the excitement of the dance and meeting me, I think something in him was awakening and nothing could stop it. He lay on the floor of their inner city apartment writhing; his arms and legs had a life of their own. Mick was obviously in a trance and while he was physically present, he seemed to be in another place simultaneously.

We gently touched his limbs so that he knew we were there for him and so as also to protect him from himself if he should go out of control. His essence needed to express itself and we were going to fully go there with him, none of us were scared of it, nor were we judging it in any way. At one stage his feet kicked out with powerful energy and incredibly in front of our eyes the video player ejected a tape, although none of us had touched it. Mick's feet were facing it, and though almost a metre away, when his feet kicked out there was enough energetic force to release the tape.

It was then I knew that this man was truly powerful inside and out. That there was something very special about him I knew already, but this display of energetic power, of knowing without knowing, being able to do such a thing without ego or awareness, was a pure expression of the power of one's spiritual self.

When we went into the bedroom together it was with the purest of intentions and we only held each other. We talked and talked and learnt about each other's lives - where we had been and where we were going. I remember being so present in that room, and so high and in love at the same time. I wanted every touch, every moment, and every precious, sacred breath to count and to last forever.

I was absolutely, unequivocally smitten, in love, in heaven, in ecstasy, as if heaven had come to earth in that small modern apartment in that ancient city. I had never heard of Dublin as being seen as the city of love but to me it was and always would be to this day - the city where I found my heart.

We could not be together straight away. The next day Sue and I returned to our lives two and a half hours away in the South of Ireland. I went back to my life, wanting to be with Mick, but I had to first leave the life I had created. A week and a half after we met, Mick was on his way to see me. He had been to his elder brother's stag party and had a spiritual experience whereby he cried and cried his heart out. He was so happy to have met me and know I was in the world, and also to know that if he had to let me go he would, but he had in that one night we had together experienced the truth of all things, of love's hold, and could never turn back. Love is so passionate and powerful!

One day when he was at the stag party I was thinking of him and his energy suddenly changed to very high (even more high than normal and that was saying a lot). I text him and said, "What did you just do, something changed in you?" and he said, "Just had a coffee."

The difference to me was so intense and tangible as if I was in the room with him or even in his very body, in fact he was in Liverpool across the Irish Sea in the U.K.

and I was in the South of Ireland. To this day if he has a coffee he is so affected by it and he gets very hyperactive and I often feel it in my own body!

When he returned to Dublin from the stag party our phones would not work properly and would keep hanging up as if the energy was too powerful around us. We were able to get some texts through however and when he was on his way to the bus station to see me, I suddenly knew that he wasn't going to get to Tramore and he was going somewhere else where I would meet him.

I managed to text him to look for the answer at the coffee shop and the rainbow would be the answer. Staring across a packed Dublin city bus terminal towards the bus terminal café, an old friend of Mick's, Paddy, walked past the coffee shop right in his line of sight. Mick called out his name and asked where he was going. To which Paddy replied, "The Rainbow Lodge, it's a retreat centre in Athlone, and some special Native American medicine people are coming over. Mick said, "Can I come?"

Then Mick went with Paddy on the next bus out of there. There was something really special about this; it just felt like destiny, an important, if not vital, part of our life journey. It was one of those pivotal moments that you know you can't miss because if you do miss it, you just know deep down that you won't be who you are meant to be; that you will miss something absolutely integral to your life's purpose/destiny.

Still our phones were playing up and I could not fully understand where he was going, we just couldn't hear each other on the phone. I understood he was going with his friend to the centre of Ireland, to Athlone but that was all I received. Within a day or two of him leaving for this spot I could feel that whatever he was doing was pure and sacred. I could feel the energy of the earth lifting high, and in my mind's eye I was shown an improvement in the energy of all things on earth because of what was happening there. I could see waves of energy lifting, expanding upwards and outwards. I just knew that something very sacred, prayerful, was occurring in this place in the centre of Ireland and I knew I had to be there.

Mick was finally able to get through to me with the address and details. It was a Native American Indian retreat and I drove there to meet him. I could feel the power in this place before I got there. I could not wait to join him; every part of me was electrified. We were still both so high from meeting each other. He had been unable to work because of it and his boss had given him some time off to come and see me.

Mick had been led by our spirit guides and his own open heart, to what would prove to be a very significant life changing course, a week-long Native American Indian retreat set in an old hotel, called the Rainbow Lodge, just outside of the ancient Irish midland town of Athlone. Dermot O'Hara, a powerful Celtic Shaman based in Dublin city, established the retreat lodge to create a space for spiritual work and healing. He organised for two very important Native American Indian elders, a Chief named Lloyd and a Medicine Woman named Nancy, to come from America to facilitate.

On arrival to the old mansion, one could see the historical mystique of the place. It was a large white building, several stories high, with large windows and the most beautiful old way about it. It had stunning greenery all around it and in the lawn in front of the house was a large, cream-coloured tepee. There was a grove of trees to the right hand side of the house; a grove that had a clearing within it, just perfect for a sacred site, and it became the location on which we built the sweat lodge.

Immediately upon seeing this place, feeling the

powerful energy held there, I again knew that my life would never be the same again.

It really did feel like my destiny had finally caught up with me. I knew something very powerful was going to happen. I was so high in spirit, grounded and present, but could feel the holiest of universal energies, the most loving and beautiful beings present within these grounds. I could feel the spirits and angels strongly in this place.

The grounds were beautiful, the hotel was haunting, but in a sacred, good way. It wasn't scary, nor did it feel like bad spirits from the past were present, just the opposite, all of the energy of the place, the old times that people might have spent holidaying, relaxing, eating, dancing in the grand ballroom, all added to our magical time.

Dermot did not know who I was beforehand, but it was evident to him upon meeting me that spirits spoke to me. I do not mean to be big headed at all, it is just that I have been described as other worldly many times and I have come to understand that people can often see that there was something about me that was indeed 'different'. During our stay there at the lodge, I had a direct line to the spirits and nothing was going to stop the information getting through to this special group of aligned people.

I remember taking everything in. The smells of the Irish summer, of beautiful foreign plants and trees and flowers that I didn't know the names of, the grass, and the breeze, that was fresh and inviting and laced with the scent of the old magnificent fir trees. There was a magical outdoor area at the rear of the hotel, behind the kitchen. At night this area became alive with the power of what felt like a living breathing earth, the wind, the moon, the stars, and something else not visible that held my attention.

My dress flowed and swayed against my skin as the wind danced around me, creating a magical mystical hand, caressing my body gently and beckoning me to dance with the spiritual people around me. I was talking to them and feeling so alive, so connected with them. It felt like I was dancing with the wind as my partner and I remember closing my eyes and feeling the whole universe around me, within me, of me, that night. I danced under the stars with the moonlight as my witness, the wind caressing me and without a care in the world.

We knew that we were all a part of something that was so important to our lives but also a part of something bigger. Chief Lloyd would tell stories in his beautiful gentle funny way, but they would speak of a depth of understanding, compassion and knowing that only comes with being an elder in a very ancient culture. He was very amusing and he laughed and smiled so often. He would tell the funniest anecdotes. We would all sit in the kitchen together, a meeting place that held special energy because of the familial atmosphere created around simple nourishing food and drink.

Medicine Woman Nancy would teach us about protecting the plants as well as the animals. She was a highly spiritual yet very grounded woman, highly educated and also a mother, she was the epitome of the powerful modern Indian Medicine Woman. It was such an honour to meet these people and to be with them. Learning from them and just knowing that they were so important to the future of the Native Indians in America was humbling and inspiring at the same time.

Channelling Through an Ancient Spirit

On a particularly magical night, the wind danced around us and felt like it was alive, enticing us and inviting the magic to come. I was almost shaking; I knew something very important was going to happen. There were about twenty of us that night and we held a powerful sacred ceremony in the old ballroom downstairs in the largest meeting room decorated with Native American Indian hangings and sacred objects, set underground in the hotel. We were singing songs that they taught us; we did a small circle ceremony with their powerful medicine tools and drums. We shared their sacred pipe that held their own tobacco, which had been grown on four sacred mountains, carefully cultivated and produced by their own Native people.

I don't know exactly when it happened. We were in a large circle; the drums were so powerful combined with the chanting/singing of the group, the beat felt directly as if it was going into our hearts. I could feel my body being taken over. I had been talking to a Native American ancestor spirit for the whole time we were there, his ancient strong energy so powerful; he was not someone you could just ignore.

I had agreed years before in conversation with this powerful being, as a teenager, when he showed me he would want to take my body to show people he was here, that it would be okay to do so. I had noted he had been singing through me and I had been becoming something else when the drums started and the medicine stick was passed to me, I became ancient, one with something so powerful, so ancient, so knowing and it felt like I was this powerful man before and now. I can't explain this – it just felt that I had been him before and that I would be again. It felt to me that he was a Native American Elder Chief who had lived before and had died. He was coming to give his people an important message.

We were in a large circle; I began to walk towards the top of the circle, towards the elders. I felt him walk in my body; it was jerky, as he hadn't walked in a physical body like this for a long time. I became a channel for him to speak to the elders. He sang a song that was unlike any other, I did not breathe for a long time and I made sounds that I did not recognise as human at all. It was so loud, so unusual and powerful, I just recall being there but sort of distant and feeling interested in the fact I hadn't stopped singing, my mouth was wide open and more importantly I hadn't breathed for some time. It felt like he could just keep doing his call endlessly and I would not need breath.

Finally, he stopped.

In an ancient tongue he spoke to the chief and medicine woman and though I couldn't understand the language, I could understand the meaning. In his words he told them to go back to the land and treat her as sacred. His power and the way he spoke could have been mistaken as anger but it was not. It was the rawest expression of power I have ever experienced. He was so strong in his message; he really needed the elders to see him and understand that they were so vital to the changes needed on this planet.

I remember he fell gently into the lap of the Medicine Woman, calling her Mother and telling her she must go to the land. She told me some time later that it was so relevant to her, as she had become somewhat academic and learned. He had much love for the sacred mother essence that she stood for and it poured forth from him, such love and profound respect.

When I came back into my body I remember feeling so shy and exposed. I shyly moved back to Mick and let him hug and hold me. Apparently the whole time I was letting the ancestor come through me, Mick was sitting in his chair shaking, with his chest open and his head back. We were both bringing spirit through. The other thing that the ancestor had said as he walked through the circle to the elders was clearly, that tonight, a soul that had once split would rejoin, that two would become one, the sacred was happening and this was their wedding acceptance and native ceremony.

Sacred Union

It was Mick and mine wedding night.

I remember the Elders nodding at the Native Ancestor Chief, (me), in understanding. It was such a profound moment, for in me I knew what was happening, that they were nodding at him, and in this nod they were acknowledging that two sacred ones were becoming one again. More importantly they had been one before, and they were now rejoining.

I had never spoken like this before, nor heard anything like it. But it was perfectly understandable and right to me. This ancient knowledge just poured through me, through the ancestor. This taught me what sacred union and sacred marriage was in a way I had never before witnessed in my lifetime, not even in a movie or in one of those fairytales that I so loved as a child.

After the ceremony, Mick and I were left alone; people were giving me some space to breathe after the big 'show'. Mick and I started swaying, moving together and a dance began between us that was like no other dance I have ever witnessed. We were both in some sort of spiritual trance. We swayed and moved; we were ourselves but it also felt like meeting ourselves for the first time. We were something more. Our own spirits danced together. There were no inhibitions or cares.

At one stage, I was lying with my back on the floor and Mick was leaning over me, we locked eyes and in that moment the world stopped completely and suddenly for a few seconds as we saw ourselves a long time ago. It was an incredible life changing moment for us both, I was an old ancient Chief and Mick was my wife, we clearly saw each other in our Native bodies, also something more, I saw the Egyptian in him, an ancient beautiful prince, who I had loved dearly before. When I say prince he might not have literally been this, but to me he was as beautiful as royalty and as holy as the most exalted priest. It really was the thing that dreams are made of.

But it was real. It felt so real and we experienced the vision simultaneously. We saw each other and our past life together and as we did, Mick moved so powerfully within his skin, that he actually physically jumped several metres into the air and away from me. I have never seen anyone leap from the floor so high or so far and I doubt I ever will unless it is a stunt on a movie created by a computer program. He landed on his feet and hands, like a cat, breathing heavily, trying to make sense of what had just happened. We both knew. We had seen each other so very clearly, and the truth of all things had opened up our souls, our hearts and our lives in a way that nothing ever had or ever would again. We were as one with each other, we loved each other before, and we would do so again.

It was a few seconds after this, that our dear wise human elders knew that our wedding night would be consummated right there and they told us to go outside into the tee pee together. The atmosphere was slightly broken, and again we were our normal, human selves. It was strange because we felt compelled; something bigger was directing us all. Mick and I separated. He went to the male room and prepared himself and I went to the female room to do the same. Though it was unsaid, we all knew we were preparing for our union, our marriage, and that it was a sacred act, accepted and seen by the spirits and blessed by the loving beings around us.

I had never done this before but as my friend helped me prepare myself, I put on my beautiful long cotton green dress, for me it was representative of the mother earth and all that is pure and true. I found myself wandering to another room, off the kitchen, a sacred dining room where our host had placed several vials of pure rose oil and sandalwood oil for use during ceremonies. I did not know what I was doing, but I felt drawn there and I placed the oils on my wrists and neck and head. I anointed myself ready for the union to come. I prayed and thanked the angels, God and my beloved spiritual brothers and sisters. They showed me how to prepare for the wedding night and what to do with the oils. Through prayer I felt ready to be married and joined with my beloved Mick.

The joy in me was palpable and everything was just so right, so special, sacred and blessed. I was calm and ready as a bride should be on her wedding night to her beloved.

Mick was in the tepee preparing the fire for us. When I entered the tepee the look on his face said it all. To him I was the most beautiful bride; I could see it in his eyes. He loved me more than any other. We had indeed found each other again.

It was a magical union. Inside the tent our bodies morphed. Our skin turned a shiny brown colour. I spoke in tongues. A Native American Indian spirit man danced round the teepee singing, we could distinctly see his shadow through the teepee. The wind blew a gale outside; whilst inside the teepee we were warm, heated through by the fire and the heat from our naked bodies. Crows sat in a row on the fence outside the house and only crowed every time we had an orgasm.

In this sacred time and space, we were married.

Our Wedding

Just short of a year later, we decided we wanted to celebrate with our Catholic families and make everything official in society's terms. We had a very unique personalized ceremony in an inner city Dublin Jesuit Catholic Church where we even performed a song. Mick re-enacted how he had proposed to me by singing me a song under the stars. That song was called 'Marry Me

Please'.

It is the most romantic song I have ever heard. Two months after we met at the Rainbow Lodge, we had gone back there for a weekend. Mick officially proposed to me under a full moon singing this song to me. He had changed one of his love songs that he had written when we first met, adding in the extra chorus at the end that repeats the line 'marry me please' several times.

It was one of those times when I didn't see something coming and one of the most magical incredible romantic nights of my life.

At the Catholic wedding, we also had a Buddhist girlfriend of ours do a beautiful and exotic dance on the altar (she was a stunning vision in a long flowing white dress). It was so enchanting that her performance made the priest forget to do the prayers of the faithful, which are quite important to the Catholic ceremony!

On the day of our wedding it was a scorching 29 degrees Celsius, a relative heat wave in Ireland. This is incredible when you consider the days leading up to the wedding, and the days following the wedding, were completely miserable, cold, wet, and raining, with accompanying dark skies! People said to us, "Only you two could have pulled this off!"

Several months previously when I was looking at the calendar trying to decide on the date, a spirit person spoke into my mind and said, "This day will be full of light." This is the phrase I kept repeating before the wedding, to anyone who would listen to me! Only a spirit could have told us exactly which day there would be a heat wave to have our wedding on! For an Australian used to the heat and much more comfortable in warmer weather at that time, it was the most beautiful and appropriate gift and blessing that the spirit world could have given us for our wedding day.

Love

Because of my amazing experiences, I firmly believe that true love exists. If I hadn't lived this incredible experience with my husband, Mick, I don't know if I could have believed as much as I do, so I share this story with others so that the truth about love can spread.

If Mick and I have experienced this, then so can and do others. Love in this form is amazing, but love in all other forms is also incredible. The love we have for our children has only added to our love for each other. We have great love for our community of friends and family and our pets also. We feel truly blessed to have experienced the love that we have in our lives. For me the love of my spirit family is also very prominent in my life, I thrive because of their constant guidance and loving support.

Once you have found such love, the world is never the same again. It is as if the true magic of the world has come to you and opened your heart, body, mind and soul. You are full, complete, knowing. You cannot turn back once you have known this love and held onto it. It is important to try to fight for this, keep it in your heart. We are meant to know such love and to experience joy and love in our lives romantically and through friendships and family and animals and the environment. These are pure and sacred ties that we have with others existing around us, alongside us.

When I was a teenager I dreamed of having many sisters and brothers. I would see them in my mind. Mick is one of six children; I believe I was linking in with this. The other thing I would do is lift my top lip up with my finger and stare at myself in the mirror. I know it sounds strange but I used to wonder if I would need to get cosmetic surgery one day to correct my lip. Mick's lip is exactly the way I used to push my lip up. It isn't common to have lips like his. His teeth show all the time, his lip is full and high. When he used to ride to work in winter in Dublin his teeth would be freezing! My children have inherited it and to me it is a highly attractive trait. I know that I was sensing him, seeing him in my mind's eye. But it was to be at least fifteen years before I would find him.

It is not to say that in this physical life you will not have your challenges, you must work on your human relationship because the stresses and strains and the choices we make influence us. But when you have such a love, in any form it is the foundation from which wonderful things can grow. With love in your life, from your family, partner, friends, you feel you can achieve everything and anything. It's just a matter of listening to that little voice within, so that you can accomplish meaningful and powerful things in your life – such as spreading love everywhere you go, to helping others, to making the world a better place just by being your beautiful, shiny, spiritually-connected self.

Chapter 9 Exercise:
Focus on Yourself as a Being of Pure Love

I try to focus on love as much as I can. I think of myself as pure love and that love is emanating from me. I feel such gratitude for my children's laughter and my husband's boundless energy, my pets and their unconditional love and I am grateful for all that is around me, my community, dear friends, my comfortable home, the presence of nature and the daily cycle of sunsets and sunrises which I find particularly inspiring. The more I concentrate on love, and what I love in my life, the better things become in my life. The more we all do this, the better, more loving and happier this world will become.

- This exercise just involves closing your eyes for a few minutes and thinking of yourself as pure love. You might envisage yourself as a pink rose quartz crystal of love or as a rainbow of colours and light or as a white ball infused with love. You might think of a puppy or kitten or a butterfly. Whatever for you signals feelings and thoughts of love just imagine that you are that love for a few moments.
- Then when you open your eyes feel calm and centred, peaceful and loving.

Know that love is always around you, within you and is you...Feel safe and loved, knowing that at all times you are a cherished being of love and light. Know that you can become this love, envisage this love, at any time during the day or night. Do it several times a day and feel the difference in your life almost immediately.

CHAPTER 10

My Family & Life After Death

THE LAST CHAPTER LOOKED AT THE IMPORTANCE OF LOVE IN OUR LIVES, this chapter and the next look at something just as important - that is knowing without a doubt, that we do not die, that our lives do not cease because this particular body dies.

Our souls are deeply complex, beautiful and multi-dimensional. We ourselves are spiritual beings and like our ancestors before us, we will shed this particular dense physical body one day. There are portholes in and out of this life and we take them so that we can join in here when it is our time and we can leave here also when it is our time.

Our spirit family wants us to know not to be frightened; we are just going back to where we came from. When we get back there we will soon remember it and we will not just be okay, we will lighten with love and joy and be greeted by loved ones who went before us. In time, we will then be there for the people we left behind on Earth!

The spirits always tell us not to worry about this, it will happen when the time is right, and thus to make the most of our lives here; to be joyous just because we are alive and to help each other while we are here.

I would like to share my family's experiences because

they are heart-warming and unique examples of the power of spirit around the death bed, which really is just a transition or a porthole to our lighter form of existence, our spiritual, subspace or celestial self.

The Stories

I have a large family and I have some very interesting stories related to dying and after death spiritual connections. It's important that we all share these with each other; they are a part of our ancestry and also our future. We mourn for those who have died, because we miss them, but in all honesty they still live and they want us to know this.

They want us to have a good life here and for us to enjoy it here while we are physical beings. They want us to know they love us but that there is no rush to be with them because one day we will join them and to them that is in the blink of an eye.

They tell us to really experience it here because this is a very special place to experience and grow – so they remind us to try to be aware and in the moment. They guide us to enjoy the cloud formations, the sunshine on our faces, the birds in flight, the little worm crawling across the path, the butterflies dancing together, the emotions and the love, the shared experiences with family and friends, all of these types of sacred physical earth moments.

I'm sure that many people reading this have their own incredible stories of loved ones returning in dreams or as angels or spirits to help you cope while you are here.

I'd love to hear your stories one day. Perhaps if you haven't had those experiences yet, reading these will help you cope with the loss of a loved one, or help open your mind to receive a special visit from them. Many people tell me they wait for such experiences but haven't had them. Yet it can take years sometimes to have such a visit from your loved one, especially when the grief is so thick and dense but please don't let that stop you communicating with them, sending them love and imagining yourself talking to them – because by doing this you keep the channels open and the love flowing and this is healing and positive.

If you hear them saying something in your mind like they used to say, or a funny way of teasing or responding to things, then they are probably talking to you in your mind and reminding you of their funny little ways! They talk to us through dreams and thoughts and sensations within our body (you might feel them nearby or get goose bumps), they might put a special symbol, number or feather in your way and you just know it's from them. Smile and say hi and let that love they are sending out to you completely fill your heart, because that's what all of this is all about, LOVE.

My Dad

My dad's name was Abraham Wone (pronounced like bone but with a w), but to his friends, he was known as Abe. And if my Dad taught me anything, it was to help others. We were in the car going for a family drive, I was about thirteen years old, when Dad stopped the car to break up a fight in the middle of the street. My younger brother was next to me and my mother was in the front passenger seat. We watched while he jumped out of the car to stop about ten big strong young men beating into another young man who was completely defenseless. If my father had not stopped them there is no telling what would have happened to this young man. This man, now nearly middle age, talked to one of my relatives when my father died and expressed how grateful he was to my Dad for doing such a brave thing because in that moment,

257

until Dad came along that day, he thought he was going to die.

Dad was not a young man when he stopped that fight, he was at least in his sixties then and he had a false leg. I remember feeling so proud of my dad and I thought he was so brave – and as I reminisce about it, the feeling is just as strong if not stronger because I'm older and understand the real risks he took to his own personal safety that day.

Another time we were on a long stretch of highway between Ingham and Townsville in North Queensland and we noticed a car broken down on the side of the road. It was late at night and there were several young people that looked like backpackers trying to flag down some help. Of all the times for them to break down they chose the right time. My dad had been a mechanic his whole life so it was only natural for him to want to help them.

He got out of the car; we stayed in it and locked the doors. Mum wasn't really impressed as I think we had grown up with too many scary American horror movies and she was terrified. My little brother and I were sitting in the back of the car wide-eyed and again wondering if dad was going to come back in one piece or not. They were a group of travelling young European backpackers. Dad got them back on the road by using a stocking to make a temporary belt for the engine and they were so grateful and so very lucky!

He also showed a lot of compassion to others and was always helping people either through money or lifts or gifts of food such as reef fish he caught on weekends or long beans that he grew in the back garden. As a mechanic he did a lot to help people by charging lower rates than average, letting people have their cars and paying off the work and doing free repairs for family and friends.

Once a young couple broke down in their bus while

they were travelling Australia and they camped in our back yard for a few weeks (possibly months, we can't remember how long!) until their bus was fixed.

Dad was not a greedy man; he had enough to make our lives comfortable, we had a little house and great food and we went for wonderful Sunday family drives together and often went fishing on weekend evenings. We had a very simple life and it was wonderful to be raised like this, running in cane paddocks and riding our bikes after school.

During the week Dad worked really hard and often did long hours getting up early to help local farmers with their tractors; Farmers are notorious for starting work really early in the morning and going 'til the sun went down.

As I became older and more comfortable with my psychic gift I shared some of my experiences with Dad. He was fascinated by it all and seemed very interested in my stories. He was a spiritual man himself, he told me he didn't believe in any one religion, but believed in being a good person and being kind to others and that he felt something would come after this life, he just didn't know exactly what. His parents were Muslims, while he was very naturally spiritual and joyful and I suppose a lot of his way rubbed off on me, which I am very proud of and grateful for.

About a year before my Dad died I had a powerful spiritual dream. Spiritual dreams are different to normal dreams because they are so real. They feel tangible, and vivid and often so very clear and powerful. You actually feel as if the events are real and those with you in the dream are also real. In the dream my father's four deceased brothers, his mother and father, and a recently deceased sister (and some other deceased loved ones I was aware of but couldn't see as clearly) were sitting on a long bench. Actually it was more like a padded comfortable couch without a back to it, so that they all sat around it with their backs facing one another. They were very solid forms. They looked just like you and I.

They then showed me that my dad would soon be joining them and they put him on the couch with them. Everyone appeared very serene and happy, including my Dad, except that Dad was shimmering and not completely substantial like they were. How interesting that he would normally be completely solid in physical form to us, but to them, he was shimmering!

For many years beforehand, I knew that Dad would die aged eighty-two. Before he died, just over two weeks short of his eighty-third birthday, he told me that his deceased family were around his hospital bed. He said his brothers and mother were there and it was as if they were real.

I assured him they were real and lovingly told him that they had come to get him. In my grief I couldn't see them, but I could feel spiritual bodies around the bed.

He said to me, "I'm not scared."

Those powerful words helped me cope with his death so much. He was such a beautiful, brave soul, in life and in death. He went into death with this conscious awareness of his spirit and his spirit family waiting for him. Not long after that he was delirious and then he went into a coma.

It was such a difficult time in my life because not only did I love and cherish my dad so much, he was my security blanket in this world. He was always there to help me out with money or physical help. He surprised me with my first car when I went to university. He paid for most of my university tuition as well. He always gave me money to buy nice things for myself. That was his way of saying I love you, because he found it hard to actually say those words.

I have come to really appreciate all that he has done

for me in my life and all that he signifies. I knew that he was not in pain anymore and that he was still very much alive and with his beloved family members and friends who had passed before him. I knew I could see him whenever I wanted by calling to him in my mind.

At the time of Dad's passing I was eight months pregnant. This compounded the difficulties for me because I was so heavily pregnant and everyone was terrified I would go into early labour. The grief was so intense, magnified by the pregnancy hormones, but my spiritual beliefs and angelic experiences got me through it. Then my beautiful son Orin came and he was an incredible baby, and I could feel my dad so strongly around us because he was visiting his new grandson.

As a sideline, and in what could be considered to be an incredible twist of fate, Dad's two best male friends in the whole world also passed away around the same time as Dad. I had visions in my mind's eye that they were all together, still telling the same old jokes and still supporting each other emotionally in the afterlife, the same as they always did in their human lives. This was a great comfort and I felt there was certain magic to it, like they had a contract to be together in life as well as in the afterlife.

Visits From My Dad

Dad has visited us many times since his passing. The most memorable was on the night that I cried to my daughter Kia that her Poppy (as he was known to several of his grandchildren) didn't get to play guitar in the last years of his life, due to a nursing accident during a hospital stay that paralysed his left arm. That night we were awoken at 1am by the guitar being strummed! Mick jumped up and said, "Oh I thought I heard the guitar strumming!" To which I replied, "It Did!"

There was no one else in the house, only Mick, Kia and Orin who was a newborn baby. We had all been fast asleep. It woke us all up! It had not happened before or since. We knew it was Dad saying I can play; I can do anything I want now!

I can only smile about Dad, I feel him all the time, especially around my children, my nephew and my Mum. He loved watching his grandchildren and nieces and nephews play. He loved teasing them and hanging out with them, not doing anything special, just being together. He has given me a lifetime of fond memories and a legacy of kindness and cheekiness that I treasure with all my heart.

Several times since his passing he has come in vivid dreams to give me important messages about relevant things in my life. I have noted them throughout this memoir where relevant. During these dreams he would come and give me answers to questions I had asked him when I was awake. He also came and told me my mum was unwell with an infected leg so that I was able to help her.

In another powerful dream, he came to show me how absolutely beautiful he was in spirit and I was completely blown away by his stunning, beautiful essence. I woke up sobbing my heart out, as he had been right in front of me, our faces almost touching. Another time, I was having a dream where we were in the kitchen together where I had grown up, he was standing by the fridge and I was by a small pantry cupboard located a few metres away. Then within the dream I actually realized that I was having a lucid dream! I said, "Oh my God Dad this is a dream, I realize it and I can hug you and feel you!"

I ran over to him in a semi-conscious dream state, I hugged him and I felt every second of it. I felt his strong chest and shoulders! I felt the warmth of his skin and his arms around me! Again I woke up sobbing my heart out;

the joy and love that I felt was just incredible!

I feel very privileged to have witnessed my dad's incredible spiritual transformation and to have enjoyed this amazing after-death relationship with him. When you get a chance to communicate with your loved one after they die it is much easier to see yourself as a spiritual being also.

My Paternal Grandmother

I will never forget a powerful sight that made me believe without a doubt that we exist beyond this physical life. I was in my teens and my brother and I had woken up early. It was Mum and Dad's wedding anniversary and we wanted to do something special so we were setting the table and making breakfast for them (nothing fancy just tea and toast but made with an abundance of love!).

It was quite early. Normally they were up earlier than us and Mum would have to drag me out of bed. I think they slept in a little that morning. As I was setting the table, I peeked in to look at my father still snoozing in the bed. My mother had just gotten up and was in the bathroom. As I glanced in I got the shock of my life when there, standing at the foot of the bed, looking down on him with such love in her eyes, was my paternal grandmother, Nenek (the Indonesian name for grandmother, pronounced ne-ne).

In front of me was a beautiful, short, smiling, rotund Australian-Indonesian woman, with soft, light white-grey hair and an even softer, loving look on her sweet brown face. She was dressed the way I always remember her in a long flowery shift dress, staring lovingly at her son. She had been dead for about ten years at that stage, so it really was a truly remarkable moment for me.

I felt so blessed. I felt in awe. I couldn't believe what I was seeing. It was only for a second or two and I looked away momentarily because I was in mid motion getting plates down from the cupboard right outside my parent's bedroom. When I looked back she was gone and Dad was alone still sleeping peacefully completely unaware of his visitor. Though I couldn't see her anymore I felt she was still there.

There was no golden or white glow around her, nothing to identify that she was a spirit person. She was exactly as I remembered her and she looked completely and utterly alive and healthy and very well!

She was such a gentle soul and I remember her soft, kind eyes and her soft body and arms as she bent over to hug us. I remember her cooking at the stove and setting the table full of food, with a happy smile on her face that reached her pretty Asian eyes. There was always the sound of many grandchildren running around playing and adults talking and laughing. There was the sound of music playing either from the radio or Nenek playing her old piano accordion.

There were dogs and cats and horses. There were curry and rice smells and seafood, sambal and chilli delights. We enjoyed exotic tropical home grown fruits for dessert. She died when I was only a little girl but I remember her well and fondly. Apparently my brother and I could speak to her in Indonesian and we would rattle away with her, however after she passed on we stopped speaking it and I haven't spoken it as an adult at all.

When my father was dying in hospital and he said that he could see his family members around his bed, it was easy for me to imagine them there because I had already seen this for myself those many years ago.

My Maternal Grandmother

My Nana, my maternal grandmother, died in my early

twenties and because I was older and had a lot to do with her as I was growing up, her death hit me hard. I wasn't doing intuitive readings yet, I was working as a psychologist and studying for my Master's and PhD in Clinical Psychology. I was so busy with work but I found it a very emotionally stressful time because I lived away from my family and straight after the funeral I had to keep working and studying even though I was still grieving deeply.

I cried so much over Nana's death. At the time of her death she was probably the closest person to me who had died, so it was a big one for me. She died of cancer and it was sad watching her die, her body slowly wasted away before our very eyes. It took several weeks for her to pass over. Her large family was by her bedside. She had nine children, countless grandchildren and her husband, my grandfather, was also still alive then. So the effect of losing her was particularly compounded because there were so many people in the room experiencing powerful emotions such as grief, loss, anger, and sadness.

Some members of the family were angry with her doctor at the time. A few weeks before she died she went into his office hopeful and came out dejected. Instead of telling her that she should just keep looking after herself as best she could, he told her there was nothing more they could do for her, and she basically gave up when she came home and within a few short weeks she was dead.

In Australia, Aboriginal people have a saying for this and it is called 'pointing the bone'. It is where someone puts a spell or hex on you and it comes true, where someone's words influence your belief system and have a 'nocebo effect' (a negative influence rather than a positive influence as in the 'placebo effect').

Before the doctor's appointment my grandmother was still making dinner for my grandfather and her live-in adult daughter (whose epilepsy meant she required assistance with daily living activities). Nana was still trying to make the most of what remaining time she had left. She had been doing puzzles and playing cards and spending time with us all. She said I love you to us, which was something she had never been comfortable saying out loud before. After the doctor's appointment however her will was broken and she just completely gave up. Proof that words are so very powerful.

As I said above, it was hard for me after her death because I was a lot younger then, I was grieving and working as a psychologist in aged care assessment, helping people get access to the right care and help in the community and doing the paperwork that was necessary if they needed to go into nursing home or hostel care. I loved my job; I cared so much about older people, and their families. Probably because I came from such a big family, I have a great respect for older generations.

I wasn't doing readings at that stage; I was a psychologist and a shy closet intuitive! But then Nana changed all that!

Three months after her death she came to me in one of the most powerful dreams I have ever had. She was younger, beautiful, and alive. She was standing at the back of her old house in Innisfail, North Queensland. I had so many childhood memories in that house, such as breaking my ankle on a skateboard, playing dolls under the house, jumping off the roof of a big old van in the back yard, and lots and lots of yummy food, dinners, cakes, biscuits, cups of icy cold cordial and involved family conversations.

That old house is no longer there because it was damaged beyond repair in a cyclone. It had to be removed and only an empty grass plot remains.

In the dream the house was still standing and everything was the same as when she was alive. Nana was in the back yard, standing underneath the clothesline, dressed in a beautiful white lace gown, with the most beautiful smile on her face.

She then showed me the most amazing, profound intense feelings of love I have ever felt in my life apart from when I was a teenager in hospital and the angel spirit came to help me. It was beyond description in human words, a complete sensory experience, a fully loaded explosion and complete immersion in love!

I was told that this feeling of love is what is waiting for us on the other side. I was told that I was only being shown what I could handle and take in. I took this love into my core, and my heart and mind healed from her physical death because I knew without a doubt that she was so fully alive and so real that my sadness was eased.

I knew without a doubt that there was no separation between us because of death, that we did in fact live on and that the love waiting for us was unbelievable. I cannot fully describe the love she showed me. It was like being love itself. Not just our normal way of sensing love, but really truly being love, a total immersion with love.

And this feeling has always stayed with me and has helped me communicate with people who have left this place for the next. It made me abler to fully understand and realise what the spiritual people say when they talk about the healing power of love and that love is the ultimate meaning of life.

My Nana waved goodbye to me and then she faded away while still waving. I was calling her and reaching for her, trying to get her to stay, but I knew she couldn't. I was crying but the tears were shed because of joy and because of the love that she had shown me.

She has come to me a few times in dreams, always powerful, but never as intense as in the first dream. That dream changed my life for the better because it was after experiencing it, that I could never again doubt the love on the other side. Though I am loving my life and feel I have a lot to do, I have to say that a part of me cherishes that one day I get to go home to that feeling of intense love and connection I was shown, I can wait, but believe me it is like nothing we can possibly experience here – it literally is love that is 'out of this world'.

My Maternal Great Grandmother

I must have been only five or six when my maternal great grandmother died. Nana Carmen was her name. She was a really funny lady, with a witty, interesting personality. She was confined to a hospital bed in the last few months of her life. I remember we would visit her in hospital and give her drinks and she would eat biscuits with her tea.

My mother loved her very much; she had been like a second mother to her, and very caring, gentle and humorous. The night she died, Mum was woken at 2am with a voice telling her that Nana Carmen was dying and that she had to get to the hospital to be with her. Mum raced to the hospital and got to be with my grandmother in her dying moments, which was very special. It was also very special because the voice was very strong and distinct, knowing that my mother loved her so, the spiritual person/angel made sure that she was with her so that they could say goodbye and know that she would still exist beyond.

I don't know how long afterwards it was, months or years, but one night my grandmother just turned up at the foot of my bed. I knew it was Nana Carmen, her brunch coat (dressing gown) was swaying in front of the fan that cooled me down at night and her presence was so big in life; there was no denying it in the afterlife. I was so scared. I was so little and I could feel her there and instead of talking to her, terrified I hid underneath the bed sheets breathing shallow and fast until the feeling that she was there passed.

I don't do this anymore! Now I talk to people on the other side but as a child it was very scary as people used to tell spooky ghost stories and make jokes of such things and not tell you how to cope with it if you actually saw 'dead' people! No one explained that these presences were just the same as us!

I think that's why a lot of children are scared of the dark because of the energies and spirits/angelic beings that they sense and it's why my husband and I used to fall sleep with our children until they learnt to feel safe and secure. My children know about spiritual matters because for us they are everyday or at least regular occurrences so we often discuss talking to my Dad or our loved ones who have passed or about predictions for the future or the spiritual things that have happened in our lives.

Intuition is a normal part of life for my family and it makes our lives happy, loving and spiritually rich. We are very connected to each other and in tune with each other's needs. We are also very honest and caring and natural and grounded. We don't force each other to be anything we are not. Which for me is an important part of unconditional love and being authentic while here in the physical world.

My Uncles

My family has very interesting stories about the actual time of death. My Dad's Brother, Uncle Mussah (or Adrian) was a gentle man. He died many years ago now, but Mum and Dad used to love telling the story of how our clock stopped at the moment of Uncle's death. His wife's clock and some clocks that belonged to other close family members stopped as well. It was a powerful life-after-death statement.

My mother's dearest elder brother, Uncle Tommy,

was a larrikin. He was a classic Aussie bloke. He had strawberry blonde hair and beard and these laughing eyes that just twinkled. Uncle Tommy died from cancer in Townsville Base Hospital in Queensland about a year after my Dad.

It was sad because he had been going to the doctor for a long time with back pain and the doctor had missed his cancer; they just kept giving him steroid injections for back pain. By the time they diagnosed the cancer it was too late and he only had a few weeks to live. Apparently just before he died he told the hospital staff and his family (his wife, his 8 siblings, his own grown child and several of his step children whom he raised as his own) that he knew where the fire alarm button was for the hospital and that he would set it off at the moment of his death!

This is precisely what Uncle Tommy did!

To great fanfare at around 2.30am my uncle died and at that exact moment the fire alarm went off in the hospital and it couldn't be turned off until the fire brigade arrived and gave the all clear. The nurse came in and exclaimed "Tom did that!" because she knew that he had said he was going to do it!

My family was crying, but through the tears they were laughing and rejoicing because he had done it and shown them that he was okay.

At the exact moment of his death it was as if a massive burst of energy came through our house and we were all awoken. I jumped up and exclaimed to Mick, "I think Uncle Tommy just died!" I could feel his energy strongly in that jolt of energy!

I remember feeling teary but feeling the absolute magic and wonder of life and so-called 'death' at the same time. The moonlight was streaming down the side of the house that was comprised of glass panels, lighting up the entire hallway and living room. There was an undeniable magic in the air, an unusual quality, like the type that comes during the eye of a cyclone, a somewhat eerie silver glow permeated, but also a calmness. We knew 'something' had just happened.

We had a dear friend staying with us at the time, sleeping up the other end of the house and in the morning she told us that she was woken by something strange at precisely the exact same time. We felt what was like a big bang and a massive swoosh of energy that went from one end of the house to the other as if something flew through it.

We all knew that Uncle Tommy had done it. He had shown us that he was still alive. Several years later I watched a man in a utility truck drive towards me and I could have sworn that the driver was my Uncle Tommy! Another time this happened with my Dad and I'm sure he was driving a passing truck! But when I looked again my Dad was gone and replaced with the person who was actually driving the truck! I wasn't imagining it – somehow they can influence these things so you can see them. Sometimes they can turn up where you would expect them, both my Dad and Uncle Tommy drove utility trucks. It was their way of saying hello!

AMANDA McHUGH

CHAPTER 11

Make Your Life Count In Honour Of Brian, Sky & Kayla Burdett

When People We Love Die

IMAGINE, LOSING YOUR ENTIRE FAMILY IN A TRAGIC CAR ACCIDENT. You are left feeling all alone in the world. Your two children and their father are suddenly gone and you are still a mother left to live in the world without your beloved family. This is what happened to my dear friend Felicity Burdett. Her family died suddenly in a tragic car accident when she was only in her early thirties.

My dear friends, Brian (Birdy) and his two beautiful daughters, Sky and Kayla Burdett were killed instantly in that car wreck. The girls were only ten and eight at the time. For several months before their deaths I kept writing the words, 'It only takes just one moment to change everything'. I made a note of it in my phone; I contemplated writing a song about it.

I couldn't shake the feeling that something big was coming, something that would affect my immediate family/friends. And then, in an instant my dear friends were gone and I knew why I had been hearing that

particular statement. I had almost finished the first draft
of my memoir at that stage but kept feeling that a chapter
was missing. It was only when the girls started
communicating with me that I knew the missing chapter
was their story.

Not long before the accident, I had written some
powerful work that felt channelled from a much higher
source; it was about acknowledging the ancient spirit of
children and understanding that sometimes children die
young because of their own soul's journey.

When the girls died, I felt that I had been psychically
preparing myself for their departure. At the time I
decided not to share some of this work in the memoir
because it was theoretical, but when they died it became
reality and I re-wrote the chapter completely because
their lives encompass everything that needs to be said.
Their story shows us that we can see things before they
happen, that psychic premonitions are real, and that we
continue to exist out of the body when we die. Theirs is
a powerful story and one to educate and enlighten us all.

Knowing the Burdett Family

Felicity Burdett is one of the bravest, conscious,
spiritually aware and inspiring people I know. She is a
constant source of strength and inspiration to others.
Felicity has an unfaltering belief that her children and ex-
husband live on in the afterlife because she can feel them
and hear them around her.

I feel very privileged to have physically known Sky and
Kayla Burdett while they were present here in their
beautiful physical forms. They were two of the most
vivacious, talented, beautiful, funny and happy little girls
I have ever had the pleasure of meeting. They were aged
just ten and eight at the time they passed over and I
cannot emphasise just how much these two girls shone

like diamonds when they were here. They were exuberant and effervescent; so present here on earth and just so completely full of life and energy.

On the 9th March 2012 their bodies died, along with their father Brian "Birdy" Burdett. It was a tragic automobile accident on a highway near Braidwood, NSW Australia, known for being a treacherous stretch of road particularly during wet weather. Felicity was not in the car and thus survived her children and her still much loved ex-husband. Sadly, authorities told Felicity that Birdy was going too fast for the wet weather and the poor road conditions. He didn't know the road well, Felicity and the girls had only recently moved to the coast while Birdy was working and living inland still at the snow fields and going to and fro to have the girls on weekends. The car skidded after going around a corner and went side on into a big powerful SUV vehicle. They were killed instantly.

My family and I had the awesome pleasure of living with the girls and their mummy for several months in 2009 when the girls were aged eight and six. Felicity and Birdy had separated by then but remained good friends.

Birdy and Felicity were both incredible musicians and they both penned catchy, powerful songs that celebrated life, family and love. Ironically, Birdy's last album was called 'Glad To Be Alive' and while that gives me goose bumps and makes tears well in my eyes whenever I hear that name, it also makes me feel overwhelmingly grateful to be alive. I know Birdy is still very much alive, and this gives me great comfort also. Felicity's award winning album was called 'Going with the Flow' which she has practiced now, like a Zen Buddhist, as she goes into her future without her beloveds. She maintains an amazing perspective and an incredible peaceful presence that she literally emits everywhere she goes.

Felicity and Birdy loved nature and living life to the full and they instilled this in their children. They made the most of every second of life. They were into singing, dancing, performing, playing different instruments, surfing, swimming, beach lifesaving, writing and any sort of artistic or creative endeavour, rollerblading, riding bikes, skateboarding, snowboarding, skiing and shopping. As a family, they loved just hanging out and having a wonderful time with friends and family.

You name it and they did it! They were just always so busy and active. The girls absolutely loved school and hanging out with their friends. When we lived together, there was always music in the air when they were around. The children were always making up games with my then six-year old daughter and one-year old son, and playing on the trampoline, dancing or choreographing a show for the adults. If she wasn't surfing, Felicity was often playing her guitar or practicing her saxophone. There was truly never a dull moment living with these amazing life-affirming people.

Predicting Their Accident

Two years before the accident, when Felicity, Sky and Kayla were still living with us, I felt that the girls were not safe in the car with their father. I knew he loved them and was generally a safe driver and would never put them at risk but I sensed the energy of the crash over two years before it happened.

At the time, I pulled Felicity aside and I asked her if the girls were safe in the car with their father. Felicity said that every time the girls went with him she worried because they were out of her control, but that he loved them and looked after them well and they were all so happy together she had to let them go. I understood this as a mother, the worry that we generally have for our children when they are out of our sight and I couldn't tell her anything else or specifics, so we just let this feeling be put aside at the time. Of course neither of us forgot that it was said.

The week before the accident, I had a very big headache and chest pain. I had not seen the Burdett family since they lived with us two years before. Felicity had asked us to visit her, however we were busy and we kept saying we would visit at some stage in the future.

We had moved across the road into a big old farmhouse about the same time the Burdett's moved to Jindabyne, in central NSW. They hadn't been to our new place and we hadn't been to theirs but we were in each other's hearts. Though we had lived in our new house for two years, we had never met the new owners of the house that we had shared with Felicity and the girls. In what might be considered an interesting 'coincidence', about a week before the girls died, the lady who purchased that house came over and said that a heifer (a female cow) had escaped and to please watch out for her.

We got talking and I told her about the wonderful little girls who used to live there with us and how in one of their amusing games, the kids threw all the shoes they could around the yard and on top of the roof while jumping on the trampoline! We were laughing about this, because one shoe, my only pair of high heels in the whole world, seemed lost forever never to be found and I wondered if the lady had come across it. It never turned up but it made for a hilarious story, and I always kept the remaining golden shoe to remind me of the fun times we all had at the house (and maybe just in case the other shoe ever turned up somewhere!). It's like I was being reminded to think about Sky, Kayla and Birdy that week, and things just kept coming up that reminded me of them.

A day or two after this woman's visit, I started reading a book called 'Every Dead Thing' by John Connelly – it is quite a scary read so it's not everyone's cup of tea. But as strange as it sounds, at the time I felt compelled to read it. It was an inexpensive book that I purchased for a few cents a couple of weeks before, from the sale shelves at the local library. I felt drawn to read it that week.

While reading the book I was in agony. I had an intense headache and chest pain. As strange as it might sound however, I felt it was important to read that book though I didn't know why and I forced myself to finish it. As I was reading it, several times I put it down and I said to myself, "There is something I am missing, this is a spiritual 'thing'." I would sob and ask myself what I was missing. It was only later, after the girls and Birdy had died, that I realised that in the book, the main character's nickname was Bird and his entire family get killed – his wife and children gone and he is the only survivor.

Of course I didn't understand the connection at the time and I only knew that I felt better and my head subsided wherever I put the book down. I laid the book down on my chest and spoke to those in the spiritual realm, "I know this is a spiritual thing, something is going to happen, you are trying to tell me something ... please tell me, I know this book is relevant somehow." I couldn't get it. It didn't come to me.

That week I also went to a wonderful night of film at the Byron Bay film festival and I saw a friend of Felicity's whom I hadn't seen in years. He said that he had seen her recently at a music festival. I remember I felt excited inside and said that yes I had to ring Felicity this week, as I had been meaning to ring her for ages. But I didn't put it immediately into my phone onto my list of things to do and it went out of my head.

On the Thursday, I was having an afternoon rest, during which time I meditated and spoke to spirit. All of a sudden I just knew that something was going to happen to someone I loved very shortly.

I literally actually asked the spirits to please tell me

who was going to die, but they wouldn't. They showed me an image of my husband's brother John. I knew he was related to this somehow, but I knew it wasn't actually him. I can't explain how I knew (I just knew) and I said to the spirits, "Okay I know it's not him, and I know you can't tell me. I know I will find out in the next day."

I prepared myself mentally and emotionally that I would find out very soon who was going to be hurt. I just had an undeniable knowing that someone I loved was going to die the next day.

I am very aware that I have profound conversations with those on the other side, and I can find it hard to explain these interactions to others at the time. I do think that one day there will be many others like me, who will come out of the closet as spirit whisperers, spirit conversers and spirit walkers. I think that's why I like to read books written by other people who are like me because it helps me feel a sense of connection with others who have embraced this journey.

I remember taking a few really deep breaths and just going into an acceptance that something big was coming. I prayed a lot and cried although they hadn't died yet. They had showed me my brother-in-law John because he had a connection to Felicity and the children, he had been visiting with his family the year we lived with Felicity and the girls, and our families had spent a wonderful Christmas together. I also found out later that he just 'happened' to be texting Mick at the same time Felicity would be texting Mick about the crash, the morning after the crash happened.

On Friday afternoon I took my two children and my daughter's good friend to the beach. I felt like crying and my head and chest were still hurting as they had been all week. I couldn't shake the feeling that something was about to happen that day and there was a deep sadness within me in preparation for this. I was literally fighting back the tears at the beach, I was very contemplative and I forced myself to be in the moment with the children.

We explored the low tide estuary at Brunswick Heads, riddled with countless crab holes and the resultant tiny crab sand balls - trying not to stand on the little sand balls was impossible but we boldly attempted it anyway. We watched schools of whiting caught in shallow pools and I dreamed of fishing once more as I always did when near the water, a lifetime of fishing with my parents and brother still very much a part of my psyche. We swam in a protected inlet, the kids running, and swimming, building forts and sandcastles, and digging holes by the water's edge. I managed to find joy being in nature and watching the children play so happily; all the while I was aware that news would reach me very soon that would forever change our lives.

Early the next morning I was lying in bed just relaxing. Mick had stayed the night at a friend's house in Brisbane, a two-hour drive north from our house, because he had a late gig there the night before. At about 7.30am Mick texted me to say that he had received a text message from Felicity saying that her little girls and their daddy had perished instantly in a car crash the night before. He texted me, because he didn't want to wake our children with a phone call to the house phone, although I also think he also text because he was in shock and couldn't speak to me if he tried at the time.

The headache was gone. But now, the concerned feeling that something bad was coming turned into intense grief and it was very, very painful. My heart hurt like it could explode and I cried and cried. Sobs literally wracked my body.

In her text to Mick that morning, to advise him of their deaths, Felicity also said that if I was to see the girls to contact her please. I knew exactly what I had to do and after crying for some time, I went into myself, into the spiritual realm, to make contact with the girls and their daddy.

Making Contact with Sky, Kayla and Birdy

They came instantly to my mind. It was incredible. The girls were able to say it wasn't their daddy's fault. It was so quick, the car slipped and he had to try to keep control. It swerved because of the slippery road and unfortunately, also because of his speed. It appears that he had overtaken a car and crossed double lines before going around a corner too fast. The girls were adamant that it wasn't his fault. Even though I know he was slightly speeding for the conditions, they were trying to say, as bad as this was, it was meant to be and not to blame him. I had seen it happen two years before it occurred – so in this way their story also speaks to us of fate, of a bigger picture that we just cannot fathom.

In my mind's eye, I could see that although they were physically dead in our sense of the word, they were very much alive. Sky, the eldest girl was very strong and present and aware and able to speak to me clearly and show herself. Kayla, the youngest, was a bit more shocked and wanted her mummy. She seemed not to be coping as well as her big sister at first, perhaps because she was probably asleep on the back seat when she died and therefore not aware of what was going on. Whereas Sky was awake and present, fully aware, sitting in the front seat next to her Daddy and going instantly in full consciousness, from this life, to the next. This is what I felt at the time regarding their deaths and the coroner report confirmed it later.

My friends, these newly born spirits, were all concerned about Felicity. Kayla was curling up beside her mummy in bed as she came to terms with the change. Kayla's energy was very intermingled with Sky's for some time; their energies were hard to separate – perhaps it was because Sky was the strong, older child and Kayla received strength from her, as was often the way when they were physically alive. Their daddy was there, shining as a bright spirit, as usual, his humour and lightness of being unmistakable. He felt awful for Felicity but he had emitted this sense to me that he knew that it was also a part of their journey for this to happen.

Birdy was always a larrikin and had a fun loving way of seeing the world, he always knew how to party and he was always the life of the party! So although he was a bit more subdued at first, he later accustomed to his new self. There was a very loving spirit lady there with them, helping the transition from this physical plane. I could sense her but not clearly see what she looked like. It felt like it could be an aunty of Birdy's but I didn't know for sure, I never got her name.

Sky clearly told me that they wanted to, "Make their lives count".

In my mind's eye it was as if I was transported through time and space and shown that this was decided upon before the girls were even born into their physical bodies. They wanted to enjoy this world completely and be a shining example for all about how to live life to the full, making the most of every single minute. The girls and their daddy wanted me to highlight to others the need to enjoy life thoroughly but to be aware of its preciousness, to slow down and not be in a rush, not to worry about being late or what people will think of you. It is better to get somewhere safe and to tell the truth about your lateness and your need to slow down to be safe, rather than to rush and risk yourself and others. It is better to enjoy your life and do what you desire to do, not to allow others to dictate and control you or to live in fear or anger or unhappiness. Too many of us feel controlled by others and by their emotions, but at any one moment we can recognize that we are alive and take back our lives as our own and live them to the full. I felt that we weren't meant to judge each other.

Sky said it was meant to be, as hard as it was for us to understand, it was part of the higher plan of things, which is why I had felt the energy of it years before, and felt something coming the week before it actually happened. As much as I wanted to, even asked to, I couldn't stop it. As painful as it was for all of us, it was not to be stopped and their passing was meant to happen in this way. Some things are meant to be and we have to put them in perspective, in the bigger picture of things, and cope with them (easier said than done of course).

The morning after her body died, Sky showed me a vision of herself that was pure angelic beauty. She was stunning. She looked like a glowing model from the pages of those magazines where you just know that the models have been airbrushed! She had long silky blonde hair cascading down the left hand side of her body, over her heart. I had not known her with long hair because when we lived together it was just below her shoulders. Two years had passed. So when I told Felicity my vision I said, "I don't know if she was planning to grow her hair or if this means anything to you?"

Felicity replied, "You hadn't seen her for several years; you didn't know she had grown her hair exactly like that, it was beautiful, so long, she would have been so proud to have shown you." That is exactly how she was, she was so beautiful, proud, so stunning, that her image had me in tears. She really was an angel.

Birdy was able to acknowledge the love for his family, and pass on a message to his beloved sister. He was able to physically describe her enough to me that I was able to recognise her at the funeral and tell her that he had been planning on spending a lot more time with her and that he loved her very much. Several months later he was able to come through to me and help her through a difficult period in her life, which was of great comfort to her.

Some of their messages were harder to put into words. The girls pointed out that many things here had multiple meanings and that we don't often see things that are right in front of our face.

One night in my mind, Sky showed me herself saluting her mother, like you would salute a captain, and I told Felicity what I saw. The next day Felicity was at a fundraiser for her at the bakery in their hometown and there was a little rowboat that kids played in just outside. At the same time four children got up and saluted right in front of Felicity.

Sky and Kayla wanted their Mummy to know that there is so much magic in the air created by the spirit people and that they would not leave but always be here for her.

They said the experience of time is so different there, so they know they will see us all soon, they understood that it was harder for us when we are here, that when we are in pain time seems to take forever. The little messages made all the difference to how Felicity coped with the girls' traumatic physical departure from our world. That they were still with us was obvious and that they were going to help us here was extremely heart-warming and wonderful for all of us who loved them.

Sky and Kayla have assured me that they will be guiding their mummy on her sacred journey here and I have to say they have helped other people I know as well by giving me messages about those people and how to help them. They told me to tell Felicity that, "South America would save their lives".

Unbeknownst to me, Felicity's girlfriend, Leanne had been there before and it was always her wish to return and live in South America. I saw Leanne playing soccer with the children in South America and she affirmed that she had played soccer all her life and it was her thing, which I did not know. I also saw she would be playing music with Felicity and Leanne confirmed she received drums for her birthday and that was their intention. Felicity had a beautiful vision/dream about healers in the Amazon and heard the name of an ancient tribe though she had never had any knowledge of it before. There was some connection to South America that had healing for Felicity and her partner, Leanne. Sometimes a connection of a place or thing, a dream or a hope can keep us going, and that seems to be what this connection to South America was. A place of healing and dreams and hope, that spirit used to help Felicity take comfort from.

A Gift from Kayla to her Mummy

One morning when I woke up, Kayla was strongly in my mind. She showed me a present in my mind (it looked like a wrapped gift box) and as I went to reach for it, it elongated and turned into a surfboard. Kayla said that her mother should have retail therapy that morning and also buy a hat. Kayla showed me a picture of her mummy's van and had a big smile and she said that she was happy that her mummy was reminiscing about the van and the girls.

I passed on this message by sending an early morning text to Felicity about the gift elongating into a surfboard, the shopping, the hat and the van reminiscing and the big smile. Several hours later Felicity rang me and said she had only just read the text but was amazed because that morning she had decided what to spend some of her daughters' bank account savings on and it was a beautiful surfboard that she would use in honour of them; hence the 'gift' from the girls that elongated into a surfboard as in my vision!

Felicity and Leanne had also gone on a conscious

shopping spree that morning as retail therapy. Leanne had purchased a hat and just as Kayla had said, Felicity had spent twenty minutes telling the man in the surfboard shop about her van and how happy she was to have taken her girls all around Australia in it. Kayla had managed to show her mummy that they were with her the whole morning and that they approved of everything that was done – even if the approval came early in the morning, before the events had even happened!

Unicorn Pictures, Perfume Oil, Love Heart Bubbles & Healing Photographs

Another time, Felicity had a dream where Kayla showed her she had a unicorn to ride and Kayla was also drawing one. I did not know about this dream but had been shopping and purchased some things for Felicity. The day after her dream I presented Felicity with a beautiful picture of a unicorn that her daughters told me to buy for her. I had not known about her dream when I purchased it for her!

Around the same time, I also purchased beautiful perfumed oil for Felicity. I felt driven to buy it for her, hearing her daughters whisper to me that her mother needed a new scented oil. I was going to give her the oil, but just before I had a chance, Felicity said laughingly that she had heard Kayla tell her that she smelled! It reminded me of the oil I had for her in my bag and I gave it to her on the spot!

There were many amazing sights and experiences that these incredible two girls were able to share with us. They were able to create love heart bubbles in a sheltered rock pool at the beach when their mummy was doing a goodbye ceremony with some special friends of hers, to scatter some of their ashes. Everyone present saw these bubbles shaped as love hearts.

When we were at the scattering of their ashes at Burleigh Heads (where their father spent much of his teenage and early adult life) I heard the girls say the word "bubble" to me and to mention it to Felicity. It wasn't until after the paddle out and the scattering of the ashes at sea that I got to see Felicity and before I could mention the word bubbles, Felicity started talking about the love heart bubbles and how amazing it was for everyone that was present. These little girl spirits were so clear in their communication with us it was astounding!

Felicity and Leanne came to stay at our house and that night Kayla said the word photo to me. The next morning before I got to mention that Kayla had said "photo", Felicity said that she had a dream that Kayla was pointing at a photo and saying she missed her body. Up until that moment it had been hard for Kayla to get through to me clearly and Sky had been doing most of the communicating.

It was then that I realised what needed to be done so I spoke to Felicity about guiding Kayla to acceptance by speaking to her in her mind and discussing the accident and that even though her body had died she was still very much alive and they could still be together and communicate, it would just be different now. Just as it was in her physical life, Kayla needed her mummy's comforting words and acknowledgement on how to cope, so that she could let go of what was holding her back.

After this Kayla was able to get through clearer to me, saying whole sentences whereas before it was like she was sitting at a desk, hunched over drawing all the time and when I tried to talk to her she couldn't really focus on me or hear me. She was able to tell me about the surfboard gift after this communication with her mother. Both Kayla and Felicity had to come to terms with the loss of Kayla's body. They discussed it together, which enabled the communication channel to become clearer.

One day in 2017 Sky and Kayla came through to me when I was in the shower (I was in a super relaxed state so it was easy to hear them). They told me that the following day I was going to meet someone who had lost a daughter in a car accident like their mummy and I felt a beautiful surge of love between us. The next day I was working at a charity shop that I volunteer at, raising money for orphaned Kenyan children to attend school, be clothed, fed and cared for. I was working when a man told me that many years ago his daughter was killed in a car accident. I paid respects to him for the loss, grateful that the girls had told me beforehand because I was prepared to support the man I was speaking to and simultaneously, I felt lovingly connected to the girls in that moment.

Another time, Kayla and Sky also showed me that the spirit people really influence our skies here and are able to paint (this is the only way to describe it) or to create rainbows, cloud formations and other such things. They can influence lights and animals as well. Immediately after their deaths two light bulbs went in our house and light bulbs never go in our place. I felt them saying to me that it was the girls testing their power and telling us they were here. Several times since their deaths, I had been expecting a visit from Felicity and was thinking of her and both times light bulbs exploded at the moment I was thinking of her. I felt the girls come and tell me their mother couldn't make it and then the bulbs blew!

Felicity told me a story about a friend who had a dream about her girls. The pregnant friend asked Felicity if her girls could possibly reincarnate as the twins that she was expecting. Felicity could feel the girls say a strong no! At the same time her bedroom door slammed shut as if in negative response to the question. Felicity said her door never slammed; there was no wind and no explanation for it slamming. She could strongly feel the girls and felt them communicating with her. She is a strong psychic and I know that this will only increase as she continues on her journey with her beloved daughters and ex-husband by her side in spiritual form.

I hadn't spoken to Felicity in some time, months and months and I was busy editing my book. I got to the section on her family and started working on it, I was very emotional about it for a day or so, I hadn't said anything to anyone about it and out of the blue she contacted me. More proof that we are certainly connected in ways that we don't fully understand yet.

Felicity is probably one of the bravest people I know. She has great integrity and strength and I feel extremely honoured to know her in this physical plane. She is a great teacher and we have much to learn from her. I advised Felicity on regular meditation and daydreaming so that she could access the other realm and communicate with her girls herself and not just through me. Felicity could feel them strongly when they were in the room and also the girls would get through to her through dreams, visions, and physical things like the clouds, rainbows, animals, colours and lights etc. and through psychic mediums such as me.

The girls and Birdy also got through to another psychic – Birdy told the psychic to tell Felicity, "That's life Babe". Which is exactly how he talked and exactly something he would say – the psychic did not know Birdy before this reading, she just lived near the accident site. He was the easiest going, loving, party-going, fantastic fellow. He had so many friends. His motto in life was surf, ski, music, fun, and love. He was always himself and I loved that about him.

Making Sense of The Hole In The Ground

One night it was as if Sky and Kayla took my arms, one on either side of me, and it felt like they were transporting me somewhere. Though I knew my body was still in the bed I was moving through space so quickly I couldn't keep up with it, it was just so quick. We stood before a massive golden city and then the next minute we were hovering above a massive round hole in the ground. Strangely there were lights coming out of it like an inverted building. I had never seen anything like it, it was such a perfect round shape and it was as if these lights were all down the inside of the walls. I hovered above it with them and I wanted to go into it but they wouldn't let me. They told me that even though my body wasn't there it was still dangerous for me to go into it.

I didn't know what to make of it, and was absolutely gob smacked when the next day in yahoo Internet news they reported a massive sinkhole in the middle of a city whereby a building had sunk down into it! It was exactly like the sinkhole they had taken me to the night before. I know I might have lived a sheltered life but before they took me to that sinkhole that night I had never heard of such sinkholes! It wasn't until the next day when yahoo news reported it that I had ever seen such a thing in this physical world.

Skype Session & A Visit From the Girls

After the scattering of the ashes, when Felicity had returned home, we had a Skype session and the girls got through to Felicity and were able to say a few things that showed they were still by her side all the time.

During the Skype session, Sky handed me a meat pie. I said, "Sky is showing me a meat pie" to Felicity, Leanne and Felicity's sister Katie, and I explained how I also heard the words, "More of this for Mummy." That afternoon unbeknownst to me, Leanne's Aunt had dropped over homemade meat pies and that is what they had for dinner. Sky was able to say that her mother needed more of this type of nourishing food to keep her strong.

Sky was also able to say what she wanted to have done with her shoes and socks, to go to classmates as appropriate, but the remainder to African children who had nothing and who would be really happy if they received the girl's belongings for they had so little. She wanted her best friend to have her rainbow-creating crystal hanging in her bedroom window and her charm bracelet. A few days before the Skype session, Sky told me that her best friend would be coming up in conversation and I knew it was important to her. During the Skype session Felicity told me that she was to going to be seeing Sky's best friend in the following few days so it was very relevant. Kayla wanted Felicity to keep her bracelet until the special person who was meant to have it was there. But she did not tell us who this was; just that Felicity would know when this person turned up.

Kayla also showed me a fast racing car zooming in my mind, like a child would do while holding it, back and forth really fast, which I relayed to Felicity. Felicity said a few days before she had a special visit from two little children and it was very memorable. She was in Kayla's room playing with the little boy and the only toy he brought with him was a racing car that he loved. He was zooming it back and forth how Kayla had described. Kayla was acknowledging this visit and of course that she was there.

I sensed a great feeling of love and compassion in relation to Felicity playing with this child through Kayla as well - the pain of playing with children but also of loving children is now a part of Felicity's life. Children are a reminder to her of her own loss, but also of the joy inherent in young souls and the love that is possible for another being.

Through all of this it became apparent that Felicity herself is a gifted psychic and a powerful natural shaman. Through her music and her beautiful strong essence, she changes energies, changes lives.

Several weeks before the tragic accident that took the physical bodies of her daughters, Felicity had been playing and chatting with her children in the bedroom. They were all laughing about what they were going to do when they were teenagers and Felicity had this overwhelming sense that her ecstatic, laughing youngest daughter would not live to be a teenager. She shook off the feeling and told herself to be right in the moment of now, of joy, and she soaked up the joy in her children, in the moment, feeling the pure bliss of laughing with her daughters. The feeling passed and she didn't think of it again. She had never done readings like this or thought of herself as a psychic person really so there was no reason for her to dwell on these types of feelings or thoughts.

As I have been saying, those intuitive feelings like the ones Felicity had are a natural perceptive sense of the human mind. We see or feel things; we know something without knowing how or why we know. We have a feeling that something might happen but no one has said anything out loud and there is no actual physical evidence in front of us but nonetheless there is evidence and it is in our knowing. There is something going on that is obviously so much bigger than us, we sense it sometimes, just like Felicity did, and sometimes it's not up to us to change it.

CHAPTER 12

Love Is...

A Chapter Written by an Angel at 3am

ONE DAY I REALISED THAT I HAD BEEN WRITING ABOUT LOVE and that I thought about love continuously, but I realised I had never defined love.

This is important for everyone out there including myself because love is a unique experience, shared yes, but nonetheless an individual experience while in the human body. I started to daydream about it one evening but I didn't get to write about it because I was busy with the family. That same night I awoke at 1am with a pressing urge to write however I ignored it, thinking I needed more sleep. The words 'Love is' were going through my mind. By 3am I was still awake and knew that this was one of those nights that I could not let pass me by, an angel or spirit person had something important to say through me.

I don't know who she was exactly, but I can say she was female and that I felt a deep sense of peace, ease, comfort and joy when she came. By the end of the encounter with her I was exhausted, but I felt amazing. I went back to bed at about 5.30am.

She felt very wise and pure. She was intelligent, kind and had an important message that she wanted to say.

Here are her loving words for us to embrace and take into our hearts. I was just then, as I was typing this intro, told to say, these words are 'From Laura':

LOVE IS...

Love is the total acceptance of another's core.
Love is the surrender of the heart to the heart of another being.
Love is the strength that we gather to carry on, that builds momentum when it is shared, given out, carried through life and witnessed by all.
Love is the one thing that you can count on to lift your spirits and heart.
Love is the sacrifice that we make for each other.
Love is the kindness and respect that we give to all other beings we encounter.
Love is the joy in our hearts shared and shown to the world, to others in the world.
Love is the immensity, the propensity, the fuel, and the creator of all things around us and within us. Without this fuel life would cease to exist.
Love is complete giving.
Love is complete sharing.
Love is complete patience.
Love is not being perfect.
Love is sometimes hard.
Love is saying to somebody that they are right and you are wrong.
Love is apologising.
Love is protection.
Love is equality.

Love is riding the golden wave together.
Love is seeing through the ego, to the personality on the
inside, to the one that needs and requires love.
Love is not taking other people personally.
Love is letting people be.
Love is trusting.
Love is knowing that you must protect the innocent
from those who do not yet practice from the force of
love and are blind to it.
Love is intelligent, kind and prosperous.
Love is all things, at all times, everywhere.
Love is the fuel for the fire, the ice in the mountains; the
love in your heart is worth more than any money or any
so-called valuable.
Love is the challenge of a lifetime, bigger than climbing
Mount Everest, bigger than swimming across any
channel or sailing around the world, love is pure and
simple, the biggest challenge you will face at any one
time.
Love is the ability to love those who hate and hurt
others.
Love is the caring grace inherent in all people.
Love is respecting and savouring the beautiful physical
differences we all have.
Love is letting others know we love and care for them.
Love is understanding.
Love is not bitter.
Love is not jealous.
Love knows no bounds but the ones that we impose so
unwisely.
Love is acceptance of life.

Love is life.

Love is the porthole through which we come and through which we return. We are love and we become love. We emit love, we share love, and we BE love in its purest form.

Love, love and more love, is the be all and end all of all things. We must embrace love. Without the love that is felt in our heart for others, for their shine, their glow, their heart, their light, we are but dull sparks - we are shiny, proud, beautiful, intelligent, glowing beings because we are LOVE.

Love we must not forget.

Love.

Chapter 12 Exercise:
Add to this list of love

1. Write down your own list of what love means to you.
2. Also write a list of all the things you love doing and that make you feel connected to yourself or others, anything from creative things to sports to cooking etc.!
3. Then make a list on what you are grateful for in your life. This list always makes me feel so happy and humble. I often think about what I am grateful for! Often I hold my heart as I do so and I end up with a big smile of gratitude on my face, sometimes I even end up in tears because I just feel so grateful for it all!
4. Make one last list about what, if anything, you would like to include in your life to bring more loving, happy feelings into your life?

I've found that when you do what you love, you shine and you bring even more positivity into your life and more chances for spirit to help you and get through to you and others!

5. Revisit these lists on a regular basis. Add more to them. Or just to bring love to the forefront of your life again. Also, practicing gratitude regularly is really important for our happiness and wellbeing.

AMANDA McHUGH

CHAPTER 13

Conclusion

*"The intuitive mind is a sacred gift and the rational mind is
a faithful servant. We have created a society that honors the
servant and has forgotten the gift."*
Albert Einstein

I HAVE SAID IT BEFORE, AND I WILL SAY IT
AGAIN, our intuitive, psychic sense is the greatest gift
that we could ever embrace and use in our lives. We live
in a psychic world, where otherworldly activity exists
within us and around us all the time. We are part of this
mystery by the very nature of our souls.

The answers to questions about where we come
from, where we go to when we die and where our loved
ones go when they die are important to us in this life.
These answers help us make sense of our world and find
meaning to life. They can help us live our lives spiritually
aware. Knowing also helps us find peace so that we can
get on with the joy of living. It can help us find
perspective when inevitably we are faced with death and
dying of ourselves and of our loved ones.

We know there are countless stories about intuitive
experiences and that the abilities of psychic mediums are
becoming more and more accepted in the mainstream. As
we continue to accept, use and develop our psychic

intuition, psychic abilities will contribute to human evolution and lead us into the future. It will advance the human race.

Parents often say their young children, such as under the age of 4, report psychic phenomena when they were very young. Children often say things about reincarnation or seeing dead loved ones and talking to them, but that after a young age, their psychic ability appears to taper off. In fact, the psychic ability always continues, but in a different way. It becomes a useful ability for human survival, one where we constantly assess and review the energy in people and things in the world.

Without structure, guidance and training, the psychic gift lacks strength and purpose, however it still naturally works in the background of our lives. Its potential power gets dulled and drowned out by our busy lives; such as financial stress, school and work pressures, health, relationship, and family and social issues. But regardless of this, intuition is simply a part of us and we use it to make decisions every day. We use it to weigh up good and bad energy of things that we have to make decisions about, without even a second thought as to the fact we are using our intuition.

Sometimes we become very consciously aware of using it though, such as when we sense something is wrong in a room we've just entered or that feeling we need to contact a loved one as something feels wrong with them or when our hair prickles on the back of our neck and we suddenly realise we've wandered into a dangerous area of a city or town. Sometimes we don't listen to our intuition and get ourselves into trouble and we can get annoyed with ourselves when we don't listen to our gut intuition (well that's what happens to me anyway!). But that's also how we learn so we shouldn't be too disheartened (and that's what I say to myself to make myself feel better when in the past I've ignored my intuition!).

I have an excellent example of this. Many years ago I had the strongest gut feeling about a company that would be a good investment. They were just releasing their shares to the public on the stock market and I loved the brand and I thought other people did too. However, I didn't listen to my strong feeling because my partner at the time didn't agree with me that these shares would be really profitable. I had $10,000 to invest but I didn't do it. I didn't listen to my own gut instinct and instead I listened to my ex-partner's opinion. Within a few short months of their release to the public, the stocks tripled in value! I would have had $30,000 had I listened to myself! It was a costly lesson to learn!

Where do we go from here?

I have no doubt it would be very beneficial for us all if we learnt about our psychic sense early and nurtured it. Each successive generation learns more from the previous generation and also adds to this accumulative knowledge. As my dear friend Donna once told us, "Follow the children", and she was right, they can show us a lot about our natural gift if we listen to and watch them carefully.

Many of us have heard that Albert Einstein was considered to be a slow child, but really he was one of the most brilliant minds of our time. Imagine how many Einsteins we could be potentially dulling down because in this generation we are quick to medicate and label special and unique souls coming through. Or what I could have done with my prior knowledge of 9/11 if I wasn't so uncertain about sharing what I could see and feel.

There are also some wonderful parents and caregivers who embrace and encourage their children's innate psychic abilities and for all of you out there thank you and I applaud you for your foresight! With your acceptance of your children's natural abilities, you are helping us all evolve!

Mystics and medicine people throughout history have reported visions, fits, trances and strange episodes and states. In our culture we tend to medicate people when they have these types of awakenings. I think we need to be more careful in the future with this. We are stifling our own psychic evolution by doing this. In my own life, I consider myself lucky that I had a degree in psychology and was able to protect myself and be strong when my intuition really awakened. I listened to the call of spirit and travelled, first to America and then to Ireland, a country steeped in old spiritual customs and mythology. I married into that country, to an Irishman, and I think that helped me to be more accepted and find more acceptance within myself as a psychic medium. Psychics are valued in Irish culture and when I lived there I officially worked as a psychic medium for the first time in my life. Then when I came back to Australia, we settled in the spiritual hub of the country, near Byron Bay.

So while I have been able to do this and able to be myself here, without shame or ridicule, I have been telling people I am a psychic medium for the good part of 17 years or so now, but what about everyone else out there in everyday society? In our world I believe that many people with strong psychic powers have been and still are held back, ignored, diagnosed and misdiagnosed, medicated, persecuted and ridiculed.

In the long term, we will have to formally embrace and cultivate our intuition, it's a big step for us, but one that is inevitable. We can't hide this ability anymore, you can see from the internet and media, it's like we just have to be ourselves. We have to share what we know and use this ability. Like all evolution, it takes on a life of its own and because of all we know now with technology and the internet and people sharing so much knowledge so readily, psychic knowledge has been widely disseminated. It's just a matter of time before it is outlined fully by science and understood more, so that we can all accept it and then we can really see what we can do with it!

Let's Embrace It!

Psychic power has so much to offer us! We could see the future to help prevent or prepare for all manner of things from environmental calamities to humankind-created disasters such as severe weather, war, and preventable incidents such as massive oil spills into the ocean or acts of terrorism etc.

We could also intuit causes from the past or see what is happening presently that might benefit from human or spiritual intervention to improve our future prospects. We could be healed of grief and fear, we could prosper from spiritual growth of all humankind, embrace a better way where we help all others in poverty or suffering, because it is our spiritual purpose on this earth.

We could create a much better earth experience for all human beings. Because we can feel the connections between each other, through our cultivated psychic sense, we care more and we make more of an effort to support each other.

Regardless of how it will evolve, our psychic sense used now can bring us so much comfort. Sometimes in life we feel very alone, we feel like we are lost or not seen or listened to. We can feel scared, invisible or bullied. But one thing I know is that this is a temporary and one-sided affair. This can be remedied at any moment, a change in perspective, situation, a move, a decision to pray to God, to the universe, to spirit or our guides and angels to ask for help and a request for love to enter your life and heart.

We can reach out to other people for love, it's one of the bravest but also important things we can do, seek true connection with others.

Recently when I was feeling down about something and clearing some deep and old emotions, I prayed to God and to my spirit family for days and days asking for love and support and guidance. Then one night, my beautiful Bibi (the word for 'aunty' in Indonesian) Masna came to me. She looked so beautiful and young and vibrant, the way she was when I was a child. She always made me laugh and feel good. She was like the gorgeous female version of my father; they were so alike. In my powerful spirit dream, she put her face up to mine and said, "You are free! You were always free! Free! Free! You are free!" I woke up with the image of her face still embedded in my mind. Well this changed my life for the better from that moment on.

All I had to do was ask for help. Just like sometimes when you get a hug or a back massage you didn't realise how much you needed it, it can be the same with spiritual connections. Until you become aware of it and nurture it, you don't realise how wonderful it can be for your life.

As human beings we also need other human beings. We need touch, true heart felt connections, and to feel important and valued by others. When we have human social support and feel part of community, we cope much better with life's ups and downs, as we have people to turn to and trust. We experience compassion and empathy for others and they experience it for us.

There are people all around us, even people we don't know on telephone help lines, even in a grocery store, or a neighbourhood centre, or hospital, or while you're out and about walking your dog, who will help us shift a bad situation or thought by giving us some attention, loving words or actions, or some sound advice. We often just need to listen and be willing to change a mindset and let their support and love enter our hearts and minds. We also need good people around us, men and women who are caring and looking out for our best interests and we look out for theirs. Animals/pets can also give and receive love and are as important to us as we are to them.

This is what the spirits want for us while we are here, these loving heartfelt connections. They also want us to have this with them, with spirit, through prayer, gratitude, meditation, creativity, art, reading and writing, and experiences in nature. They just love knowing we acknowledge them and are listening out for their messages.

Since I was a little girl I used to do a meditation that involved a pure white room. It was completely white. A white chair, walls, floors and ceilings and I would be pure white too, like the whitest brightest light. I would sometimes see guides in the form of a Socrates type person, a Native American Indian Chief, a Samurai warrior and as I got older women, ancient mothers, aunties and grandmothers who helped me learn to be strong, loving, patient and kind, especially to children. Sometimes it would be an animal guide that would give me love and guidance. At other times, I would also fly high into a star filled sky, floating in the cosmos. Beautiful beings would give me reiki or healing by placing their hands on me or holding or hugging me while I floated. I would come from these sessions so grounded and also feeling very loved and strong psychically and physically.

People go around the world often not smiling or interacting with others. They don't know who to trust or if the person's kindness is for real or a trick. We can become wary of others. We can lose faith in people and in our ability to discern good from bad, trustworthy and safe from negative and unsafe. I suppose I would say to listen to that little voice inside.

Being connected to your higher self and the spirit

dimension through prayer and meditation will help strengthen your ability to hear that inner voice. I have a policy of always being loving, kind and approachable but also having a sphere of powerful God light protection around me at all times. This protection is gained through prayer and visualisation of this protective aura. I always believe we are protected by a loving God force.

I'm not saying things won't happen in life that hurt, but we are in a greater plan for the universal growth and I trust this plan. Remember too that being in nature, having walks in forests or along the ocean, is important to cleanse and strengthen us, leading to better thoughts and stronger discernment when dealing with others. Most important, having a safe and stable home to go at the end of the day is important for our body and spirit to replenish after being immersed in other people's energies out in the world!

Some people don't realise how obvious it is to others that they can be read like an open book. Once I did a reading for some young people in Dublin. To one of the boys I said, "You were drinking last night and then you stole some things." One of the girls who with him, hit him on the arm, and said to him, "I told you so! I told you not to steal! See!"

He was mortified that I could see into him! He just kept staring at me, and I told him that we can see things about people and we can make other, better choices for our lives, or else we can end up in jail and in other bad situations. I got to tell the young woman that I could see her successful, with lovely business clothes and she was very happy with that. She had big dreams for her future that did not involve being a street kid and getting into trouble.

So, in relation to this, I have to say one last thing before I sign off and it is about our ability to hear other's intentions, deeds and thoughts. We do this more than we realise and it's a very important gift that needs developing. If we had cleaner, clearer, and more positive thoughts and intentions we could really help the world's energy clear also. Several examples from my life come to mind.

One morning I thought of a friend I hadn't seen or thought of in many years. That evening I received a message from this friend. He had been thinking of messaging me to ask for my opinion on something. So before he had a chance to message me, I had picked up on his thoughts directed towards me. Secondly I was in a shop when I bent to look at some interesting items. I heard a voice in my head that said, "That's mine." I ignored it. Next minute a lady called out to me, "That's mine there."

"Sorry," I said. I then told her I heard a little voice in my head say, "That's mine," before she said it. And she said, "Yep that was me!" It was one of those funny moments you share with a stranger. And moments like that happen to me constantly. Sometimes I just nod and smile when people say things to me, as I've already heard it in my head moments or sometimes a day or more before. I just don't like to be a know-it-all as my mother calls it, so I don't say that I've already had this conversation with them.

Just imagine all of the countless thoughts floating around in the world! These thoughts are connected with energy that we leave in the world. There is an amazing example to share here.

It happened when I was living in Tramore with my friend Sean. Sean was sitting on the lounge chair and I went to put something in the bin under the kitchen sink. I literally felt a wave of thick, dark grey hatred come flying out at me. It wasn't the first time this had happened when I went to use the bin. But for some reason it was really noticeable on this day and I said to Sean, "I don't know why but every time I open up the cupboard to put something in the bin, a wave of hate flies out at me!" Sean replied, "Oh my God, I'm so sorry, every time I go to use the bin, I think to myself 'I hate this bin being in here'!"

Energy can accumulate if thoughts have been directed at something long enough. This energy can accumulate on objects, places and living beings.

Another interesting example is when Mick and I were sitting together at our home in the hills of Byron Bay. He got up, walked down the hall, to the kitchen, got something, went back up the hall again and then sat close to me. On his return I said, "You smell like Dublin."

He said, "I was just thinking of Dublin when we lived at the IFC (Irish Financial Centre) and how this felt like that time."

He told me how he had really gone into the memory of us living in Dublin when we first met and were totally crazy for each other and how he re-created it in his mind, in his thoughts, feelings and with his senses. I was then able to smell it off his breath and sense it off him as he was sitting very close to me. I could feel Dublin in my own body, as if I had just been thinking about being there. Before he walked down that hall we had not been chatting about Dublin or Ireland at all. We were talking about an entirely different topic. His thoughts created a tangible physical change that I was able to read like a book.

We all have this powerful gift. If we try, if we listen to the finest of sensations that we experience, we could be much more aware of what we are all putting into the world and also what we are sensing. Our thoughts potentially have a lot of influence on us, on what we are feeling, thinking and experiencing and on others' experiences too. I feel this is something that is important to think about and ponder as we go about our daily lives and into the future. It has ramifications for all levels of life and for child care and education, government, relationships, mental health work, service provision, business, health and healing, and energy work; there are just countless ways this infiltrates and influences our lives.

I think this is why I have been getting a lot of benefit and comfort from the modern Hawaiian Ho-oponopono prayer that Hew Len and Joe Vitale outline in their book 'Zero Limits' (I mentioned this book previously). When I have negative or uncomfortable feelings or thoughts, or when I'm particularly tired, I find their prayer, "I am sorry. Please forgive me. Thank you. I love you", helps me to cleanse and feel uplifted. When one has these forgiving and loving emotions within oneself, negativity can't exist simultaneously and just quietly slips away. It is believed that this is a prayer to the Divine and that the Divine heals what needs healing within you as you reach out to spirit asking for forgiveness, love and transformation.

A Final Angelic Gift

As we are nearly finished our time together for this book, I must share this final beautiful experience with you. I hope you've made it this far and I thank you sincerely for sharing this intuitive journey with me.

This is a particularly powerful angelic encounter, though it is also very sweet and simple. One day I was speaking to my dear friend Katie on the telephone. Katie and I lived on opposite sides of Ireland, I lived in Dublin and she lived in Ennis. Suddenly, much to my delight, several beautiful little beings showed themselves to me in my mind's eye. They looked like small flying angelic cherubs with wings and chubby little bodies. Just like you see in cartoons and books on cherubs. They were so delightfully happy and joyous. Meeting them was such a pleasant surprise!

The sweet little cherubs spoke to me and told me to tell Katie that the maroon-coloured book she was reading with the pink ribbon was really beautiful and it was helping the world heal. They wanted Katie to keep reading this book and other beautiful books like it, with continued focus and sacred reverence. They said it was good for us to read beautiful spiritual texts and books about angels and the spiritual/angelic world and about miraculous acts etc., without human bias and interpretation, but with the love and sacred, positive intention in which the words were originally intended.

They said that these works kept us connected to our spiritual/angelic nature and to loving, positive energy. I understood that the sacred words were not for judging, segregating, ostracizing or ruling over other people, but to be held in loving regard, and we are meant to bring that loving, sacred feeling and positive intention from the angelic or other world, into our physical world.

Katie started crying because at the time she was reading her MAROON-COLOURED BIBLE WITH A PINK RIBBON as the page marker!

So books like the bible, and this sacred memoir, are treasures to hold close to our hearts, minds and spirits. They tell the loving truth that the angels want us to hear and want us to feel while we are here. I don't mean to advertise any particular religion per se, but I think the angels want us to read and engulf our minds and thus our souls in beautiful works of love and light. They want us to thrive and shine here and there are some beautiful works of art that channel such divine energy for us to connect to the transcendent while we are 'playing in the physical realm'.

Final Words

We are all a bridge to the divine. Whether or not we see it or choose to be a conscious, living bridge that actively connects this side and the next, we are all bridges by our very nature, our existence.

These final words came to me from the whisperings of an angelic spirit and I hope they will be of great comfort to you, as they have been to me:

You are seen
You are loved
and
You are never alone.

I repeat these words to myself and think about them if I am ever in need of solace. We are seriously so loved, so valued and so seen.

I hope that of everything you have taken from this book you can really see and feel that. It is love that spirit wants us to feel and take with us and share with everyone else.

Love is our destiny and I hope that this book has shown this love from the other side and that we are not what we appear to be. We are like the river or the iceberg, people can see the top part, but when they get through and dive into the water and really look around they see the abundance underneath, the whole of life that is teeming and flourishing just below the surface, revealing the magical, beautiful, and amazing beings that we truly are!

A Parting Meditation

Read this through once, then close your eyes and go deeply into the love.

- In your mind say the words to yourself, "I am seen and I am loved". Slowly and calmly repeat these words to yourself several times, along with slow, deep breaths. Know fully in your whole being that you are seen and loved.

- Imagine the love slowly filling you up, feel it and see it going all the way from your head, down your body, to the tips of your toes. You are full of love.

- You might see beautiful angels or beings or loved ones with their hands on or around you sending the love into your body. Breathe these feelings of love fully into your being for a few beautiful, deep, love-filled breaths. Any negativity that you have is expelled from your body on the out breath.

- Feel the love expand outwards from you in a beautiful aura or shield, it might be white, pink, another colour or full of sparkles or silver or gold or like a rainbow.

- Know that you are love and you emanate love. You breathe in love into your whole self. You are love. Know this fully and utterly right here, right now. And with this know that you are never alone. Know that at all times you are loved and seen fully by the angels and that we are all one.

- You can do this meditation in ten minutes or one minute or for as long as you like, whenever and wherever you like, on a bus, in a shop, in a classroom, in the park, in your bed. It will lift you and put you in the right frame of mind, body and spirit to undertake your life with spiritual awareness and love in this physical world. Always put your physical safety first if you do this when you are out in public.

You are connected to the divine and you are grounded to our precious earth when you do the sacred meditations in this memoir. We are beautiful sensitive, psychic, sensory, intelligent beings and we are part of a greater mysterious psychic world.
Never forget that you are LOVE
and that you are LOVED.

AMANDA McHUGH

AUTHOR'S APPENDIX

A Bit Of History & Background To Intuition

I THINK YOU WILL AGREE THAT, after reading all of the stories in this book, that our minds and spirits are truly amazing.

I originally had this appendix as a chapter in the book, but it is much more about educating about intuition, so I thought it best as an appendix. I wanted to share this information, but it can be a bit on the educative side, rather than on the side of sharing interesting psychic stories from real life. I hope it's of some use and interest to you about the overall topic of intuition in our world.

Intuition & History

We all possess the ability to harness our intuition and put it into use in our everyday lives. Unlike what we were told as children in primary school, we definitely have more than five basic senses!

Every single one of us is born with intuition, which allows our minds to tune in to the knowledge that exists beyond our physical world. As we get older, this intuitive voice is often drowned out or dulled down by the noise of living and we may stop using it altogether. We aren't taught about it in our Western public school system or by our parents because they weren't taught about it! In fact, others often tell us not to trust our own intuition.

I met an Israeli woman who had been living in Australia for several years. She took one look at my eyes and fiercely hugged me very close and she said that she missed meeting people like me from her old country, people who had the sight. It was a lovely recognition of my pure ability and it was her culture that enabled her to recognise it and speak freely about it.

Throughout history there have been many accounts of psychic phenomena that defy normal explanation. These examples can be found in the Bible, the Koran, Buddhist teachings, Hinduism, in the oral histories of the Indigenous Australians and Indigenous Peoples around the world, and in modern parapsychology.

Yet, in most Western societies, it's quite a fringe thing to talk about because our culture tends to be traditional, conservative and religious. Some religious interpretations do not allow for the psychic gift to be accepted as a natural part of ourselves but reserved for a special select few such as Jesus, Saints or Yogis. In the Bible there are countless stories of angel visitations and prophecy, and many of the saints and sages received guidance this way.

Sometimes it is just the use of the word psychic that people don't like. Our psychic intuition has been mistaken for many things in the past such as devil worship or witchcraft! It's only a natural gift we all share, but us humans can be a superstitious bunch! You might find this hard to believe, but as late as the 19th century a person was accused and burnt as a witch! I really could go on about this, I think that this time in our history really effected our ability to be honest about and freely use our psychic abilities. We shut them down so that we would be safer in society.

In the modern world, science hasn't yet caught up with all of the scientific proof about the validity and power of psychic intuition. There are actually a lot of studies showing that intuition exists and also a lot of research studying famous and powerful psychic mediums, however it has yet to fully reach mainstream science, particularly Western medicine and psychology.

Spiritual matters remain still separate, although many can attest to miracle cures through spiritual means, much of mainstream psychology and medicine prefers to label this as fringe, placebo, one-offs or, sad but true, as psychiatric disorders or episodes.

In some cultures, a profound awakening to spirit is often what is considered to be a breakdown or a manic phase in the Western world. Hopefully in the long term we can grow wise to this and stop labelling that which is natural to the spirit. People having awakenings are often labelled and medicated. This is sometimes necessary if the person is a danger to themselves or others, however sometimes it is to make other people more comfortable in the person's presence.

There are cultures who allow such awakenings to work through their natural course. They don't deny or medicate, but embrace the person's spiritual path. They have found that when the person gets through the episode, they are often healers, teachers, spiritual leaders, or medicine people. They can also bring valuable information from the spiritual realm. There are some Western centres of healing enabling this process to complete itself, but they are very limited.

I remember reading about one American family who were so desperate to help their son who at 14 years of age was labelled as schizophrenic and put on heavy medications. After treatment did not work and only made him worse, they knew they had to seek alternative help and they sent him to an African community where such episodes were embraced. The teenager was immersed into the community and his life took on new meaning. Within a few short months he was healed. It became apparent that he was a healer and he took on a healing role in the community. He returned to America and went to college and became a very successful psychologist (See Malidoma Patrice Some's 1997 book "Ritual: Power, Healing and Community").

In new age terms this sort of incident is often called 'The Dark Night of the Soul' and it often leads to transformation and spiritual growth on profound levels. Seers, healers and teachers are born from this process. This can be an important part of our awakening, and if we have people who understand around us, we can really grow and thrive after these experiences. But if we continue to label, medicate and stereotype we may not be helping the person to rediscover their new stronger and wiser self. Sometimes people believe the labels they receive from the medical people, and they think something is really wrong and bad with them. This then has a negative effect on their self-esteem and sense of self-worth. Meanwhile in my world, it means that your higher self is trying to help you learn and grow.

Developing Our Intuition

Intuition doesn't have to arise after a crisis though. Like anything, developing intuition can take practice, especially when it has been closed off or asleep. However, the more we use our intuition and learn to trust our 'gut feeling', the more often our intuitive instincts will kick in and the more our psychic channels will open. Our psychic channels will expand when we learn what is possible.

Also the more that we practice prayer, gratefulness, mindfulness and meditative states of peacefulness, the more information from intuition can get through to our consciousness. This makes sense as a person whose mind is full of clutter, negative self-talk or constant worry will find it more challenging to hear that positive, inner, intuitive voice.

Relaxation and meditation are particularly important to developing intuition. There have been a lot of studies showing that relaxation and meditation actually increase productivity, concentration, alertness, calmness, develop new synaptic brain pathways and reduce anxiety, depression and blood pressure.

The same can be said of prayer, which I consider to be another form of meditation, and I pray a lot. I thank the Divine and my spirit brothers and sisters for all that they do for us and for the beautiful world around us and all of the blessings in our lives. I have a deep and genuine sense of gratefulness for life.

I also concentrate on certain positive and empowering words or affirmations such as the word and energy of "love" or phrases such as "I am pure love and light". Simultaneously I imagine myself as a being of pink loving light, with a large aura of loving light surrounding me. These beautiful affirmations and visualisations help centre, ground and bring spirit into the forefront of our lives and our essence. When you are in a state of grace and gratefulness you cannot also be angry. This peacefulness and openness of mind lends itself to receive spiritual information more readily.

I read snippets from a book written by another psychic medium, who had her brain waves measured while she was giving psychic readings. Her brain waves were like those of someone who was in a deep sleep or coma, but she was talking and fully engaged! She felt that she was able to shut off from self-related activity, give her ego a rest and allow information from other sources to come through her for others benefit. Like myself, she thought we might be able to teach others to turn this switch on, enabling others to access this area of the brain to use their intuition at will also. Thus this is another indication that one of the keys to unlock or enhance intuition could be through meditation. (For your information, the book is Laura Lynne Jackson's 2015 'The Light Between Us').

Maybe some people are more naturally intuitive than others or maybe they've just learnt to access that part of the brain that is intuitive at will. Just as some of us are naturally gifted musicians or sports people, perhaps there are people who are born with a more heightened "sixth" sense or psychic ability. Throughout history there have been amazing examples of psychic ability, such as spirit mediums who can speak different languages when they channel deceased people from different countries. When they are not channeling they cannot speak those languages.

Interestingly, psychic abilities are not new. Psychics have been the leaders, healers, shamans, and medicine men and women of Indigenous cultures all over the world for centuries.

Psychics, medicine men, shamans, oracles, seers and Australian Aboriginal clever men have been utilized by people in positions of power such as tribal leaders, kings, queens, pharaohs and emperors etc. These shamans and clever men were naturally gifted psychics, who were able to travel to the spirit world to glean important information and act as a bridge between worlds to enable healing and spiritual growth for their people.

Yogis in India and Buddhists have been shown to be able to do incredible things, from levitation to controlling their temperature, so that even when they are unclothed and sitting in the snow they don't feel the cold. They can even emit steam off their bodies while in the snow! Yogis have also been known to be able to appear in two places at once. 'Autobiography of a Yogi' by Paramahansa Yogananda is an excellent book on this topic and as I read it I felt waves of powerful energy flowing through me. I don't know if it would do this to everyone, but it is still a wonderful read!

When I studied the history of healing and Indigenous healing at university we explored these incredible psychic healers and their amazing powers. And yet I know there is still fear and skepticism levelled at modern-day psychics like myself. So while I do talk about my gift openly, I am careful about the words I choose to describe my experiences because I know that some people can take me the wrong way or have preconceived ideas about what I do. Telling my stories openly with people can also lead to them sharing their own incredible psychic stories.

As an example, a few years ago I was at a friend's 21st birthday party when my friend's grandfather asked me what I did for a living. He was a humble farmer, and I didn't want to alarm him or put him off. I told him I was a writer but that there was more to me than that.

I said, "Sometimes I just can't help it, it's natural to me, but I talk to people who have died or see things before they happen. It's just something I do. I can't stop it; it has just always happened to me."

I was very sincere and honest with him. He looked deep into my eyes for a few seconds without any apparent judgment and then he began to share his own special story.

He told me that many years ago he was piloting a small plane, carrying several passengers. He was unable to see into the distance to navigate and couldn't make out the land because dense fog was blocking his view. He had to rely on the plane's controls and compass and a physical paper map with a layout of the land to navigate. As he was looking down at the control panel, a voice called out loudly into his ear, "Look up now!"

He looked up and immediately saw a looming mountain peak coming out of the fog. He knew instantly that he was piloting the plane directly into the peak.

His survival instincts kicked in, he reefed the controls

back to lift the plane higher into the air, the nose angled up sharply and he cleared the peak just in time. Without the warning from the voice, he and his passengers would have crashed into the side of the mountain top and died.

He said, "I've often wondered why me?"

I was very touched by his story and it meant a lot that he shared it with me. He was a very down to earth man, a farmer living in rural Australia and yet his story shows that any of us could be privy to messages from the other side. It also shows that if we listen to them we can save ourselves.

The voice is there for all of us, and each one of us has the potential to hear and listen to the voice, to follow through when we are warned about something or when we feel something just isn't right. Sometimes the voice is as loud as the one my friend's grandfather heard, while other times it's just a niggling feeling or it may come through in a dream or a vision, or through someone else. I wanted to explain this to the farmer, but as I was gathering my thoughts to speak coherently, he was pulled away for family photos. We had a mutual knowing about something deep, something that as humans we can grasp, but not necessarily put into words.

As humans we feel something is there, but we don't know exactly what. We live our lives in a physical, tangible way and sometimes, every so often, life changing 'spiritual' occurrences happen, like the voice that warned my friend's grandfather to pull the plane up at the last minute or the twins who died at birth that were able to show themselves to me, so I could let their mother know they were around her.

We each have our own stories to tell, and if not our own stories then we know other people's amazing stories. These types of stories abound in our world, if only we decide to open our ears and our eyes to them. If we add together all of our 'one-off intuitive stories', we get an amazing pattern of a strong and valid intuitive sense - one that is very much alive and being used in our everyday lives. We also come to understand that there is a lot more going on in this world than we can see with the naked eye, that there are beings living in what we call a 'spiritual' world, that exists alongside our own.

We can communicate with and work together with the loving beings in the spirit world to make our worlds a better place – if you think about it, their world improves when ours does!

The spiritual world will be an easier place to navigate for those of us who are already familiar with it before we get there. Bridging the gaps between our world and the next is a wise move for our evolution both here on the earthly plane and there in the spirit world. It also helps us cope with loss, change, grief and death because we comprehend without a doubt that we are not alone, that we are loved and supported from the other side, and that our loved ones never truly leave us, and importantly, that we ourselves never truly die.

The Usefulness of Psychics

Psychics have been used for a long time by law enforcement, though they generally don't advertise the fact! Psychics pick up on energy imprints from objects and crime scenes and can give intuited information and leads to police that are uncanny and invaluable to solving crimes. I have also contacted police about things before, as you will read in the memoir.

Psychics can use their ability in other streams of work. I went to an author's reading of her book. As she was telling the audience the storyline of her book, and how she wrote it in one sitting, as if it almost wrote itself, I felt that it sounded like a channeled piece of work, much like my own work. When it came to question time, I told her

I was a psychic medium and that the book sounded channeled to me. I asked her if she felt that her book was channeled to which she replied yes. She said it hardly needed editing at all. She then explained that after she had written the book an old friend came back into her life. Amazingly, her friend's intriguing life story was exactly the same as the story that the author had written about in the book! It was quite a unique and unusual story, so the odds of it being a coincidence were minimal. Perhaps through some continuing energetic connection with her friend, the author had managed to tap into her friend's powerful life experience.

I know of other authors' whose partners or relatives have died and they have channeled the writing of their deceased loved ones.

I know of strong energy readers who are incredible in sales. They are good at thought projection and getting people to buy products off them!

In terms of the animal kingdom, we know that animals possess intuition. They seem to know when bad weather is coming and they make for high ground or leave the area that's about to be hit. They read their human counterparts and understand moods and thoughts.

My little mini Maltese Shih Tzu dog, Sparkles, had this incredible knack for running the other way when I used to just think that it was time to give her a bath! On the other hand, there were times when I was thinking about giving her a piece of fresh meat and before I've had a chance to call out to her, she's run into the room and stared at me!

Sometimes it can take a near death experience or traumatic event to open up our intuition and heighten our psychic connection. Regardless of where you are on your journey, this book will open your mind to the infinite potential that exits inside every one of us and at the very least enhance the positive energy in your life. We can all learn to tune in and choose to listen to the signs that are in front of us.

Are there others who share these views?

As a trained psychologist, I know that there has been a lot of research into instinct and intuition, particularly in the field of neuroscience, quantum physics and parapsychology – although I also know it's still very much on the fringes of mainstream. Reading about this research is a fascinating new world that many people have just not ventured into.

There are many psychologists, psychiatrists, neuroscientists, physicists and other medical professionals who share similar views to me but we are only just glimpsing the field of possibilities. Doctor John Lermer worked in palliative care for so long and witnessed so many amazing things that he came to believe in life after death and in angels. Doctor C. Norman Shealy works with a medical intuitive, Carolyn Myss, and together they established schools to teach people how to read the energy that is emitted by the body to diagnose illnesses. Neurosurgeon Dr Eben Alexander died and went to heaven and had incredible experiences with celestial beings in the afterlife. He was revived, survived his ordeal and is a strong advocate that the soul lives on after physical death.

Parapsychology is the school of psychology dedicated to the study of paranormal abilities. Dean Radin is a famous parapsychologist with at least five published books on the field, showing that psychics and mediums have proven themselves time and time again in thousands of controlled lab tests. Radin's book, 'Entangled Minds' (2006) looks at the physical, scientific and rational explanation behind intuition. He explains how psychic phenomena are a part of the interconnected and entangled physical reality we live in. Albert Einstein called this entanglement, "spooky action at a distance", it is where two objects remain connected through space and time, without communicating in conventional ways, in a relationship that continues long after their initial interaction has occurred. Radin looks at how a similar entanglement of minds explains our psychic abilities. He believes it's only a matter of time before mainstream science catches up with all the evidence for psychic abilities.

Nancy Du Tertre is an American attorney who became a psychic detective who helps police solve crimes. She was a true skeptic and still calls herself 'The Skeptical Psychic'. In 2010 she published a book about her experiences called 'Psychic Intuition', where she outlines that intuition is not a fantasy and that it is a natural and trainable sense. She discusses how most mediums have been women and summaries some of the physical sensory reasons why this might be so.

Canadian Chris Carter wrote a great book on the history of science and the afterlife based on 125 years of research by the British and American Societies for Psychical Research. He reviews some fascinating cases of life after death communication between deceased persons and mediums, as well as numerous powerful and validated cases of reincarnation.

Irish psychic Lorna Byrne has captured her experience of talking to angels in several books, while John Edwards, Lisa Williams, James Van Praagh, Alison Dubois and Australians Charmaine Wilson and Mitchell Coombes are just a small selection of many famous and highly reputable psychics with fascinating books and films about their psychic experiences. Doreen Virtue is an extremely famous psychologist who has become a world expert on angels and talking to angels and healing through their spiritual care. She discusses at length the many times she herself has heard angelic or spiritual voices, and how those voices have helped her and others time and time again.

As you can see there are excellent books in this field, and amazing brave, wise psychics and mediums who are daring to share their gifts with the world in the hope that we all benefit from this wisdom.

With all the evidence amassing, and more and more prominent psychic people becoming accepted in the mainstream, I dream that one day there will be standard community-taught and 'approved' courses on how to use our intuition/psychic abilities to benefit our lives here.

It makes sense that we would do this, a next step in our evolution. It takes a great deal of calmness and awareness to be consciously psychic on a daily basis, so any such study would involve the teaching of mindfulness and meditation also.

As I've said before and will probably say again, regular practice of relaxation, meditation and mindfulness, puts the mind and body in a state that is conducive to receiving messages and being able to hear them. There is so much going on in the world at any one time that we need to calm ourselves to hear the messages and the information that can help us.

Having said this, we also need to trust that we receive the information when we are meant to, from sources who care deeply for us. These sources assure me that they are always there for us and they will always come when asked (even when not asked they are always with us).

Sometimes we might not sense them or what they are doing, but in time, their good will and actions can come to fruition. We have to learn patience, and must trust that they are working alongside us for the good of us all.

One example for me is that the spirits always come through for people when I am doing readings. The spirits guide me in a psychic healing session and they never let me down. They have helped me in the past with my nervousness beforehand by telling me that they will always come and help. I never have to fear that I am alone when I am doing readings for people. It is a collaborative effort between spirit and our world at all times. The psychic is the bridge for the information to flow freely between the divide.

I have experienced so many magical spiritual occurrences in this life, times just like those I've summarized above. It is during these times that I've experienced a great sense of oneness with all things and universal love fills my being so strongly, that I almost feel like I am glowing or walking on air! I feel so shiny inside and out!

I am not high; I am not off seeking spirituality in India or South America or somewhere exotic like that. I am a mother, a wife, an active community member, for many years the secretary of my children's school Parent's and Citizen's Association, a young woman who loves writing, music, comedy, walks on the beach and living a wonderfully blessed life with my beautiful family.

I am also a lighter of candles, a feeler of subtle energies, a beautiful being of light that is connected to all things everywhere. Some might call this a connection to God, while others may call this a connection to something different; the universe, the divine, spirit, the angels, or the higher self; for me it is all the one.

I am grounded and present. I believe that there are a lot of people like me out there, people accessing and living the sacred here and now, not waiting for a guru to show us the way or for death to turn us into spirits or angels. We live as sacredly and as consciously as we can, in the here and now.

The normality of this life for me is that one moment I can be making food for my children, cleaning up my kitchen or folding freshly washed clothes, working on my book, telling jokes, texting my friends, having a dance or writing a song or watching a good movie, and the next minute I am talking to someone on the 'other side' of this physical veil, feeling the spirits connected to me, feeling bliss and love and receiving answers and guidance from them to help us here.

Questions?

People ask me a lot of questions. Can you turn this on and off? Do you have to try hard? Do you have to practice? Aren't you scared?

I could say yes to all those things. But I can also say no because I don't always have to try at all, and while practice does make it easier, like practicing does for other types of skills, it is natural and it will come through anyway.

I could turn it off by not listening, but in my experience it's best to listen and act on advice I receive because it always leads to helping someone. I have to be honest here and say that when I haven't listened I've learned the hard way that I should listen, I will get hurt or someone else will because I haven't followed through on spirits' advice.

I used to be scared when I was young, I'd hide under the covers at night scared of my nightly invisible but loud visitors, as I had no guidance on how to use my intuitive abilities. I'm not scared anymore because I have learnt how to use my gifts and I feel loved and protected from loving beings on the other side and also very supported by my family and friends now.

Over the years I have read lots of books by people who have skills like mine and I know I am not alone in what I can do. As my children have strong psychic gifts as well, I choose to be a strong role model and teacher for them, so that I can guide them to be comfortable with their intuition. They can then use their gifts in a powerful and controlled or 'aware' manner to benefit their lives and others' lives also.

Because people always ask, I want you to know that if I ever sense anything negative, a negative spirit or energy, I ask for the protection of God, of the Light, of Love and of the angels, of loving spirits and guides. I feel protected by the good in this universe. It has happened where I have had to call on God when a negative energy has come into my space, and immediately that being was forced out.

We all choose how much we want to listen to the other world alongside us. I choose to consciously live in both simultaneously and you can too.

We can appreciate that intuition is a valid and important sense that we use every day, generally without consciously realising it. We assess every person, thing, being, and situation as it comes into our sphere. We instantly just 'know' if there's something funny about another person or if there's 'bad' energy in a room the instant we walk in. We can 'feel' something's wrong with our loved one even though they are a fair distance away. We feel a niggle telling us to stop and not continue with that business deal, our gut tells us something is wrong, though the head might fight this and say otherwise.

Just as we can all turn this off if we choose to, I have to ask why would we? It's of such benefit to us, why don't we make learning how to use our intuition more accessible to us all?!

ACKNOWLEDGEMENTS

Thank you dearest readers and fellow beings on this journey – I send you all my love and well wishes that you have a beautiful life filled with angels and love.

Thank you to the otherworldly, loving beings (such as spirits, guides, angels and ancestors) that live alongside us, always helping us, often without acknowledgement, unseen and unknown, spreading love wherever you go.

To my Dad, and all my Relatives and Friends in Heaven, thank you so much for continuing to love and guide me, especially in my dreams, you help me so much, I don't know what I'd do without your continuing support.

Thanks to my Mum and Dad who taught me about spirituality and kindness and for giving me a beautiful childhood.

Thank you to Indigenous World Peoples for teaching us about ancestors and mother earth and for continuing to protect all that is sacred and true.

Thank you to my family and friends and for all the people whose stories are in this book and for those dear ones who read the memoir and gave support and advice – Mick, Misha Sim (the most patient editor ever), Felicity, Despina, James, Aisling, Fiona, Azriel and Mark.

To my hubby and my children, you are the best and you prove to me that love heals all and that we can live our dreams here on earth. Love you forever and ever.

ABOUT THE AUTHOR

Amanda Wone McHugh grew up in the cane paddocks and beaches of Far North Queensland, Australia. She is from a very large family and grew up in a multicultural environment - her father's parents were Asian Muslims and her mother's parents were English/Irish Catholics.

Amanda always felt that spirituality was not to be found in any doctrine or building, but in your heart and mind and your own relationship with the sacred and spiritual that you could sense and feel within you and all around you. She could feel God in everything and everyone. Her father once said that he felt being kind to others was his spirituality. This felt right to her too.

Since she was a young girl she dreamed of writing books that would help others, she didn't know how she would do that, but in her mind's eye she saw that she would write many books that would help people and make the world a better place to live in.

Amanda lives in the hinterlands of Byron Bay in New South Wales, Australia, with her Irish singer-songwriter husband, Mick McHugh and her two children, Kia and Orin, a little old lady doggie named Sparkles and the feline managers of the house, Minty and Little Kitty.

Amanda has always been a psychic medium. She is also a trained psychologist, counsellor, songwriter, poet, dancer, photographer, filmmaker and dedicated mother, wife and friend.

Please email Amanda at the contact page on her website www.amandamchughauthor.com if you wish to add your story to her next book of psychic stories to inspire the world! Thank you.

AMANDA McHUGH

www.ingramcontent.com/pod-product-compliance
Lightning Source LLC
La Vergne TN
LVHW011343080426
835511LV00005B/110